Crosscurrents/Modern Critiques/Third Series

Edited by Jerome Klinkowitz

A Constant Journey

The Fiction of Monique Wittig

Erika Ostrovsky

Southern Illinois University Press
Carbondale and Edwardsville

Copyright © 1991 by the Board of Trustees, Southern Illinois
  University
All rights reserved
Printed in the United States of America
Edited and designed by Jill Butler
Production supervised by Natalia Nadraga
94 93 92 91   4 3 2 1

Les Editions de Minuit has generously given permission to use extended
quotations from their copyrighted publications of *L'Opoponax*, *Les Guérillères*,
Le Corps lesbien, and *Virgile, non*.

Library of Congress Cataloging-in-Publication Data

Ostrovsky, Erika.
    A constant journey : the fiction of Monique Wittig / Erika
Ostrovsky.
        p.   cm. — (Crosscurrents/modern critiques. Third series)
    Includes bibliographical references.
    1. Wittig, Monique—Criticism and interpretation. 2. Feminism and
literature—France. I. Title. II. Series.
PQ2683.I8Z8   1991
843'.914—dc20   89-49482
    ISBN 0-8093-1642-0   CIP

The paper used in this publication meets the minimum requirements of
American National Standard for Information Sciences—Permanence of
Paper for Printed Library Materials, ANSI Z39.48-1984. ∞

To my daughter

Contents

Crosscurrents/ Modern Critiques/ Third Series

I n the early1960s, when the Crosscurrents/Modern Critiques series was developed by Harry T. Moore, the contemporary period was still a controversial one for scholarship. Even today the elusive sense of the present dares critics to rise above mere impressionism and to approach their subject with the same rigors of discipline expected in more traditional areas of study. As the first two series of Crosscurrents books demonstrated, critiquing contemporary culture often means that the writer must be historian, philosopher, sociologist, and bibliographer as well as literary critic, for in many cases these essential preliminary tasks are yet undone.

To the challenges that faced the initial Crosscurrents project have been added those unique to the past two decades: the disruption of conventional techniques by the great surge in innovative writing in the American 1960s just when social and political conditions were being radically transformed, the new worldwide interest in the Magic Realism of South American novelists, the startling experiments of textual and aural poetry from Europe, the emergence of Third World authors, the rising cause of feminism in life and literature, and, most dramatically, the introduction of Continental theory into the previously staid world of Anglo-American literary scholarship. These transformations demand that many traditional treatments be rethought, and part of the new responsibility for Crosscurrents will be to provide such studies.

Contributions to Crosscurrents/Modern Critiques/Third Series will be distinguished by their fresh approaches to established topics and by their opening up of new territories for discourse. When a single author is studied, we hope to present the first book on his or her work or to explore a previously untreated aspect based on new research. Writers who have been critiqued well elsewhere will be studied in comparison with lesser-known figures, sometimes from other cultures, in an effort to broaden our base of understanding. Critical and theoretical works by leading novelists, poets, and dramatists will have a home in Crosscurrents/Modern Critiques/Third Series, as will sampler-introductions to the best in new Americanist criticism written abroad.

The excitement of contemporary studies is that all of its critical practitioners and most of their subjects are alive and working at the same time. One work influences another, bringing to the field a spirit of competition and cooperation that reaches an intensity rarely found in other disciplines. Above all, this third series of Crosscurrents/Modern Critiques will be collegial—a mutual interest in the present moment that can be shared by writer, subject, and reader alike.

Jerome Klinkowitz

Acknowledgments

I wish to express my gratitude to Nathalie Sarraute for encouraging the writing of this book and for the insights she gave me into Wittig's work during our conversations in Paris. I also want to thank Monique Wittig herself for speaking with me about her past, present, and future work with such openness and for providing me with invaluable first-hand information. I am deeply indebted to them both.

A Constant Journey

Abbreviated References

B: *Brouillon pour un dictionnaire des amantes.* With Sande Zeig. Paris: Editions Grasset and Fasquelle, 1976.

C: *Le Corps lesbien.* Paris: Editions de Minuit, 1973.

G: *Les Guérillères.* Paris: Editions de Minuit, 1969.

O: *L'Opoponax.* Paris: Editions de Minuit, 1964.

T: "The Trojan Horse." *Feminist Issues* 4, no. 4 (1984), 45–49.

V: *Virgile, non.* Paris: Editions de Minuit, 1985.

Prologue

"TOUT GESTE EST RENVERSEMENT"
(*Les Guérillères*)

*R*enversement, in all its multiplicity of meanings—upheaval, overthrow, reversal, and subversion—can be considered the key to Monique Wittig's writing. From the very start, Wittig's use of this concept has spelled the annihilation of existing literary canons and the creation of highly innovative constructs. Renversement is already evident in her first work, *L'Opoponax*, published in 1964 during the heyday of the "new novel" in France and during that period's impact on writers from many other countries. Instantly recognized as an event that constituted "l'exécution capitale . . . d'une certaine littérature"[1] and that marked the advent of a new wave in writing (without a label, this time), *L'Opoponax* was judged unquestionably avant-garde.[2] Perhaps most important of all, it showed that Wittig was engaged in a combat against all literary conformity and that she had embarked on a path totally her own—a path she would follow, consistently and without concession, "in splendid solitude."[3]

Not that *L'Opoponax* lacked acclaim. On the contrary, the work received the coveted Prix Médicis, and the radical nature of Wittig's undertaking was recognized by the most discerning of her contemporary writers: in France, Marguerite Duras, Nathalie Sarraute, and Claude Simon; and in America, Mary McCarthy. A rare tribute indeed, considering that *L'Opoponax* was the first work by a writer who was, until then, totally unknown.

In the twenty years or so that followed, Wittig continued to write fictions that won her international renown, that were translated into numerous languages,[4] and—even more sig-

3

nificantly—that confirmed her initial stance, her enduring capacity to subvert literary traditions and recreate them utterly and to do so with increasing audacity and inventiveness: *Les Guérillères; Le Corps lesbien; Brouillon pour un dictionnaire des amantes; and Virgile, non.*[5] The critical reception of her writings, on the other hand, did not always show sufficient appreciation of her aims or recognition of their revolutionary properties. While at times the criticism was characterized by fine insight,[6] at other times it erred by confining her fictions to an extremely narrow category,[7] or it even contented itself with showing outrage at their "scandalous" nature.[8] Evidently then, her work remained highly controversial and was in dire need of clarification. Perhaps this prompted Wittig herself, in 1984, two decades after the appearance of *L'Opoponax*, to utter her convictions regarding the nature, aims, and functions of avant-garde literature—and thus, of her own work.

These appeared in a brief, little-known text, "The Trojan Horse." A scant five pages long and not easily available,[9] it is nevertheless a key document that provides fundamental and invaluable insights into her entire work. Here, Wittig states her basic outlook, unequivocally defines her stance as a writer, and destroys a number of misconceptions that have frequently flawed discussions of her fictions. As a backward glance by an author at his/her own writing—after having reached maturity as an artist—it is as valuable for the critic as, for example, Céline's *Entretiens avec le Professeur Y*, Ionesco's *Notes et contre-notes*, and Sarraute's *L'Ere du soupçon*. Yet Wittig's pronouncement instantly and significantly distinguishes itself from these texts, for "The Trojan Horse" was originally an oral communication, delivered to students of various American universities,[10] and only afterwards published in written form. It thus already demonstrates one of Wittig's fundamental aims (apparent in her fictions from *L'Opoponax* to *Virgile, non*)—to subvert established categories, destroy past models, and renew the literary adventure by means that are themselves new. While being a writer and of French origin, she addresses herself in English to a youthful American audience, rather than publishing, in French and in France, a written statement directed to a more traditional public or to the literary establishment.

Even more than this striking choice however, the nature of the text itself constitutes its principal originality. Incisive yet simple, it expresses Wittig's fundamental convictions in terms that, free of jargon or specialized terminology, are immediately accessible to a general audience. It thus clearly expresses the desire to destroy literary elitism, and it attacks the pervasive tendency to indulge in theoretical discourse (which could be considered a type of establishment). Instead, she chooses to appeal to the imaginative potential of her listeners. This is evident in her recourse to imagery in order to speak of literature and, first of all, in her recourse to the arresting image of the Trojan Horse (redefined, as one might expect). Her pronouncement begins thus:

> At first it looks strange to the Trojans, the wooden horse, off color, outsized, barbaric. . . . But later on . . . they want to make it theirs, to adopt it as a monument and shelter it within their walls. . . . But what if it were a war machine?
> Any important literary work is like the Trojan Horse at the time it was produced. Any work with a new form operates as a war machine, because its design and its goal is to pulverize the old forms and formal conventions. . . . It will sap and blow out the ground where it was planted. (*T*, 45)

Instantly then, by the use of her simile, she defines the avant-garde work of art (and, incidentally, her own) as an engine fashioned to destroy outmoded, inefficient, traditional forms that, she adds, have become "incapable of transformation" (*T*, 45). At the same time, she emphasizes the constant need for refusal and renewal, lest such a work be accepted (or adopted) by the establishment and thus lose its potential for overthrow. She also insists that, just as with a battering ram, a landmine, or the more artful construct of the Trojan Horse, the demolition power of a new work constitutes its primary value. To pulverize, to explode existing structures and even the most fecund inventions of the past is thus its major goal.

Of course it can be argued that Wittig is not alone in recommending a scorched-earth policy in order to prepare the ground for new growth. Every avant-garde movement has proclaimed the need for such action. Each has carried it out in its own way. In our century, it was probably the Dadaists who resorted to the most drastic means. But it remained for a poet to say it all in three lines:

> Perdre
> Mais perdre vraiment
> Pour laisser place à la trouvaille.[11]

What distinguishes Wittig's Trojan Horse "war machine" are the clarifying notions that she adds instantly. She affirms that her statement is not a manifesto nor a proclamation of commitment to a particular ideology. In order to differentiate a literary work that functions as an agent of violent upheaval from committed literature, she dissociates the two terms and states her own position, refuting the notion that fictions are vehicles for political or ideological expression. In doing so, she appears to criticize those critics (and they are fairly numerous) who have treated her work primarily as militant feminist propaganda:[12]

> Committed literature and *écriture féminine* have in common that . . . they throw dust in people's eyes by amalgamating in the same process two occurrences that do not have the same relationship to the real and to language. . . . In the expression committed literature phenomena whose very nature is different [are] thrown together. Standing thus, they tend to annul each other. (*T*, 46)

It therefore seems evident that Wittig, although she has made some ideological pronouncements,[13] does not wish these to be confused with her literary works and considers herself first and foremost a writer of fictions. This is borne out by her writing, which is, overwhelmingly, in the fictional domain, and also by the major portion of "The Trojan Horse," for the latter is devoted to the writer's craft and the elements that are essential to its exercise.

The first of these elements, according to Wittig, is the study of the history of literary forms and the relationship of the writer to the vast corpus of texts, past and present. In other words, she does not reject the literary heritage per se, and indeed, her works show her extensive knowledge of past and present texts. However, while this is deemed a necessary base, she insists that in the final analysis a writer is confronted with only two choices: "Either reproducing existing forms or creating new ones" (*T*, 46). It is quite clear that she herself has not only refused the first of these choices but has even advocated the violent destruction of existing forms. On the other hand, the desire to create new forms is basic to her entire fictional enterprise. It informs every aspect of her work and can be seen in her treatment of literary genres; the structure of the text; fictional time and space; the problem of protagonists; the choice of symbols, numbers, and colors; mythological figures and myth patterns; semantic, syntactic, and grammatical considerations; and the nature and function of language.

It is on the last of these elements that Wittig chooses to concentrate in the central portion of "The Trojan Horse" (just as she makes the destruction and recreation of language paramount in her fictions). Here again, as in the instance mentioned above, Wittig shows a profound knowledge of current explorations and practices of critics and writers in this domain. However, her treatment of the question of language has the merit of simplicity and absence of jargon that characterizes her entire communication, and she appeals, once more, to the imaginative potential of her public.

To begin with, language is defined as the primary ingredient of the writer's craft (that is, his/her "raw material"), and as such, it is comparable to the sculptor's clay, the painter's colors, or the musician's sounds. In order to differentiate words from these other raw materials though, Wittig again uses the key image of her text:

> Words are, each one of them, like the Trojan Horse. They are things, material things, and at the same time they mean something. . . . They are a condensate of abstraction and concreteness, and in this they are totally different from all the other mediums used to create art. (*T*, 47)

Then—returning to the distinction made earlier between historical or political discourse and the literary text—she goes on to explain the use of words in the latter (the domain that obviously concerns her most):

> In history and politics words are taken in their conventional meaning. . . . In literature words are given to be read in their materiality. . . . But one must understand that to attain this result a writer must first reduce language to be as meaningless as possible in order to turn it into a neutral material—that is, a raw material. Only then is one able to work words into a form. (*T*, 47)

The meaning of a finished work of fiction, she goes on to state, derives directly from its form, that is, from the manner in which the writer has "worked words"—by taking each word and "despoil[ing] it of its everyday meaning in order to work with words, on words" (*T*, 48). This is a striking pronouncement and one that illuminates an important aspect of Wittig's treatment of language in her fictions.

It would be wrong, however, to regard her as believing that the writer's aim is primarily to demonstrate virtuosity in the handling of language or to strive for unintelligibility. Something else is at stake. This becomes clear if one continues to follow Wittig's development of the goals of the "word work" she has described. The main one is to produce a "powerful vision of words" by means of a characteristically violent form of renewal: "I would be perfectly satisfied," she states, "if every one of my words had on the reader the same effect, the same shock, as if they were being read for the first time" (*T*, 48). Destruction and recreation are thus intimately linked by Wittig, in the area of language (as in every other domain of literature).

But she goes on to expand her previous statements by explaining that this "shock" of words, their impact comparable to that of a "perfect war machine," derives also from "their association, their disposition, their arrangement, and by each one of them used separately" (*T*, 48). This pronouncement is highly significant, for it reveals something that critics have not always seen in her fictions: Wittig's view of language is primarily that of a poet. This insight is vital for the understanding and interpretation of her entire oeuvre, for rather than vehicles for the expression of an ideology, militant treatises, or *romans à thèse*, her fictions are—essentially—poetic constructs and should be viewed as such.

Another extremely revealing statement is contained in the final portion of "The Trojan Horse." It deals with a key concept that is also demonstrated in Wittig's works of fiction and seldom noted by her critics. Here she discusses what she considers one of the "most strategic" parts of a writer's task: universalization of the author's point of view, especially if that point of view is highly individual or singular (*T*, 49). As an illustration, she uses Marcel Proust. This choice is, of course, significant, for his point of view (that of the nonheterosexual) is shared by Wittig. However, while adhering to her point of view as firmly as Proust had done, she—as much as Proust—refuses to limit herself, or be limited, to a certain outlook—either militant feminist or lesbian (labels that critics have often attached to her work). Most importantly, she aims at universalization in her fictions, just as he did.

This is expressed quite clearly in the concluding paragraph of her statement where she defines the ultimate task of the avant-garde writer (and thus states her most fundamental concerns):

> To carry out a literary work one must . . . know that being gay or anything else is not enough. . . . It is the attempted universalization of the point of view that turns or does not turn a literary work into a war machine. (*T*, 49)

Considering all that Wittig has elucidated in "The Trojan Horse," it seems only fitting that any discussion of her work should honor the intentions and convictions voiced there. Thus, the pages that follow will treat her fictions accordingly: as poetic constructs rather than as committed literature; as centered on the various formal aspects of the writer's craft and the innovations found there; as attempts at the universalization of a particular point of view; as highly original examples of avant-garde writing—in other words, as the appropriate avatars of "The Trojan Horse."

1

The First O

*I*t all began with *L'Opoponax*. On the surface the work seemed innocent enough. It could be (and was) placed within "the familiar category of the autobiographical novel of childhood"[1]—a genre not in the least unusual for a young author, and one that critics tend to consider a predilection of women writers.[2] In reality however, *L'Opoponax* was the first of Monique Wittig's Trojan Horses—a veritable declaration of war. The work destroyed a literary form whose well-established attributes and boundaries made it the perfect target for attack, the initial line of defense to be shattered by her "war machine." So well did *L'Opoponax* overthrow an existing genre and "blow out the ground where it was planned" (*T*, 45), that Marguerite Duras called it "un chef-d'oeuvre [car] c'est l'exécution capitale de quatre-vingt-dix pour cent des livres qui ont été faits sur l'enfance."[3]

To truly appreciate the perspicacity of Duras' statement, the revolutionary nature of *L'Opoponax*, and the extent of Wittig's success in her "execution" of past models, it is necessary to consider the particular characteristics that traditionally appear in this type of novel. Only then does it become apparent how Wittig subverted (or reversed) each and every traditional characteristic before proceeding to its recreation—and this, from the very outset of her literary career.

The initial example of *renversement* is the work's title. *L'Opoponax* has nothing in common with the titles usually found in novels of this type. Nowhere is there an allusion to the author's self or to her past life, such as one sees, for instance, in Simone de Beauvoir's *Mémoires d'une jeune fille rangée*, Colette's *La Maison de Claudine*, Maxim Gorky's *My Childhood*, James Joyce's *Portrait of the Artist as a Young Man*, George Sand's *Histoire de ma vie*, and Nathalie Sarraute's *Enfance*. Instead, the work's title is an enigmatic term whose only link to the author might be the three-fold repetition of the letter O (*Opoponax*), a letter that also appears in her first name (Monique), and that may be a very indirect reference to her past, since it is the initial letter of the word *origin(s)*. Consulting the dictionary provides no clue, for there "opoponax" is defined as a medicinal plant of the Mediterranean region, which produces a gum-like substance that can be used as perfume[4]— a definition that nowhere applies in the novel. Also, the definite article that precedes the term seems to refer to a particular opoponax and thus further removes any possibility of a dictionary explanation. A reading of the work reveals that the term providing its title has multiple meanings that vary considerably: a force that propels the text;[5] the opposite of a civil identity; power and defiance; the love that dares not speak its name;[6] prohibition and transgression; a kind of numinous power that suggests the terror and delight of sexual desire;[7] a cryptonym (a name that hides and, by hiding, shows that it hides).[8] By its very complexity, the word both outdistances and destroys the expectations habitually associated with a title. Instantly then, it marks the opposition of *L'Opoponax* to other works in the same category, and it is evidence of Wittig's penchant for renversement before the book is even opened.

Also from the very outset, *L'Opoponax* distinguishes itself from the first person singular narration and/or subjective point of view typical of the genre. Wittig succeeds in telling the past "as if it happened to *somebody else*."[9] She thus totally reverses the habitual notion of a personal viewpoint and desubjectifies a traditionally subjective narration. This emotional distancing is achieved by several innovative techniques instantly discernible in the text—the refusal of the pronoun *I*, and the substitution, not of *she*, but of the impersonal pronoun *on*. This is an arresting choice, for *on* (almost impossible to translate into English, the closest approximation being *one*) has numerous connotations. It is indefinite, neutral, neuter, indeterminate, and guarded; but it is also collective, generalized, "both oneself and everybody"; (thus suggesting universalization). This pronoun—which pervades the text of *L'Opoponax* from start to finish, giving way only at the end of the final sentence— is "a key that unlocks more doors than expected." It marks (among other things) "a neutral relation between the author and her material"[10]—a quality most unusual, if not totally absent, in most autobiographical novels of childhood. And since it also suggests a group, a collective, it further removes the narrative from the singular/subjective point of view and thus again indicates that vast distance established between this work and others of the same genre.

A further innovation immediately noticeable is her use of multiple protagonists, rather than of one "heroine" as would be traditional. Indeed, so great is the number of protagonists that Duras compared them to "une marée d'enfants" or, more precisely, "une marée de petites filles."[11] The choice of the term "marée" is felicitous, for not only are the little girls numerous, but they tend to merge, to flow in unison, as if they constituted the movement of a tide. This is achieved, first of all, by presenting their names in long lists (first and last name, as in school, but at the same time also serving to distance them), and by an innovation in punctuation, that is, the omission of commas. Enumerations such as these appear in the text:

> Laurence Bouniol Julienne Pont Marielle Balland Noémi Mazat Marguerite-Marie Le Monial Nichole Marre. (*O*, 227)

> Marielle Balland Nicole Marre Laurence Bouniol Julienne Pont Marie Démone Anne Gerlier Denise Causse Anne-Marie Brunet Marguerite-Marie Le Monial Marie-José Broux Sophie Rieux. (*O*, 269)

By refusing to use commas conventionally to separate the children's names, Wittig achieves many ends: the overthrow of a long-established tradition; the destruction of boundaries or distinctions; the negation of a name's usual function as indicator of an individual entity or civil identity; the production of an incantatory (or poetic) effect through the sound chain that the names constitute; and an emphasis on naming—or rather, renaming—as a form of creation. Most importantly though, this device reinforces the removal of *L'Opoponax* from the traditional presentation of a single protagonist. It is thus also in accordance with Wittig's pronouncement in "The Trojan Horse" concerning the necessity for universalizing a literary work if it is to be a true "war machine." So successful is she in this enterprise of universalization that, for Claude Simon, reading *L'Opoponax* resulted in the following experience: "Je ne suis plus moi, je ne suis pas non plus une certaine petite fille: je *deviens* l'enfance."[12]

"Childhood itself," moreover, is represented in a unique manner in this work. While *L'Opoponax* treats the evolution from the early school years to adolescence and, in this, resembles another well-known genre (the bildungsroman), its very structure shows an approach that is quite different from one that typifies this kind of novel. Wittig's text does not proceed by clearly marked stages or divisions. True, it is possible to distinguish seven parts in the work, but these parts seem to have a purely symbolic significance (as the study of numbers in her fictions will show), and they do not follow the usual pattern, in which such divisions function as temporal indicators or markers of the various stages in an individual's formation. Within each part of the novel, the text appears as a continual flow. It is uninterrupted by paragraphs, breaks, or even punctuation marks that distinguish descriptive material from dialogue, what is told from what is said. The lack of distinctions is moreover reinforced by repeated use of the ingeniously ambiguous phrase "on dit," which can be translated, alternately, as "it is told," "it is said," "one says," "they say."

The continuity of the text also achieves a performative level, for it has, itself, duration and fluidity, an absence of boundaries or evidence of fragmentation. In this, it perfectly renders the child's perception of temporal flux as opposed to the adult's insistence on chronological measurement and segmentation. Although some critics attribute Wittig's treatment of fictional time primarily to a refusal of "phallocentric" linear concepts,[13] it seems more appropriate here to consider her obvious preference for a use of temporal notions that characterize childhood and are in contrast to those of adults. The latter, it has been pointed out, are inevitably associated with loss, degeneration, decrepitude, death, or what has been described as the "fall into time,"[14] while the child's experience emphasizes duration, continuity, endlessness, and an eternal present.

In Wittig's novel, this experience is rendered simply, yet powerfully, by her exclusive use of present tense verbs (maintained until the final phrase of the work), which creates not only a sense of the present but also of presence—both of which are characteristic of childhood. Perhaps this quality answers the question asked by Claude Simon when speaking of *L'Opoponax:* "Après tant de récits où tant d'adultes ont vainement essayé d' 'exprimer' leurs souvenirs d'enfance, comment Monique Wittig a-t-elle réussi, elle, à *dire* l'enfance?" His own answer was that the work "nous *restitue* l'enfance. . . . C'est à dire que celle-ci n'est pas racontée mais proprement recréée"[15]—and this recreation is achieved by the means just described.

If continuity, fluidity, and absence of boundaries represent the temporal experience of childhood, the same seems to be true for spatial considerations. Places move as the child does, distances are not measured in miles, and movement is accomplished with ease. In the text of *L'Opoponax,* these notions are expressed in a treatment of space that parallels that of time. Rather than having distinct settings, scenes shift, merge, and refuse all demarcations or separations. Sometimes this switch or merging occurs so swiftly as to pass almost unnoticed, with nothing in the text (neither a break nor a punctuation mark) to indicate a displacement or distancing. For example, a scene set in school gives way, in the very next sentence, to one in the countryside, or the interior of a church suddenly becomes a field in winter, even though the action in both scenes would have taken place months and miles apart (*O*, 86, 88, 95, 187, 223). Such treatment establishes a time/space continuum that echoes the notions of flux and unity already noted in Wittig's handling of protagonists and their names. And if, as one critic has noted, it creates a text that can be compared to a "child's letter,"[16] it also shows again how well she succeeds in "*telling* childhood" (to use Simon's phrase). Perhaps even more importantly, it is additional evidence of the renversement to which Wittig subjects various traditional aspects of fiction.

Among other fairly obvious reversals found in the novel is the treatment of established religion. Once again, at first glance nothing seems unusual about *L'Opoponax* in that domain. Most of the work is set in a Catholic school—a commonplace in France and thus an apparently traditional setting. But there the adhesion to habitual portrayals stops. As Duras has noted, the nuns are "toutes pareilles, anonymes comme la matière même de l'adulte" (and therefore opposed to the world of childhood). Also, "à l'ombre de leur dévotion se passe la scrutation païenne,"[17] the secret, ritualistic, subversive life of the children. The antagonism between the adult world and an established religion (Catholicism) and the world of childhood and paganism is here paramount. It already foreshadows the renversement that Wittig undertakes in later texts, in which pagan rituals as well as the subversion of established divinities and myths play a dominant role. In *L'Opoponax*, the renversement is marked both by the activities of the children and by the appearance of several figures from pagan mythology: Romulus and Remus, an unidentified female divinity of Gallo-Roman origin, Artemis, and Orpheus and Eurydice (*O*, 141, 177–78, 210, 251). The last three of these figures assume increasing importance in Wittig's later works but already are markedly present here. In addition, there is a refusal of significant doctrines and practices that characterize Catholicism: sin and the Devil, life after death and the judgment of souls, and the sanctity of church services and various sacraments. But here again, Wittig's principal aim is not to attack or promote a particular ideology or point of view, but to engage in combat against traditional forms and orthodox practices—whether in literature or in any other domain.

This is also true for a stereotyped view of children as— Dr. Freud notwithstanding— innocent, pure and, most especially, asexual or presexual. In *L'Opoponax*, this notion is instantly demolished. Sex rears its head in the very first sentence, where a premature exhibitionist offers all and sundry a view of his "quéquette," an infantile term for penis (*O*, 7). And it is certainly not an accident that his name is Robert Payen (pronounced in the same manner as "païen," meaning pagan), thus immediately linking him with forces that are antitraditional and un-Catholic. Another behavior of a similar nature also occurs in the novel, but is, however, of far greater import and occupies a much more prominent place: the growing sexual desire between young girls. While a representation of such desire is not particularly unusual in literature—and even a must in pornographic texts, which almost invariably include a lesbian sequence—in this context, it is a transgression or overthrow of Christian doctrine, in which such desire is a sin of no minor consequence. Much more important than this, however, is the manner in which this desire is treated in *L'Opoponax*. This constitutes the true renversement of establishing notions and thus merits close attention.

Although desire is an important element, the relationships between young girls in *L'Opoponax* are love relations and, in that sense, not limited to what Wittig calls "being gay" (*T*, 49). They have a much broader meaning. Also, although the relations are primarily between two named protagonists (Catherine Legrand and Valerie Borge), these two figures have emerged from the "marée de petites filles" and are thus representatives of a group rather than particular individuals. Most certainly, they are not meant as representations of a personal experience. Instead, they function in the portrayal—characterized by universalization— of young love, or even of love itself.

The awakening of this feeling is linked to puberty. This is rendered in the text by having it occur past the middle of the book. Valerie Borge, the beloved, makes her appearance when the children (as is evident from their activities) have reached this age. At first she is there only as a name among other names (*O*, 157), but slowly she emerges with greater frequency and clarity. The way she is introduced is significant. The initial glimpse of her occurs during a lesson on Italian painting and follows a reference to Raphaël's madonnas, "si brillantes de jeunesse de fraicheur" (*O*, 166).[18] She is thus instantly associated with youth, beauty, and art. But she is also immediately linked with transgression, for she is seen while engaged in a forbidden activity[19]—cutting designs into her desk with a penknife. A later view of her, this time the result of long and careful scrutiny by Catherine Legrand, again combines an awareness of her beauty (in more sensual terms now) with transgressive actions. She is now seen tracing the outlines of a coin in her prayerbook during a solemn requiem mass in the convent chapel (*O*, 190–91). Another characteristic of Valerie Borge is that she writes poetry but keeps her work a secret (*O*, 189). Initially then, she combines important qualities of the beloved (which will reappear in later works by Wittig)—beauty, poetry, secrecy, and transgression. Perhaps even more importantly, she constitutes the equation between art and transgression or overthrow, thus incarnating Wittig's central concept of renversement.

As the love relationship slowly evolves, poetry as a form of expression increases in importance. Poems constitute the means of communication between Catherine Legrand and Valerie Borge (*O*, 197–98, 201). And a line of Latin verse—"lento me torquet amore"—haunts the former, finally conjuring up visions of the beloved that cause the text to erupt with a lyrical intensity unprecedented in *L'Opoponax*:

> Elle est à plat ventre sur un cheval sauvage noir blanc gris . . . ses cheveux non attachés sont sur le vent on la voit les doigts dans les crinières et les genoux nus, toute couverte de sueur . . . la bouche ouverte, les dents à l'air . . . elle est ailleurs, tirée par les mouvements d'étoiles elle dérive, on la voit s'éloigner, c'est un gel brillant qu'on regarde tourner sur soi, elle voyage à la place d'une galaxie.[20] (*O*, 216–17)

This passage, foreshadowing parts of *Les Guérillères* and much of *Le Corps lesbien* in form, tone, and content, shows that Valerie Borge is more than a fictional representation of the beloved, for she engenders a text that has all the hallmarks of love poetry. As a matter of fact, the writing attains a paroxystic quality in sharp contrast to the predominant character of the novel, which is noteworthy (according to Duras) for its rigorous use of "un matériau descriptif pur" and a single tool, "le langage objectif pur."[21]

However, love in *L'Opoponax* does not only produce emotions such as those expressed in the passage cited above. Its "slow torment" also arouses violent feelings, foremost among them that of jealousy. This is the case when Catherine Legrand sees Valerie Borge engaged in a sensual exchange with Anne-Marie Brunet (*O*, 227). The result is not love poetry but the creation of the opoponax. It is highly significant that the term giving the entire work its title first appears precisely at this juncture, for evidently, it is born of a vehement emotion and is a dangerous force—a kind of "war machine." Also, it is the creation of Catherine Legrand. Note that she initially attempts to draw the opoponax. When she fails in doing so, she decides to replace the visual image with words (*O*, 179). The opoponax is thus instantly and clearly linked to fictional creation. This is further accentuated, for she inscribes the word in her notebook in capital letters: "O P O P O N A X." This is followed by a colon and the phrase "peut s'étirer" (*O*, 179).[22] Indeed, both the meanings and the actions of the opoponax are stretched or extended throughout the text. Furthermore, the first definition of the term (or impossibility of definition in the sense of limitation) is provided here, for Catherine Legrand goes on to write:

> On ne peut pas le [l'opoponax] décrire parce qu'il n'a jamais la même forme. Règne, ni animal, ni végétal, ni minéral, autrement dit indéterminé. Humeur, instable, il n'est pas recommandé de fréquenter l'opoponax.[23] (*O*, 179)

It is thus an enigmatic, fluid, protean, threatening force—very much like the work of fiction in which it appears or like fiction as conceived and defined by Wittig.

The text goes on to illustrate that the opoponax has multiform and manifold power. It menaces those whom it would convince, intimidate, or eliminate. It even frightens its own creator, for so great is this force that, once liberated, it is difficult to control. Moreover, since the opoponax is capable of constant change, it can become a sound or a shape, and it can cause a blurring of contours, even a loss of the most elementary certitudes (*O*, 180–81). But its primary function is to express an intense feeling—without, however, naming it. As a cryptonym, it attains its full strength by an absence of enunciation—by hiding and showing that it hides. It thus works in secret, in undercover fashion, to mine that which it aims to destroy.

In this instance, the object for destruction is a rival love. This can be inferred from the fact that the opoponax reappears in the text when jealousy erupts again. This time though, it takes the form of a direct threat in a message sent to Valerie Borge. Written in vermillion ink (the color of passion and violence) and accompanied by a drawing consisting of circles and sharp angles (geometric shapes expressing parallel emotions), the opoponax is now a text addressed to a reader (the beloved) and designed to have a particular effect—to force this reader to have a desired response (*O*, 230–31). Once more, a comparison could be suggested between the opoponax and the work of fiction as Wittig conceives it.

The third appearance of the opoponax, again in the form of a written text, is accompanied by a coincidental event of a dramatic nature—a fire (*O*, 240–42). It thus combines a verbal threat with a physical one—death in flames, a fitting metaphor for consuming passion. This time, the opoponax is victorious. It has succeeded as a "war machine." The hated rival, Anne-Marie Brunet, is overthrown, and the beloved, Valerie Borge, now promises to communicate (secretly) with Catherine Legrand, by means of correspondence (*O*, 247–49). The acceptance of a love relationship thus manifests itself in an exchange of written texts.

Once this battle has been won, the opoponax has accomplished its task. It now disappears from the scene—and from the text of *L'Opoponax* itself. It remains, however, as the title of the novel, a reminder of its importance regarding the central combat in the text (and combat as the aim of Wittig's texts in general).

As the lovers encounter each other, the violent emotions aroused by jealousy subside, but the intensity of feelings manifests itself in other ways. This intensity is now characterized by secrecy and silence. For example, Catherine Legrand shouts all the names of her classmates but leaves out the name of Valerie Borge (*O*, 235). This blank, this absence of enunciation, is far more eloquent than speech. The name of the beloved remains hidden, unspoken. It is thus allied with the unnameable and the ineffable, which suggests that it is sacred. It also has the allure of the forbidden, of taboo, of transgression (characteristics already evident in the initial portrayals of Valerie Borge, and a motif that reoccurs, in its most powerful form, in a later work by Wittig, *Le Corps lesbien*).

The secret, surreptitious pleasures of love are again described in a scene in which Catherine Legrand contemplates the bed of Valerie Borge in the convent school's dormitory and steals a handkerchief impregnated with the latter's perfume—which, incidentally, might be "opoponax"—hiding it in her smock (*O*, 239). Gestures here speak more powerfully than words, as do odors and tastes. Not only does Catherine Legrand's look conjure up the body of the beloved (on her bed), but she also notes the handkerchief's "suave odeur mais goût trop amer,"[24] which parallel her feelings—a mixture of voluptuousness and torment. Also, the line cited above comes from Maurice Scève's *Délie*, a famous love poem. Thus, the expression of an emotional experience by means of the senses is doubled through an allusion of a literary nature. Since the line of Scève's poem occurs in Wittig's text without the use of quotes, however, it is hidden from the average reader's view and can only be detected by someone who has a thorough knowledge of Renaissance poetry and who can recognize the source of the phrase. This again reinforces the sense of secrecy that prevails in the treatment of the love relationship portrayed here.

The evolution of the love relationship is also indirectly related through descriptions of works of art (which reinforce the initial representation of the beloved by means of a link with the paintings of Raphaël). For example, Wittig's text mentions an illustration of a passage in the *Georgics* by Virgil (who will reappear, even though negated, in a later novel by Wittig, *Virgile, non*). It is a bas-relief in which the two lovers Orpheus and Eurydice appear. In the text they are described in the following manner:

> On voit Orphée tourné vers Eurydice et lui prenant
> la main, leurs têtes leurs joues rondes se ressemblent,
> leurs cous ont le même courbement pour se tourner
> l'un vers l'autre, le bras d'Orphée qui va au-devant
> la main d'Eurydice est incurvé devant un des seins.[25]
> (*O*, 251)

This description suggests that Catherine Legrand recreates the mythical couple by substituting two seemingly female lovers (or at least, an androgynous Orpheus) for the male-female lovers, Orpheus and Eurydice. It can be interpreted as an oblique reference to Valerie Borge and herself. But it is also the prefiguration of the more audacious reversal and recreation of the Orpheus myth that occurs in several of Wittig's later works, such as *Les Guérillères* and *Le Corps lesbien*.

The last sequence in *L'Opoponax* depicts the climax of the love relationship between Catherine Legrand and Valerie Borge. This is indicated in the text by the linking of their names, which states their union (*O*, 256, 269, 277, 280). The fact that these appear alternately as "Valerie Borge Catherine Legrand" or "Catherine Legrand Valerie Borge" suggests their position as equals in this relationship and not as subject and object—a subtle but efficacious way of indicating a renversement of the traditional situation, and one that is developed in much more complex fashion in *Le Corps lesbien*.

The sequence itself is entirely orchestrated by Baudelaire's "L'Invitation au voyage," a well-known love poem and thus a fitting accompaniment to the actions of the two lovers. However, this poem is here subverted or at least reoriented. While it is generally accepted as an address by a male speaker to a female love object, in this instance it is used to underscore the love of two young girls. Baudelaire's work is therefore both destroyed and recreated—in very much the way that the Orpheus and Eurydice bas-relief was treated. And while the title of the poem applies very well to the final sequence of Wittig's work, the "voyage" it announces is of a different kind, with the difference in the voyagers. In the same manner, the initial sentence of the sequence (which is also the first quatrain of Baudelaire's poem) takes on a new meaning as a result of this renversement: the words "mon enfant, ma soeur" demand another interpretation. This is true also for the dream voyage with the beloved to a utopian "là" where, as stated in the poem's refrain, all is but "ordre et beauté, luxe, calme et volupté." It is significant that this refrain of Baudelaire's poem is not used by Wittig. Several interpretations of this suggest themselves. Considering the importance of what is not said—the name of the beloved, for example—this lacuna may represent the notion that the utmost intensity is achieved by the absence of enunciation. Also, the lack of precision might allow the setting to maintain its dream-like, utopian quality to the fullest. Or the absence (or deletion) of the refrain may indicate an objection to the words "ordre" and "calme," which do not coincide with Wittig's portrayal of love.

Another interesting treatment of the Baudelairian poem is its placement in Wittig's text. The former is interspersed, and yet perfectly integrated, in the latter. This is accomplished by an innovation that has already been noted in the case of Scève's *Délie:* the lack of any marks of punctuation (such as quotation marks) to distinguish Baudelaire's text from Wittig's own. Equally striking is the phenomenon of separation and joining (which will assume great importance in Wittig's later texts). While the two texts blend, they are also distanced from each other by the fact that most readers (especially if French) will instantly recognize the Baudelairian quotes. And because the quotes are separated from each other—the various stanzas occurring many pages apart in *L'Opoponax*—their original unity is destroyed. Yet, the relationship between Valerie Borge and Catherine Legrand that the quoted passages underscore is parallel to the development of the poem and thus reconstitutes its unity, even if only indirectly.

This is perhaps most clearly seen through the placement of the portions of "L'Invitation au voyage" in this sequence of *L'Opoponax*. The first quatrain appears at the very outset of the sequence and constitutes, in the poem and in Wittig's text, the call to the beloved, an invitation to dream and love together (*O*, 254). This is followed by the second quatrain, inserted in a passage that evokes a landscape similar to that of the poem (*O*, 268). The third stanza appears during a voyage that seems, to them, like an endless journey (incidentally, the title of one of Wittig's most recent works, a play, *Le Voyage sans fin*) (*O*, 270). The final tercet of Baudelaire's poem coincides with the penultimate sentence of Wittig's text (*O*, 281), just as the first quatrain constituted the initial sentence of the sequence. Thus, the text is encircled by Baudelaire's poem, yet, as we shall see, it gives Wittig (and another poet) the last word.

The final interweaving of the two texts is certainly the most significant. Together they create an intense sense of presence by their parallel use of the present tense—a presence and a present outside of time. Both coincide in the feeling they produce—one of plenitude, harmony, and serenity. In

Wittig's text, however, a juxtaposition occurs that adds complexity to the emotions elicited. While the last tercet of Baudelaire's poem evokes a setting of peace and splendor, a dreamlike atmosphere in which the colors of purple and gold predominate and sleep descends on a world bathed in gentle light, the scene in Wittig's text is set in a cemetery during the burial of an old maid,[26] and the ambiance is one of solitude, abandon, and sterility (*O*, 277–81). This provides a powerful contrast between abstinence, lack of fulfillment, absence of love, and death, on the one hand, and the blossoming love relationship of two young beings at the peak of life, on the other.

The end of Baudelaire's poem, however, is not the end of Wittig's text. It is followed by a dramatic shift to another text (by Maurice Scève) and a different love poem (*Délie*), which contains a passionate statement about the beloved: "Tant je l'aimais qu'en elle encore je vis."[27] It is certainly significant that the words "je vis"—the last words of the verse and of Wittig's novel—are a triumphant affirmation of life, especially since they are pronounced in the presence of death. Also, in the ultimate phrase of *L'Opoponax*, verb tenses change from present to past ("aimais") to present once more ("je vis"), thus linking usually separate categories of time and affirming the power of remembrance. The impersonal *on* also gives way to the personal *je*, thus imprinting on the text the speaking subject who has emerged finally and for the first time.[28] The end can therefore be seen as a new beginning, repeating an eschatological pattern found in many other domains in Wittig's fictions. And the very fact that the voice of a male poet (Scève) is appropriated by a female speaker constitutes a consonant act of destruction and recreation.

Of all the areas where this pattern is operative in the work of Wittig, none is more fascinating than that of language. Its annihilation and renewal is her central concern and her most revolutionary enterprise. This "work with words, on words" (*T*, 48) preoccupies her from the very outset of her literary career and is already quite evident in *L'Opoponax*. As previously mentioned, this novel destroys certain expectations and conventions by its sole use of "un matériau objectif pur" and its choice of a single tool, "le langage objectif pur."[29]

While this observation is quite true and constitutes a striking innovation, it has also been shown that—at times—this "purely objective language" gives way to forms of expression that are intensely lyrical (such as the previously quoted passage depicting Valerie Borge. Perhaps this use of "purely objective language" in the majority of the book and this sudden eruption of lyrical passages heighten the effect of the objective language itself and draw attention to its singularity.

At any rate, Wittig's striking treatment of language has attracted the attention of critics and has distinguished *L'Opoponax* as standing apart from, or being opposed to, most novels of its kind. Some have compared her technique to that of the "new novelists" and have even accused her of avoiding the expression of emotions in comparable fashion.[30] Neither of these statements seems valid however. It might be better to compare Wittig's approach to that of the poet Francis Ponge (especially the latter's *Le Parti pris des choses*) in its close and intense scrutiny of ordinary objects or everyday occurrences. However, Wittig's aims distinguish her work from that of any of these writers and her treatment of language is highly individual—in fact, hers alone. It is actually an attempt to create a new language. This, according to her beliefs, necessitates disintegration of certain habits, dismantlement of established patterns, and experimentation with new forms and approaches.

One main area of her experimentation seen in *L'Opoponax* deals with pronouns. It begins with the very first word of the novel, *on*. Besides its other characteristics, this pronoun has no gender or number. It thus instantly breaks down habitual limits or categories. Even more important, as Wittig states, "*on* has been the key for me to the undisturbed use of language, as it is in childhood when words are magic, when words are set bright and colorful in the kaleidoscope of the world, with its many revolutions in the consciousness as one shakes them."[31] Also, since *on* most frequently appears in the phrase "on dit," other familiar distinctions are eliminated, such as what "is said" from what "is told"—that is, enunciation from narration, the spoken from the written. In a seemingly purposeful ambiguous fashion, Wittig uses a formula in writing that also refers to the oral quality of the text. The latter serves to emphasize the power of the word wielded by those who are in possession of it. This notion is further developed in Wittig's later works, such as *Les Guérillères* and *Le Corps lesbien*. In the case of *L'Opoponax*, this power seems to manifest itself mainly in the appropriation of language (either by the children or by the author herself) and in the opposition to existing language (either that of adults or that of the literary establishment). Such conscious attack on and alteration of language shows that, from the very start, "word work" is the central concern of a writer, especially this writer.

Another of the various ways language can be altered (broken down and/or recreated) is by means of neologisms. An important device frequently used and highly developed in Wittig's later fictions, the use of neologisms is already present in *L'Opoponax* in an embryonic state. The prime example is, of course, the word *opoponax* itself. Not a true neologism that exists as such, it does not, however, correspond to its dictionary meaning. Thus it immediately pits itself against an establishment or existing authority. It is also the fulfillment of what Wittig describes as a necessary step to be effected by the writer on the language in his/her work—that is, to "despoil [the word] of its everyday meaning" (*T*, 48). Besides, the opoponax is an invention of Catherine Legrand, as well as a personal symbol that explains all that the dictionaries do not explain about the world that she, herself, is experiencing.[32] By being dissociated from its usual or accepted meanings and by having a new meaning invented (or created) for it, the word approaches the state of neologism—without, however, an actual change in the word itself. It does, nevertheless, foreshadow what Wittig does in later texts.

The same is true for her treatment of proper names. While in later works these are subject to true renversement (resulting, for instance, in "Ulyssea" or "Ganymédéa"), here they remain intact and are only unusual in the manner in which they are used: in long lists devoid of commas, which create a rhythmic flow or which form a chain combining first and last names in unexpected fashion; joined to form a unit (as in "Catherine Legrand Valerie Borge"): despoiled of everyday, social meanings indicative of civil identity; in the creation of an incantatory effect; and not pronounced, but particularly powerful as a result of this silence or absence of enunciation.

The last of these, what is not said (or written), is an extremely important part of Wittig's work with language. *L'O-poponax* does not, as some critics have stated, avoid the expression of emotions by its predominant use of objective language, but on the contrary, emotions are rendered more intense because they are not directly inscribed in the text (except in very rare instances). Thus, for example, the numerous deaths that occur in the novel are treated—in terms of language—in purely objective fashion. This however in no way indicates emotional flatness or indifference. As a matter of fact, the feeling content is heightened by means of this technique because the opposition of language and emotion contrasts with what is expected (or traditional) and because (as has been shown before) what remains unspoken is of the greatest import and produces the most impact. Other examples of the same kind—in case death might be considered something so far removed from children as not to be moving to them—include incidents of brutality by adults, which are also treated with objective language, but which obviously have strong emotional content (for instance, *O*, 223).

Other interesting examples of Wittig's work with language can be found in her use of verbs. In *L'Opoponax*, as has been seen, these are all in the present tense (except for one instance in the very last phrase). And whereas in a later work, *Le Corps lesbien*, she experiments with intransitive verbs and the passive voice, here the verbs are predominantly transitive and used in the active voice. This is a fitting choice since these verb forms aptly render the atemporal quality of childhood and the active nature of a child's life. Once again, while the innovations in this domain become increasingly complex in Wittig's later fictions, they are already noticeable in this, her first novel.

This is equally true for the vocabulary found in *L'Opoponax*. While the work refuses the language of adults (since its predominant lexicon avoids abstract terminology and consists of words that express the direct, concrete experiences of children), it does not yet declare war on the words/worlds of the

opponent as does, for example, *Les Guérillères*. As a matter of
fact, the pronouncements of the adults are incorporated into
the text on a number of occasions. However, because Wittig
(perhaps affected by the work of Nathalie Sarraute) has eliminated the use of quotation marks or any other markers that
differentiate what is said from what is told or that indicate a
change in speaker (such as the dash in French), even the
pronouncements of the adults can be considered to be filtered
through the language of the children, and thus appropriated
by the children. But of course, appropriation is not yet annihilation. This does not occur until the next stage of Wittig's
experimental expedition.

Already quite developed in *L'Opoponax*, however, is her
use of various registers of language or even several languages.
This is done mainly by the inclusion and interweaving of other
texts (poetic, historical, ecclesiastical, and so on) within the
primary text of the work. Their presence seems quite natural
given the convent school's curriculum. And since Latin is also
an important part of the study and religious practices there,
the appearance of Latin phrases in the text is not surprising.
It is striking, however, that these other texts and this language
(different from the predominating one in *L'Opoponax*) appear
in the primary text without any markers to distinguish them—
either punctuation marks, typography, or any other device
that signals a difference (for examples, see *O*, 188–90, 216–17).
The placement and frequency of these other texts, moreover,
is a subtle and skillful indication of the evolution of the protagonists, for these texts occur with much greater frequency in
the latter portion of *L'Opoponax*, when the children have ad-
vanced in school and are exposed to, or aware of, many more
written or recited texts. In that sense these other texts are also
filtered through the children and to some extent appropriated
by them. But the most extensive example (as we have seen)
occurs in the last sequence of the novel, where one of Baudelaire's poems and a line from Scève's *Délie* furnish a musical
accompaniment to Wittig's text and/or are so inextricably
linked with her text that they seem totally incorporated into
it—that is, part of its very body.

A more minute examination of Wittig's "work with
words" reveals that her particular lexicon is already partially

present in *L'Opoponax*. First of all, her vocabulary is concrete and sensual—as is fitting in a recreation of childhood, where sense experiences play such an important role. It is filled with terms that relate to life in the countryside and to close contact with nature as well as with those that designate various activities at school, thus constituting a vocabulary that echoes the principal domains of the child's life. There is nothing unusual or shocking in this lexicon (though there is in Wittig's later works). It only reveals certain predilections that reappear in many of her fictions: the use of concrete terminology, which arises from the experiences of the various senses and visceral in character; frequent mention of flowers and plants as well as other references to nature; and a penchant for certain colors (especially violet or purple). The fact that all these are not limited to *L'Opoponax* shows that her lexicon is not simply an appropriate choice considering the subject matter of the novel, but an enduring selection that will only deepen and grow as her work progresses.

Probably the only unusual part of the vocabulary in *L'Opoponax* relates to war and to the hunt. Among the children there are a number of play battles, filled with fitting terminology, which not only occur among boys (as would be expected) but involve girls as well. As a matter of fact, many of the latter could be considered future "guérillères." Even more untraditional is all that concerns the hunt, an activity usually reserved for adults. Introduced by the mention of Artemis, the Greek divinity whose province it is known to be (a divinity who reappears prominently in later works by Wittig), the hunt is secularized in those discussions between Valerie Borge and Catherine Legrand that center on the rifle the former has received from her father and has learned to use with great skill (*O*, 266). And a gift of three bullets constitutes a token of affection—a rather surprising detail considering that the donor and the recipient are two young girls (*O*, 267). Battle scenes, female warriors and hunters, as well as a related lexicon (including neologisms) assume great importance, of course, in *Les Guérillères*, but all these are already present here, although in lesser form and magnitude.

While Wittig's experimentation is fundamental for the creation of her "war machine" or of an avant-garde literary work, there is still one more domain of importance to be considered, which she herself has defined as one of "the most strategic" tasks of the writer: universalization.[33] This has already been alluded to in connection with her use of multiple protagonists and the indefinite pronoun, and with her portrayal of the love relationship in *L'Opoponax*. It is apparent however in other areas as well. For example, since various scenes are not located in any particular place (but only in the country, in a school, or in a house), they could take place anywhere or everywhere. Place names are not given except in two instances: *Fougerolles*, where one of the teachers will be buried (*O*, 278), and *Rivajou*, the destination of an excursion (*O*, 269, 270). Both of these, by their evocation of plants, a river, and joyful games,[34] seem to have a very different purpose than traditional place names and are obviously invented for their evocative charge. Moreover, for the overwhelming majority of the scenes in the novel, no precise description of the setting is provided, which seems to be the first prerequisite for any attempt at universalization.

The same is true for the treatment of time. Not only does everything seem to take place in the present, but this present is not even located in any particular period. True, there are certain indications that we are in the twentieth century (for there are trains, automobiles, rifles, and so on) but nothing more precise is given. Moreover, by including texts from the Renaissance and antiquity, as well as Latin phrases (spanning a long period of time), a temporal continuum is established that defies or eliminates chronological measurement or categories. This technique is further developed, and in even more striking ways, beginning with *Les Guérillères*, but it is already noteworthy here. It too provides a base for universalization.

The most difficult feat in this domain is to present the love relationship between Catherine Legrand and Valerie Borge in a manner that exceeds the limits of a personal or particular point of view, and to accomplish this despite the fact that the overwhelming majority of the protagonists of *L'Opoponax* are girls and that the desires depicted are not heterosexual. Universalization does occur, however, first because an attraction between members of the same sex is a rather common experience in adolescence, and second because what is described is not only the awakening of love between two specific individuals but of young love itself. An examination of the various stages in the growing relationship between Catherine Legrand and Valerie Borge (even by substituting a boy's name for one of the girls' names) shows how general these experiences are. And perhaps the use of texts from the love poems by Baudelaire and Scève serves also to expand this view of love by adding a heterosexual dimension, thus making it more universal.

It is important to establish Wittig's attempt at universalization in this particular domain and its function in *L'Opoponax*, for it will become increasingly difficult to do so in discussions of her later novels (in *Les Guérillères* and, especially, in *Le Corps lesbien*) since other considerations tend to obscure it. Nevertheless, only by understanding that this very aim and its realization turns a literary work into a "war machine" or an avant-garde creation, as Wittig has affirmed in "The Trojan Horse," is it possible to honor her intentions or hope to arrive at an interpretation of her fiction that avoids a central misunderstanding.[35]

The final and most fundamental aspect of universalization can be discerned in the pattern underlying all of Wittig's work; that of destruction and creation. This is indeed a universal phenomenon that exceeds the concerns of literature. It is evident in the sea's ebb and flow, in catabolism and anabolism, and in death and birth—that is, in the life cycle that pervades all that exists from the gnat to the galaxies. This pattern then is far greater than something that applies to writing alone, although writing is, of course, Wittig's central concern. It implies the recognition of a universal law and is thus the farthest removed from a limited, personal point of view. This is perhaps what is meant by her remark that "one must be humble" (*T*, 49), for indeed, humility results from measuring individual concerns against the vastness of the universe. Any one single experience, no matter how singular, is "not enough" for the creation of a vision of such magnitude (*T*, 49).

This vision, though, may be expressed in simplest terms. This is the case at the end of *L'Opoponax*. There, the life cycle is depicted in its most concentrated form and with the greatest economy of means. The scene is set in a cemetery, at the

moment when a coffin is lowered into the earth. Death, however, is paralleled or balanced by life, for the life forces surge
in the two young lovers. Even more important than this,
however, is the emergence of the speaking subject that occurs
at this instant. It is a birth, linked to a claim to the birthright
of creation (or a creation—the text before us). And it is surely
significant too that the last words of *L'Opoponax*, spoken by a
voice that merges with that of a poet long dead and that speaks
for the first time in its own right, are "Je vis" ("I live").

In looking back at all that Wittig has accomplished in her
first novel, it is evident that the work already contains (either
in embryonic or in quite developed form) most of the innovations that establish her as an avant-garde writer. In that sense,
L'Opoponax could be compared to the cornerstone upon which
her entire literary edifice rests. A better image, though, considering her own predilections and the quasi-organic growth of
her fictions, might be that of a seed that continues to mature
into many more fully developed fictions, with shapes and
capacities only dimly visible, although already present, at this
early stage.

The first of these fictions, five years in unfolding, is the
fulfillment of that seed's promise: *Les Guérillères*.

2

From O to O

*A*s childhood ripens into womanhood, so does *L'Opopo-nax* evolve into *Les Guérillères*, a more fully developed fictional creation. The roots of the latter can certainly be traced to the former, and in that sense there is continuity in Wittig's work. Yet perhaps even more striking is a notably strong penchant for overthrow. This affects even the forms that Wittig herself has chosen to use (such as the novel of childhood in *L'Opopo-nax*)—forms which, once explored, are abandoned.[1] Even before her pronouncement in "The Trojan Horse" that a writer must choose one of two paths (either to repeat existing forms or to create new ones), she herself makes this choice in regard to her own past forms, no matter how avant-garde these were. Since she obviously favors the second of these choices, she refuses to repeat anything she has done and moves on to fresh explorations and new forms. As a result, both unity and schism characterize the body of her work, and there is continuity in her insistence on the discontinuous.

This is immediately visible in the genre chosen for her second work of fiction. *Les Guérillères* is an epic, which consti-tutes renversement on two counts: the genre is clearly differ-ent from that which Wittig has previously used, and its use by Wittig overthrows the traditional notion (reiterated in stud-ies of women writers even today)[2] that the epic is the exclusive property of males as authors, protagonists, and readers, and that women are excluded from the genre on all these counts. Wittig's choice is thus doubly audacious. She has relinquished a form that proved highly successful (the one used in *L'Opopo-nax*), and she has decided to write an epic in which heroes are replaced by heroines and a male public by a female one. As a result, *Les Guérillères* is an even more violent "exécution capitale" than Duras judged *L'Opoponax* to be. And while the new work is not totally different in orientation—that is, in its desire to destroy an established order—it is certainly more daring. *Les Guérillères* is literally a declaration of war. It occupies, pillages, and vanquishes a territory hitherto considered to be taboo, or at least to have unassailable boundaries.

Oversimplifications can result from such a view however. *Les Guérillères* is too easily and too often classified solely as an "epic of sex warfare" or as a "battle of the sexes fought in Women's Liberation terms."[3] Statements such as these are reductive. They minimize the scope of Wittig's undertaking and ignore her complexity as a writer. The work goes far beyond feminist propaganda or a sensationalist bid for militant action. Indeed, such aims are disclaimed in "The Trojan Horse," where committed literature and *écriture féminine* are defined as contradictions in terms. Even more significant, upon closer examination *Les Guérillères* proves that it is so intricately and artfully constructed, and so multidimensional, as to belie any simple (or simplistic) explanation.

This is already evident in its title. While it is possible to interpret *guérillères* superficially as a term that merely indicates or accentuates women's bellicose role—that is, as a cross between *guerrières* or female warriors and the feminine plural of *guerilla*—thus reducing the subject of the book to a war between the sexes, on other levels of interpretation this title has far more complex meanings. The word itself can be compared to a "war machine" that destroys an existing order or a traditional view: that of women as passive, submissive, peaceful beings. In this, it is reminiscent of, and comparable to, the refusal of the dictionary meaning of *opoponax* in *L'Opoponax*. *Guérillères*, however, goes further than *opoponax*, for it is a true neologism. This makes it the perfect vehicle for achieving a number of Wittig's central aims. Its use destroys old forms (and words) that have become worn, petrified, or "incapable of transformation" (*T*, 45) and gives us a new-born term that "[creates] the same effect, the same shock, as if [it] were being read for the first time" (*T*, 48). The word can also be seen as a symbol for the reinvention or recreation of a new word/

world, thus providing a key to the fundamental subject of the work that bears it in its title. Moreover, the coining of a new word affirms the power of naming—and of the namer. And finally, *guérillères* is a poetic word in that it does not designate any existing thing. It thus proves that, as Mallarmé has said, "la fleur poétique est absente de tous les bouquets," which here could be rephrased as "la guérillère est absente de toutes les guerres."[4]

Just as the title of Wittig's second novel goes further than that of her first, so is the general format of *Les Guérillères*, even at first glance, more striking than that of *L'Opoponax*. The work is tri-partite in structure, with each of its three parts introduced by a large **O**. The central portion of the text (consisting of numerous short prose passages) is encircled by a poem in capitals and is interrupted every six pages (except at the end of the three main parts) by long lists of women's names in larger capitals. All of this results in an arresting appearance that instantly causes the discerning reader to register more than surprise and to wonder what the purpose of such innovations in format might be. Ruling out the possibility that these features are either mere decoration or a series of clever but contrived experiments that have no other value except novelty, the almost immediate conclusion is that the typographical variations, the numerical patterns and geometric shapes, and the rhythms and breaks in rhythm are part of a network whose patterns are closely allied and highly pertinent to the book's subject. Indeed they are all an integral part of the novel's meaning, as might be expected given Wittig's artistry in *L'Opoponax*, where nothing was gratuitous and where each innovation was essential to the work's interpretation.

Also from the very outset, *Les Guérillères* signals its innovative character by beginning with a poem. This poem, however, is not complete. It does not reach a conclusion until over two hundred pages later. As a result, it frames the central text—although again incompletely, for the end of the poem does not constitute the end of the book (just as Baudelaire's poem, "L'Invitation au voyage," did not coincide with the end of *L'Opoponax*). Moreover, the poem's meaning does not become clear until the entire work is read, although part of that meaning can be grasped in a narrative passage in the latter part of the text (*G*, 164). By means such as these, Wittig invites, indeed forces, active participation on the part of the reader, whom she entices, disconcerts, and directly involves in the work. In this, she joins various contemporary writers who have chosen to overthrow traditional notions of the author-reader relationship (for example, Gide, Céline, Sarraute, and Robbe-Grillet), but the manner in which she accomplishes this overthrow is strictly her own.

The use of a poem to provide entry into the work is significant on other counts also. It suggests a poetic emphasis and interpretation, which is (once again) in accordance with Wittig's aims as stated in "The Trojan Horse." It also underlines the epic nature of *Les Guérillères*, since it echoes famous works in this genre that begin with a poetic invocation. In the case of Wittig's work, however, the echoing of this convention does not indicate acceptance or submission to the rules of the genre. Indeed it flaunts its appropriation by an author who would traditionally be excluded from its use. It thus signals subversion and overthrow, the occupation of a forbidden territory. Indeed, even a rapid glance at the initial portion of the poem reveals a series of key words associated with such notions—"RÉVOLUTIONS," "MORTES," and "CRIS" as well as the all-important phrase, "TOUT GESTE EST RENVERSEMENT" (*G*, 7). The latter is repeated at the end of the poem in only slightly altered form—"SANS RELÂCHE / GESTE RENVERSEMENT" (*G*, 205). The combination of these words and phrases already suggests that the work deals with violent action and is a "war machine" (as *L'Opoponax* was before it, yet probably in more pronounced fashion or at least more overtly so than the earlier novel). From other key words in the initial portion of the poem—"PHÉNIX," "LACUNES," "VOIX CHANTANTES"—it is also possible to infer that *Les Guérillères* deals with renewal after destruction, or that death and rebirth follow a cyclical pattern, that language and the various stages it must undergo are a central part of the eschatological action, and finally that renversement is the most fundamental concern of the work—as signaled by the repetition of the phrase "GESTE RENVERSEMENT" and its placement at the conclusion of the poem.

Indeed, so intense is Wittig's desire for reversal that she

subjects even her own past innovations concerning language to such treatment, either by abandoning them entirely or by introducing considerable alterations. Thus, despite the fact that *L'Opoponax* was judged outstanding by Duras for its use of "purely objective language,"[5] this highly successful technique is largely discarded in *Les Guérillères*. It gives way to poetic prose, strongly emotional language, sumptuous imagery, and lyrical passages. And while *L'Opoponax* could be described as neutral in tone, *Les Guérillères* is striking in the multiplicity of its tones. These vary from the derisive to the euphoric, from the analytic to the empassioned, and from the comic to the tragic. On the one hand, this can be seen as an expansion of the elements already apparent in the former work, and as an indication of continuity and growth. On the other hand, it suggests a penchant for new exploration at the expense of past discoveries, no matter how well they have been received (or perhaps even precisely because they were well received and thus risk being no longer efficacious as innovations).

One of the constants of Wittig's art, however, is that some of her most audacious ends are accomplished by what appear to be simple means. Thus, for example, the multiple protagonists of *Les Guérillères* are female. While multiple protagonists in an epic do not constitute a striking renversement of this genre's conventions, the fact that they are not male is indeed revolutionary. Moreover, these protagonists are designated by the pronoun *elles*, which is as difficult to translate as was the *on* of *L'Opoponax*. *Elles* is the plural of *she* and is a radical departure from the neuter, neutral *on* since *elles* is defined and might be considered feminized. It is not Wittig's intent however that *elles* be translated as "the women," as it is in the published English translation. Instead, she wishes to destroy the categories of sex in language and also to undermine a convention where the masculine pronoun *ils* (and never the feminine *elles*) is the bearer of universal point of view. The use of *elles* thus constitutes both an assault and an innovation.[6] And while in *L'Opoponax* the world of children predominates, in *Les Guérillères* the major part of the text is inhabited by "elles," and only in a few instances in its latter portion do "ils" appear. This, of course, is not only a striking change in the use of pronouns, but it suggests a renversement of a situation that exists in most societies where both children and women are in positions characterized by submission rather than domination. At least in the context of *Les Guérillères* they occupy a place that is diametrically opposed to that assigned to them in most parts of the world.

Elles[7] (already present as an anagram in part of the title—*Les Guéri/llè/r/es*) is used as extensively in this work as was *on* in *L'Opoponax*. It only gives way to the first person plural pronoun *nous*, in the last sequence (*G*, 207–08), very much the way *on* changed to *je* in the final phrase of the earlier novel. Frequently also, it appears in the phrase "elles disent," seemingly an expansion of the "on dit" that pervades *L'Opoponax*. However, in "elles disent" the impersonal quality of "on dit" is gone. It can no longer be interpreted as meaning "it is said" or "it is told." The phrase has become more assertive in nature and indicates a pronouncement made by a speaking subject—or rather, subjects. In other words, it denotes taking possession of an act of speech. This is in itself an important victory. Indeed, the central victory (it will be seen) that is won in *Les Guérillères*.

Elles is also clarified and rendered more powerful by the long list of names in large capitals (much longer than the groups of names in *L'Opoponax*), that winds its way through *Les Guérillères*, binds and breaks the central narrative, and creates both continuity and discontinuity. It contains hundreds of elements, all of them female, and consists of first names only (not first and last names as in *L'Opoponax*). This choice could be interpreted in a number of ways: as a sign of intimacy, as a way of indicating that the fame of those named makes only the mention of their forenames necessary, or as a refusal of the patronym (and thus, of a male-determined lineage). Wittig herself makes an arresting statement concerning this choice of forenames: "CE QUI LES DÉSIGNE COMME / L'OEIL DES CYCLOPES / LEUR UNIQUE PRÉNOM" (*G*, 15).[8] She thus establishes a comparison between the names and the distinguishing feature of the cyclops—their single eye. Many interpretations of this comparison suggest themselves: The attributes of the Cyclops, mythological creatures of gigantic proportions, confer grandeur upon those with whom they are compared. The Cyclops are known for their ferocity (especially as portrayed in another epic, *The Odyssey*) and thus add to the aura of violence that pervades much of *Les Guérillères* and reverse the traditional view of women as peaceful beings. The association of the male Cyclops with the female figures enumerated, and the simile employed, suggests a gender confusion, fusion, reversal, or elimination. Since the Cyclops's single eye (*oeil*, in French, thus calling attention to the letter *O*, as well as to the oval shape of the eye), their distinguishing feature, is sufficient for identification, so is—the author seems to say—the sole forename of the women. And finally, the emphasis on the eye, the organ for perception and apprehension of the world, emphasizes the notion of women as active beings and, moreover, suggests a link with the Eye Goddess, a renowned female divinity.

Upon looking more closely at the actual list of women's names in *Les Guérillères*, it becomes evident that the names come from every part of the globe and from all periods of time. In this they are an expansion of the names that appeared in *L'Opoponax*, which were all French and appeared to be contemporary. As the following examples show, their diversity is so great that it suggests universalization:

FLORE ZITA SAVÉ CORNÉLIE
DRAUPADI JULIENNE ETMEL
CHLOÉ DESDÉMONE RAPHAÈLE
IRIS VÉRA ARSINOÉ LISE
BRANDA ORPHISE HÉRODIADE
BÉRÉNICE SIGRID ANDOVÈRE.
(*G*, 21)

AUBIERGE CLARISSE PHÈDRE
EUDOXIE OLIVE IO MODESTE
PLAISANCE HYGIE LOUISE
CORALIE ANÉMONE TABITHA
THELMA INGRID PRASCOVIE
NATHALIE POMPÉIA ALIÈNOR.
(*G*, 51)

Aside from universalization, Wittig achieves a sense of timelessness in this list by the use of many names adopted from literary, historical, legendary, or mythological figures, and by the linking of various time categories. Spatial distinctions are also eliminated, thus creating either a blurring of contours, a loss of traditional boundaries, an overthrow of familiar categories, or a continuum in which all barriers are broken down.

Besides suggesting all these important notions, the list of names provides an incantatory effect. Already notable in *L'Opoponax*, this effect has increased in depth and breadth in *Les Guérillères*. The incantation that appears here could be variously interpreted as a song, a litany, a dirge, a hymn, an invocation, a battle cry, a ritual recitation, a magical formula, and so on. Indeed, it serves all these functions in the work. Moreover, the list's incantatory quality produces the feeling of an oral delivery—almost as though it were recited by a bard. It thus creates a *mise en abyme*—an epic within an epic. And yet, since the listed names are inscriptions (in the literal sense, inscribed), they are reminiscent of vast funerary steles or commemorative tablets that, as written word, affirmed the victory over death and annihilation as well as the power of the scribe who wrote them.

Besides, accentuating the act of naming through this striking accumulation of names achieves an effective counterbalance for the lack of naming that results from extensive use of the pronoun *elles*. *Elles* suggests a collectivity that is quasi-universal (or at least, representative of one half of the world's population), yet it remains impersonal. The names (although also universalized by their scope) give a powerful identity to this collectivity. Perhaps the most important aspect, though, is the naming itself, which is universally paramount to the act of creation.

Thus, three fundamental motifs that pervade all of the work are suggested by the list of names—motifs which are all centered primarily on language and most particularly on writing as a means of destruction and recreation. It does not suffice, however, to see this list only as a unified whole. It is necessary to examine its individual components, and especially those that occur at the beginning and the end of the list, for further clarification. The list starts with the name "OSÉE." It is thus instantly linked with the leitmotif of the work because of the name's initial letter, which plays an important role in *L'Opoponax* and acquires even greater significance in *Les Guérillères,* and because of the name's meanings—that is, "she who dares," and also the Old Testament prophet "Osée" (Osea, in English). Since in French this word has an ambiguous ending that could be that of a woman's name, this prophet is turned into a prophetess—a suggestion reinforced by the appearance of the word in a list of women's names. The penultimate name, on the other hand, (repeated twice and thus emphasized), is "ANTIGONE," the Greek heroine famed for her daring revolt against the religious and political establishment. Together these two names constitute an overthrow so audacious as to amount to heresy: the renversement of the alpha-omega sequence and, by extension, of the one and only Almighty (male) God. At the same time, "OSÉE" and "ANTIGONE" affirm a sense of unity in the list of names by underlining the fact that the list contains the names of all those "elles" who have dared, dare, and will dare. Among them—although not named—the author, MONIQUE, might well take her place.

Another apparently simple device that accomplishes a complex end is Wittig's use of present tense verbs throughout *Les Guérillères*—which only gives way to the imperfect in the last prose sequence, just as it did in the final sentence of *L'Opoponax.* But in this work the present tense is more striking and indicates notions that are more involved. While in the earlier novel it created a sense of presence and of a temporal flow that encompasses the evolution from childhood to adolescence, in *Les Guérillères* there is not even the suggestion of chronological progression. Here, past, present, and future are presented in anachronic fashion, and leaps in time (both forward and backward) occur constantly. The use of the present tense in all of these sequences, although it has been interpreted by some critics as creating a "utopian" ambiance,[9] might more fittingly be described as yet another illustration of Wittig's penchant for the overthrow of existing rules and established categories—such as chronological distinctions or the use of verb tenses as temporal indicators. It might also be considered as a means of accentuating a sense of presence or active participation on the part of the reader. But the use of the present tense for all sequences also accomplishes something further. It gives unity to a text that is fragmented (both visually, by the disposition of the numerous short sequences, and temporally, by the leaps in time). It thus contributes to the continuity-discontinuity motif that pervades *Les Guérillères,* and it relates to the book's fundamental subject—the struggle against fragmentation for unity.

A similar concern seems to motivate Wittig's treatment of space. At first this might seem paradoxical, since settings in *L'Opoponax* were simple and realistic (the school and the countryside, for example) while those in *Les Guérillères* are extremely varied and include ancient and futuristic, rural and urban, industrial and legendary, and even totally imaginary sites. Also, in the first novel spatial distinctions were blurred or obliterated by a lack of separation between settings, while in the second they are visibly separated (by spaces in the text), and the changes from one to the other are extremely abrupt: scenes shift from mud huts to space habitations, from factories to sacred monuments, from the seashore to mountain tops, from a battlefield to a flowering orchard, from a child's garden to the outer reaches of the solar system, and so on. This fragmentation or discontinuity, however, is effectively counteracted (or at least modified) by the constant presence of what could be called a "tide of women," which corresponds to a more mature version of the "tide of little girls" encountered in *L'Opoponax,* and which sweeps through all these varying settings. Spatial differentiation or fragmentation thus becomes multiplicity, or even universality, and paradoxically unifies rather than divides.

It has become evident that what is quite complex in *Les Guérillères* appears simple on the surface. And yet the work has too often been treated in oversimplified fashion. Nowhere is this more evident than in statements concerning its subject. Part of this erroneous treatment is probably due to the time of its publication and to the subsequent exploitation of sensationalist opportunities by publishers.[10] But even discerning critics are sometimes misled and make judgments such as calling *Les Guérillères* "une nouvelle *Histoire d'O*"[11]—and this, despite the well-known fact that this famous pornographic novel depicts women in a totally submissive and exclusively masochistic role. It is far more fitting, as a matter of fact, to speak of *Les Guérillères* as an anti-*Histoire d'O* (notwithstanding the frequent use of the letter, sound, and symbol *O*) since it overthrows all the elements of this "classic" of pornography. Wittig might even have had this aim in mind, considering the many serious (and humorous) attacks upon traditional genres and classics of literature at which she excels.

In actuality, *Les Guérillères* goes beyond most, if not all, definitions of its subject matter. Its multiplicity of levels and its extremely large scope preclude any reductive interpretations. The most obvious proof of this is that, to begin with, no aspect of human experience has been omitted here. In broadest terms, the work encompasses tragedy and comedy, war and peace, nature and artifice, dream and reality, the temporal and the eternal, the finite and the infinite, destruction and creation. It contains fairy tales and great myths, dirges and songs of joy, curses and eulogies, verbal proliferation and silence. It links the rotation of a child's hoop to that of the spinning suns, the gyrations of a top to the motion of the spheres, the nucleus of the atom to the outer reaches of the universe.

And yet such vast scope does not preclude unity. Once again, it is by seemingly ingenuous (yet actually quite intricate) means that Wittig unifies all the varied aspects of her work. She does this by means of symbols in *Les Guérillères*. Symbols (which here make their first appearance) coincide admirably with her major aims and fundamental notions, for it is in their nature to shatter existing structures or to bring about "une rupture de plan, une discontinuité, un passage à un autre ordre."[12] This makes them the perfect vehicles for overthrowing established forms and for effecting a metamorphosis that leads to another state of being. In the sense that "le symbole est vraiment novateur [et] appelle une transformation en profondeur,"[13] it is the ally of innovation and transformation, both of which are paramount in Wittig's literary enterprise. Moreover, symbols have the particular ability to separate and unite, to combine contradictory elements, to bring the most diverse provinces of life into contact with one another, and to allow one to see the unity in multiplicity.[14] It is evident that these notions are also in complete accord with Wittig's major concerns. Last but not least, symbols are a "language universel"[15] and thus lend themselves admirably to the central pre-occupations of Wittig: language and universalization.

The specific symbol that is immediately visible in *Les Guér-illères* is the **O**. Its very size (for it takes up half a page) instantly indicates its importance. The fact that it appears three times in the work (*G*, 8, 71, 138) and creates a tri-partite structure is also quite striking. Its meaning is at first unclear. This induces the reader to wonder, to question, to search, to enter actively into the text—all of which are obviously some of Wittig's aims. For those who know *L'Opoponax*, the symbol is not entirely new. The **O** seems an expanded version of the O that appeared in the earlier novel. However it is not until *Les Guérillères* that the O assumes its full dimensions by becoming a **O**. This suggests a development, a growth that has occurred from the earlier novel to the present one. Yet, the O has not entirely disappeared here. It has joined a larger group of symbols and acquired a wider range of meanings. The group in which it is now found is, in itself, quite complex:. It includes the O, the zero, the circle, the sphere, and the spiral. All these symbols have ancient meanings yet are as vital as ever today. And because they are constants of the human imagination, they are universal in scope. Seen separately, each one is already rich in meaning. Together, they form a network that is astounding in its complexity and unity.

Concerning these symbols there is much that needs explo-ration, especially since Wittig has both adhered to and sub-verted their meaning in every instance. And because these symbols are each rich in their own meaning, they should be considered one by one, beginning with the O. Of course, the significance this letter has in *L'Opoponax* (signaled by its three-fold repetition in the title and the importance of *l'opoponax* in the text itself) carries over, to a certain extent, into *Les Guéril-lères*. The letter *O*, moreover, is one of the most widely used symbols in alchemy (whose fundamental aim is transforma-tion) in which it has a great variety of meanings, many of which are inversions or reversals of the same sign, such as night and day, or sublimation and purification.[16] This certainly parallels some of Wittig's fundamental notions. Yet her inter-pretation, as it initially appears in the novel, is highly original and lends itself to lengthy consideration. It appears in an early sequence of *Les Guérillères*. There, the O is a sound produced by the song of a siren, "un O continu" (*G*, 16). Since the siren is a mythological being endowed with powers of destruction and creation (a song that lures and kills), the sound O is linked to Wittig's particular view of art and to the central thematics of *Les Guérillères*. Furthermore, since sirens live in the sea, the O here suggests its homonym *eau* (water), another important element in Wittig's fictions and a major, universal symbol in its own right. But the same passage goes on to state that the song itself "évoque pour elles, comme tout ce qui rappelle le O, le zéro ou le cercle, l'anneau vulvaire" (*G*, 16).[17] As a result, the O, the zero, the circle, and the vulval ring are linked as symbols, and the range of their meanings is extended. Also, as will be shown, the meanings of the symbols arise from the definitions (or redefinitions) that the "elles" choose to give them. This emphasizes the power to recreate even symbols that have transhistoric and transcultural interpretations.

Even in the case of the most concrete meaning given— that of O as evoking the vulval ring or female sexual orifice— an interesting redefinition has taken place. In contrast to age-old and quasi-universal symbolic representations of the female as that which contains (a vase, a vessel, an urn, and so on)[18] and of the opening of that container as the birth canal, Wittig chooses to subvert these symbols and to emphasize the vulva over the womb—the site of pleasure over that of reproduction. This is, in itself, a radical overthrow of the ancient and wide-spread view of woman as primarily, and often exclusively, a means of procreation and as having no value except for this function. It is also the transgression of a taboo that prohibits women from feeling and/or acknowledging sexual pleasure, especially if such pleasure is unrelated to reproduction. More-over, Wittig also associates the O with another orifice, the mouth (in what could be considered an upward displace-ment—a lusory reference to one of Freud's theories). It is not only suggested by these means that the O is an organ of pleasure, but also that it is the organ that utters song or produces words. In that connection, one critic has compared the shape of the O to that of "une bouche qui parle et qui jette sur le papier les mots vivants qu'elle donne à entendre."[19] Thus, the singing, speaking orifice assumes an active role (comparable to that of a writer, especially this writer) that is equal to the sexual one. And the O affirms powers that are usually denied women in both domains.

The second symbol included in this initial group, the zero, has even more complex meanings. Though its association with the vulval ring reinforces the importance of this orifice, the symbol simultaneously recalls the opposite (traditional) notion of its lack of importance—or its zero value. Evidently however, the latter is attacked and, indeed, nullified. Many of the ancient and universal meanings of the zero coincide admirably with Wittig's central concerns in *Les Guérillères*, which suggests that she is fully aware of these meanings. In kabalistic doctrine, for example, the zero stands for "infinity . . . boundless being, the *fons et origo* of all things . . . the solar system in its entirety; hence universality . . . [also] the universal paradox, the infinitely great and the infinitely small, the circle of infinity and the point at the center of the atom."[20] These meanings link the symbol perfectly to several of the important notions referred to earlier. Its relevance will become even more apparent as one delves further into the work. Other interpretations show that the zero can be related to a number of key motifs that appear not only in this novel but in all of Wittig's work and that center on reversal, cyclical rebirth or recreation, and nothingness and totality that is, "l'instant du renversement. . . . la régénération cyclique . . . l'intervalle de la génération."[21]

The circle (probably the most important element in the group) is recognized as one of the four fundamental symbols—the alpha and the omega, and the sign of harmony and unity. The most perfect of all forms, without beginning or end, it is also the sign of the absolute. In Jungian terms, it is the archetypal image of the totality of the psyche frequently depicted by the mandala.[22] All these meanings coincide with significant motifs in Wittig's text, many of which will be fully developed in later sequences. However, since the circle appears as a prominent visual sign and constitutes the first impression made on the reader as he/she opens *Les Guérillères*, Wittig calls attention to it from the very start and accentuates its importance.

As the circle also serves to create a tripartite structure in the text, the question arises whether the number three has meanings associated with this symbol (as well as with the zero, related to it by Wittig). Investigation proves that this is indeed so. Three is considered the perfect number, the expression of totality, and symbolizes synthesis or union. It also refers to the phases of evolution—purgative, illuminative, and unitive. Moreover, the numbers three and six (Wittig's text is also structured by the lists of women's names that occur at intervals of six pages) are considered the figures of a dynamic process enabling the totality symbol to manifest itself, and triadic situations indicate the dynamic flow of events.[23] It is clearly evident that all these meanings fit admirably into Wittig's central scheme in *Les Guérillères*. Thus she achieves desired ends by subtle and (deceptively) simple means once more.

Another symbol, although not mentioned in the initial group of the O, the zero, and the circle, is an extension of the last of these, the spiral. Another very ancient and universal symbol, the spiral connotes cyclic continuity but of a progressive kind. It is linked to the cosmic symbolism of the moon, the erotic symbolism of the vulva, and the aquatic symbolism of the seashell. It indicates the center of life and denotes equilibrium in disequilibrium, involution and evolution.[24] There is a striking parallelism between the symbolism of the spiral and that of the group of symbols that Wittig associates with the O, and this parallelism suggests that the spiral (not named there and therefore probably most significant—as we have seen from other examples in the past) might be a hidden center of concern. This seems to be confirmed by the fact, already mentioned, that the spiral connotes cyclic continuity but of a progressive kind. In the largest sense, *Les Guérillères* is based on a cyclical pattern that moves from annihilation to creation in an endless series but with a progressive orientation. In this the work differs from *L'Opoponax*, which evolved as a temporal flow rather than a cyclical pattern. And it is closer to Wittig's pronouncement of her central aims in "The Trojan Horse." Moreover, not only does the spiral's cyclical but progressive pattern demonstrate the symbol's link with all those mentioned earlier as well as with an eschatological aspect (which she sees as the essential characteristic of a work of art), but it is also the fundamental pattern in the universe as found in the birth and death of stars, the round of the seasons, the diurnal and the nocturnal, and the life cycle of every animate being—and of the female body. The last of these, with its menstrual cycle in particular (traditionally not mentioned in literary works, but which—in another renversement—plays an important part in *Le Corps lesbien*) is probably part of the underlying importance of this particular symbol and the structuring principle of the text.

The stages of the cycle are evident in *Les Guérillères* in the work's most general and in its most specific terms, in the entire architecture of the work and in its minute details. The cycle is perhaps most clearly seen, however, in the dual treatment of the group of symbols spoken of earlier or, more specifically, in the triadic configuration of destruction, interval, and regeneration. Each of these symbols in turn (and sometimes several of them linked together) demonstrates this cycle and illuminates details in the text that would otherwise be almost impossible to interpret.

The negative stage of the cycle is primarily associated with the O, the zero, and the circle as symbols of nothingness or tabula rasa (which incidentally confers yet another meaning to the three O's of *L'Opoponax*—a triple negation of an existing form). In *Les Guérillères*, the circle is linked to the mirror as a trap or prison (G, 40) or as an icy arena where "elles" hover on the point of death (G, 87). Rather than being associated with wholeness, harmony, or unity, it symbolizes the very opposite. In dimensions also, it seems to have shrunk to a zero, denoting nullity or the descent to the lowest point, the nadir.

Zero, however, is also a turning point, the interval that precedes renewal, the instant of renversement. This can clearly be seen in the sequences where it represents a springboard for a new beginning (G, 38, 88). It is interesting to note that the same symbols and the images associated with them now change in meaning. The circular mirror becomes both a shield that reflects the rays of the sun (the sun being another symbol that, as we shall see, Wittig reverses entirely) and also a fiery weapon (G, 173, 37). The (circular) female breasts and the sexual orifice acquire a brilliance, an almost blinding splendor (*G*, 24). The O turns into two formidable weapons—the "ospah," which resembles a bullroarer and creates a circular field fatal to enemies (*G*, 149), and a futuristic, spherical ray-gun (the sphere being a three-dimensional version of the circle) that consumes all obstacles (*G*, 155). And since the destructive stage of the cycle has now reached a turning point, the "elles" (who were formerly depicted as victims) now appear in the guise of agents of destruction or "guérillères"—a reversal of their former state, but also a destruction/recreation of the word that designates them. They have become unified too. They have formed a "coalition des O" (*G*, 150), which incidentally is a subversion of a traditional scene in (male) epics—the lineup of warriors for battle. This coalition unites "les Ophidiennes les Odonates les Oogones les Odoacres les Olynthiennes les Oolothes les Omphales (another allusion to an allied symbol of the circle, that is, the *omphalos* or world naval) celles d'Ormur celles d'Orphise les Oriennes (*G*, 149). Among the many interesting facets of this coalition, the names of all these tribes (or nations) of women are neologisms and thus, in themselves, constitute the destruction and recreation of words. And to accentuate the cyclical pattern of annihilation and regeneration, the battle that is fought by this coalition—while it is the most dramatic and devastating—is preceded and followed by others. The "O's" are only one in a chain of vast armies of women who, although unnamed, have in the past, and will in the future, contribute to the reversal of the negative stage of the cycle.

The positive stage, on the other hand, is the most skillful and intricate of Wittig's achievements in this novel. This in itself suggests that creation (more than annihilation) is the ultimate object of this work—and of the work of art in general. It is here that the symbol of the O, expanded into the **O** and its variants (the sphere, the spiral, and the mandala), reaches its greatest dimensions; for it is toward unity, wholeness, and an integrated vision (which all these symbols denote) that Wittig's entire enterprise can be seen to move. This unity and integration is evident, if not in mimetic terms or in the progression of individual sequences (for, as we have seen, the latter are not presented in chronological order or in a developmental pattern), in the form and thematics of *Les Guér-*

illères. And it is achieved (to recapitulate) by its tri-partite structure; by the use of the numbers three and six; by the circular time-flow that unites past, present, and future; by the lists of women's names that contribute to this flow and to the sense of integration; and by the final unification of males and females.

This unification is particularly interesting, for it accomplishes a number of ends, all of them positive: the joining of formerly hostile beings, at war because of a dichotomy based on gender differentiation or because of an outmoded structure of dominance-submission (both of which needed to be destroyed); the creative (or recreated) stage of an androgynous state; and the union of male and female or the blending of the two into a genderless, hermaphroditic being, symbolized by the flower "hermaphrodis" (incidentally, also a neologism), whose shape duplicates that of a mandala (*G*, 99). The third of these coincides with Wittig's pronouncements concerning the need to move away from, or beyond, terms that designate categories of sex (*men* and *women*).[25] This concern later leads her to use the term *lesbian* and to define it in particular fashion, but here the concern is revealed in a form that suits the fictional context.

Unity, wholeness, and harmony are even more powerfully represented in a vision of cosmic proportions where the creative forces manifest themselves in the most minute as well as in the grandest manner—in the gyrations of the vulvae and the comparable rotations of suns, planets, and galaxies (*G*, 86). It is a vision ultimately synthesized in the image of "la sphère infinie dont le centre est partout, la circonférence nulle part" (*G*, 87).[26] The progression toward unification and creation is represented repeatedly by the circle, the sphere, and the spiral. This representation is most clearly shown in the futuristic sequences of the novel, which in themselves denote development or progression by being projected into the future. In these scenes there are beehive dwellings made of cells that resemble eggs or sarcophagi (and which are thus linked respectively to birth, death, and rebirth) and that also resemble the letter *O* (*G*, 122–23). But the symbolic representation is most spectacularly developed in the sequence in which Wittig depicts stupas, dagbas, and chortens—found in Bud-

dhist, Far Eastern, and Lamaist religious tradition and designating shrines for sacred relics—all of which have a basic
design: the circle "dans toutes ses modalités" (*G*, 195).[27] These
mounds containing relic chambers surround a central edifice
in the form of a hemisphere, which is traversed by circular
paths that lead upward in the direction of the sun, pass the
four cardinal points, and reach the zenith where one can hear
the music of the spheres (*G*, 195–96). It can be seen that
this structure resembles several things: a three-dimensional
labyrinth (another form of the spiral), leading, however, up
into the light (rather than to darkness and death); a mandala,
when extended into the third dimension; and an ascending
spiral from whose summit the entire unified world, indeed
the cosmos, can be seen—and heard in the form of music. It
is in this vision that Wittig has truly achieved a synthesis
of mythologies, of scientific and alchemistic notions, and of
psychological and mystical insights. And she has created an
image of such totality that it could only be described by the
timeless and universal symbols she has used.

Complex as it is, her work with symbols is but one of
Wittig's major accomplishments in *Les Guérillères*. The fundamental motif of renversement and recreation occurs in numerous other domains as well. One of the most striking is her
treatment of well-known myths. In this work, the first example is that of the Phoenix, which appears in the initial pages
and instantly announces the destruction-rebirth pattern. It
itself is also destroyed and reborn, for it appears in the midst
of several female figures and is, by contiguity and association,
feminized. Such reversal prefigures the treatment of numerous other mythological characters and situations in the work.
These are taken from a wide variety of mythologies: Egyptian,
Greek, Hindu, Japanese, Mexican, Roman, and so on. Such
diversity and scope seems to be a result of Wittig's interest in
universalization rather than a display of erudition for its own
sake. Yet her equally strong penchant for unity is evident in
her tendency to superimpose various myths, in a manner not
unlike that of Gérard de Nerval in *Les Chimères* and *Aurélia*.

The penchant for reversal, however, is Wittig's own.
Sometimes she applies this reversal to those "lesser" genres
into which great myths have descended—legends and fairy

tales. For example, Sleeping Beauty is (humorously) recreated (*G*, 62–63), as is Snow White and Rose Red (*G*, 64–65). The legend of the Holy Grail and the Knights of the Round Table is subjected to a similar fate (*G*, 61–62). The last of these instances is especially interesting since the renversement concerns a legend linked to Judeo-Christian mythology and is thus quasi-heretical. Moreover, the feminization of the Arthurian cycle and its symbolism is a startling alteration of the legend and gives it an entirely new meaning.

Well-known mythological figures are sometimes also treated by this relatively simple method. For example, Dionysus, Prometheus and Hermes are given female attributes (*G*, 30, 62, 204). Eve, on the other hand, seems to merit more complicated treatment. She is represented alone in Paradise, without Adam, and certainly not created from his rib. Instead, she is shown accompanied by her favorite serpent, "Orphée." Since this name has an ambiguous ending in French that might make it the name of a female (as was the case for "Osée"), the serpent's gender is uncertain. It might even be androgynous or a prefiguration of the hermaphroditic state that is achieved when the war between the sexes ends and when a new version of Paradise comes into being. Moreover, by the linkage with Orpheus, who was known for the powers of his artistry, the serpent companion of Eve bestows similar powers upon her. She herself, rather than causing the Fall and her expulsion from Paradise (as in the Old Testament version), attains superhuman stature and the joyful knowledge of a solar myth that all the texts had obscured (*G*, 72–73). This overthrow and recreation of one of the most famous incidents in Judeo-Christian mythology—and one from which the vilification of woman that lasted for so many centuries was derived—is certainly more daring than the previous examples given.

In other instances, the reversal undertaken by Wittig concerns not only the functions or actions of mythological figures but their very names as well. For example, both the traditional attributes and the names of two famous female divinities from Egyptian mythology undergo a drastic change: Hathor becomes Othar and carries the sun instead of the moon disc on her head (*G*, 183); and Nut becomes Out and, rather than supporting the heavenly vault, shatters it (*G*, 183). In each case the new name begins with the letter *O*. Moreover, in the same passage, these female divinities are joined by others from all over the world—such as Garuda, Esée, and Itaura (who resembles Kali in her incarnation as the Terrible Goddess)—with whom they are united to form a composite deity. We thus witness the destruction/recreation of a variety of myths as well as the birth of an entirely new myth of Wittig's own creation.

But probably the most audacious renversement of existing myths concerns the oldest and most widespread symbol of the female divinity: the moon. From the beginning of time, and in almost every culture, woman have been associated with the night sky, primordial darkness, and the underworld, and with the attendant negative symbolism (deprivation of light, dependency, passivity, and death). Wittig negates this *Ur*-concept, and—in a sweeping gesture of reversal—creates an entire pantheon of sun goddesses, drawn from a variety of mythologies: Amaterasu, Cihuacoatl, Eristikos, and Koue Feï (*G*, 34–35, 37, 31, 92). Moreover, these solar goddesses are not only the incarnations of light, autonomy, and life, but they are also powerful forces of destruction, righteous rage, and retribution. And in this, they are the supernatural counterparts of the "guérillères."

More pervasive, though less evident, is Wittig's use and treatment of the Amazon myth. It appears in the background of much of *Les Guérillères* and is, of course, already suggested in the work's title. And while it seems an oversimplification to speak of the entire book as an "utopie amazonienne,"[28] this myth—and its subversion by Wittig—is of great interest and merits detailed consideration.

Known to be of Greek (and, specifically, Athenian) origin, the myth is the product of a patriarchal and male-dominated society. According to the myth, the Amazons (whose name derives from a practice attributed to them—the ablation of one of their breasts) are of foreign birth (from Persia, Phrygia, and Colchis) and are thus strangers, outsiders, and "barbarians." Their life-style and religion are in direct opposition to the "normal" (patriarchal and matrimonial) system in which women are housebound, submissive, and limited to the role of wife and mother (especially mother of sons). They are portrayed as female warriors who govern themselves, live outdoors, mate solely with strangers and in random fashion, raise only their daughters (killing or blinding any male offspring), and fight on horseback with bow and arrow (not on foot with axes as do Greek warriors). They worship Ares and are thought to be the daughters of Ares and Aphrodite; but they also adore Cybele, the Great Mother, and Artemis. Most of all, they are thought to be "killers of men." And they reflect the specter of an uprising of women against men and a desire to substitute themselves for men (or to confuse the categories between male and female), in a type of *coincidentium oppositorum* that makes them both monstrous and numinous.[29]

It is not difficult to see that Wittig's "guérillères" resemble the Amazons of this myth in a number of ways: Most of the multiple protagonists of her work live in a place that, although undefined, appears removed from civilization. They frequently appear in outdoor settings and are in close contact with nature. They are autonomous and their society consists solely of female members (little girls, and young and old women). They often engage in bellicose activities and rebel against the male establishment (especially domination by men). And they finally do confuse the traditional categories of male and female and move toward an androgynous ideal (or a *coincidentium oppositorum*). In all these respects, Wittig adheres to the original myth. However, she seldom specifically alludes to it, and she uses precise references to Amazons sparingly (*G,* 121, 147)—probably in order not to limit the scope of her undertaking, which would preclude universalization.

Much more striking than the parallels just shown, is the way Wittig subverts the Amazon myth, and especially the details that she chooses either to omit or to change drastically. The first of these is the condition that gives the Amazons their name. The women portrayed in *Les Guérillères* are not A-mazons—*a* (without), *mazos* (breast). Nowhere is this auto-mutilation said to be practiced by them. On the contrary, their breasts are intact, luxuriant, and threatening or protective (weapons or shields). They worship Minerva, "la guerrière," called the most courageous of goddesses (*G,* 133); Dionysus (in female form, as has already been noted), whose followers, the Bacchantes, are known for their savage actions (*G*, 132); as well as various female divinities belonging to diverse mythologies (formerly discussed). Thus they are more eclectic in their religious practices than the Amazons of the original myth. Moreover, they are not portrayed in exclusively bellicose activities. There are innumerable sequences in the work where the protagonists are shown in peaceful contact with nature or during agrarian occupations, games, festivities, and celebrations. Most striking of all (and in direct opposition to the original myth) are the sequences in which they depose all weapons and live—something like the Flower Children of the 60's—in pacifist bliss with the young men who have joined them, and in a world filled with harmony and laughter (*G*, 178–80, 184).

Indeed, laughter is perhaps the most arresting renversement to occur in regard to this myth, to the genre chosen, and to Wittig's work in general. Nowhere in the original (verbal or pictorial) representations of the Amazons is there anything but violence, horror, and death: Theseus rapes Antiope, Achilles slays Penthesilea, and so on. The epic genre is generally singularly devoid of laughter. And yet the "guérillères," when the vast battle that rages in this work is ended, affirm that they now want to learn to laugh (*G*, 180). Indeed, this initiation to laughter is probably the greatest form of victory. It is the ultimate expression of freedom and of the true liberation of women—a spontaneous sign of strength and vitality.

Laughter itself is, of course, a complex and fascinating phenomenon—as Baudelaire, Bergson, the Surrealists, Freud, Ionesco, Beckett, and others have shown. In Wittig's work it appears in all its facets, yet it has surprisingly passed almost unnoticed. If it is commented on at all by critics, it is generally relegated to the category of irony or satire,[30] a limitation and oversimplification. In examining *Les Guérillères*, it becomes evident that the range of laughter found there is quite large and that its functions are manifold. It can signal rebellion and the refusal of certain stereotypes (*G*, 66). It may constitute a sweeping denunciation, a powerful catharsis that vivifies and liberates (*G*, 180). At times it appears in the form of black humor—bitter, grotesque and full of self-mockery (*G*, 64, 112). At other times it is a sign of survival, a life force that erupts to vanquish apathy and despair (*G*, 122, 140). It can express simple joie de vivre and be playful and childlike (*G*, 10, 11, 194), or it can express pure whimsy—such as in the invention of the delightful creatures named "glénures" or "juleps," which constitute Wittig's bestiary (a collection of creatures expanded in her later works) (*G*, 26, 28; 79–80). But it may also be a gigantic, roaring laugh that sweeps away debris and opens the way for a new plenitude (*G*, 122, 129–30). Whether harsh or joyous, violent or lusory, desperate or revitalizing, destructive or creative, laughter in *Les Guérillères* is a sign of newfound expression, of something long denied and finally affirmed. And most importantly, it is claimed no longer only as "le propre de l'homme" (*G*, 180)—a well-worn adage—but also as the birthright of "la femme."

It must instantly be added, however, that the term *femme* is subjected to destruction in order for renewal or reformulation to take place. It is obvious that, in order to move beyond the categories of sex—something of great import according to Wittig[31]—the designation of "man" and "woman" must disappear from language and, first of all, from the text. In *Les Guérillères*, this is achieved by the almost exclusive use of the pronoun *elles*, reinforced by the fact that the terms *woman* and *women* have almost entirely vanished. There are only several mentions of "petites filles," that is, female beings who have not yet reached the stage at which they are designated as "women" and defined by society as wives, mothers, or dependent creatures. While the term *homme* or *hommes* appears more often, it is generally present in passages that accuse, mock, or denounce male domination and in those sequences that depict the unification of males and females after the war won by the latter. In the last instance, however, there is the implication that, in the future or ideal society, such designations will disappear.

More important than the indications just cited, numerous passages in the text are devoted to the existence, annihilation, and rewriting of works called "féminaires." The word itself, of course, attracts immediate attention, and it also succeeds in stating a great deal. Since it obviously echoes the word *bestiaires*, it is a reminder of bestiaries, those pseudo-scientific works of the past that described strange, exotic, fabulous beasts. But it is also a reminder of the age-old, derogatory association of women and animals and of the emphasis on the animality (or bestiality) of women. However, since the term *féminaire* is a deviation from *bestiaire,* the word refuses these very associations. Most importantly, since *feminaire* is a neologism, it emphasizes both destruction and creation and illustrates Wittig's "word work" at its most economical and effective.

Examining the text of *Les Guérillères* reveals that the "féminaires" are central to Wittig's concerns, concerns that go beyond this particular work. They represent traditional notions of a particular kind that must be annihilated and reformulated. But here there is also a question of texts, books, even literature in general at stake, for these "féminaires" are written works, something akin to dictionaries (*G,* 17–18). This is in itself significant, for the dictionary—like the epic genre—has been the exclusive creation and property of males and thus constitutes the possession of an establishment. This state of affairs is visibly challenged, attacked, and destroyed in *Les Guérillères,* (and is subjected to total renversement and recreation in Wittig's later work, *Brouillon pour un dictionnaire des amantes*).

Moreover, the "féminaires" define women in traditional fashion, and their authors, judging from the contents, are obviously male. Most of the definitions there center on women's bodies as objects and concentrate on their genital organs, thus reducing women to their genitalia (*G,* 29, 41, 66, 111, for example). Descriptions of the latter often take the form of metaphors, geometric shapes, or letters of the alphabet (*G,* 66–67). Some of these representations coincide with the symbols already mentioned (such as circles, ovals, and rings). This can be confusing until it becomes clear that Wittig suggests that the same symbols can have a negative and/or a positive use, or that traditional meanings must be destroyed in order for new ones to be created. She also shows that, initially, women have been cowed into accepting symbolic representations of themselves or have passively submitted to, and even incorporated, such representations.

The revolt against these symbolic representations takes place slowly and necessitates a number of stages. The first stage is an awareness of their existence (*G*, 29, 41, 43, 60, 61, 66–67) and the beginning of a critical attitude toward these representations that manifests itself by objectivity, amusement, and mockery (*G*, 41, 66, for example). Then follows the judgment of them as outmoded, meaningless, and even incomprehensible (which parallels the action described in "The Trojan Horse" concerning forms of literature) (*G*, 66). The next step is the refusal of those definitions or forms, especially if they are negative—for example, those that compare women to that which is humid, somber, does not burn, and is vanquished without battle (*G*, 11). This is accomplished by a refusal of the "elles" to use such definitions in their own utterances, and it is accentuated in the text by the repetition of the phrase "elles ne disent pas" (in opposition to the much repeated phrase "elles disent"), which constitutes resistance even if it is, at first, only a passive sort (*G*, 86, 93). The next stage is a total refusal by the "elles" of all symbols relating to their bodies, since these risk continuing the link with "une culture morte" (*G*, 102). It follows that the products of this dead culture must be destroyed. This is accomplished through violent action—the burning of these books, the "féminaires." The "féminaires" are subjected to "execution" in public squares, in a great auto-da-fé (*G*, 68, 102). This can be interpreted as an allusion to the same fate suffered by witches and inflicted by those who were also the authors of works resembling the "féminaires"). After such destruction, an interval of silence or zero enunciation takes place. This is followed by the creative or recreative stage, which is concerned with the necessity and desirability of new books—books that are quite different from the "féminaires."

First of all, these new works will be created by "elles" themselves, who, rather than being objects as they formerly were, have now become subjects. Moreover, these texts will be joint creations in which they all participate (*G*, 106). The resultant new book (opposed to the Book), as it is described in *Les Guérillères,* is extremely interesting. It resembles a register or a dictionary, except the characteristics of the latter have been overthrown. This can be seen from the following passage:

Il est inutile de l'ouvrir à la première page et d'y chercher un ordre de succession. On peut le prendre pas hasard et trouver quelque chose par quoi on est concerné.[32] (*G*, 74)

That the work does not follow the usual order (alphabetical or sequential) is significant on several counts. It destroys the traditional arrangement of the dictionary (which is one of its distinguishing features). And it affirms chance over logic and reverses the notion of rational order by its insistence on disorder or chaos, thus constituting a *renversement* that goes beyond that of a particular work or genre and attacks traditional notions of far greater magnitude. This description fits *Les Guérillères*, in which sequences are also not arranged in sequential fashion. Thus it furnishes an important key to the meaning of this work's particular structure. Moreover, the lack of sequential arrangement is another instance of a *mise en abyme* (as the epic within an epic mentioned earlier). And it subtly points to the newness of Wittig's own book, the avant-garde nature of her undertaking.

A related action of destruction and reinvention centers on women's "histoire" (meaning both story and history), also habitually told or written about them by men. The revolt against this "histoire" follows stages similar to those seen in the revolt against the symbolic representations of the "féminaires"—awareness, refusal, overthrow, and transformation. In the awareness stage, "elles" realize not only that they have been robbed of knowledge (and knowledge of their own past) but also that they have been turned into beings who do not speak, write, or even exist. Worst of all, their "histoire" is filled with stories of defeat, depicting them as vile, fallen creatures (*G*, 159).

The refusal of, and revolt against, this depiction appears in Wittig's text in the form of a staccato enumeration of the various objects associated with women's "histoire," and of the abject roles that have been assigned to them. These objects are then gathered and subjected to the destructive and purgative action of fire, as had been the "féminaires." And like the "féminaires," these objects, once destroyed, are recreated. Thus, spindles, looms, sewing machines, knitting needles, ironing boards, pots and pans, brooms, vacuum cleaners, washing machines, brushes, and so on, are reduced to ashes, or exploded. The remains, however, or the objects that have not been consumed or disintegrated are treated in interesting fashion:

> Elles les recouvrent de peinture bleue verte rouge pour les assembler dans des compositions grotesques grandioses abracadabrantes auxquelles elles donnent des noms.[33] (*G*, 104)

Thus, submission and vilification are annihilated in order for new (pictorial and verbal) forms to be invented. Such action repeats a pattern, familiar by now, which necessitates the descent into nothingness before a new beginning can be made (*G*, 88–90, 164, 121). But in this particular instance, the creation associated with this beginning also resembles avant-garde art forms and thus, once again, points to one of Wittig's central concerns.

While in the case just cited these art forms happen to resemble sculptures, Wittig's main preoccupation remains, of course, with language. In this domain the eschatological pattern appears in its most developed form and is given the most extensive treatment. It follows the same stages as those seen in previous instances. The first realization, obviously, is that language (as it exists) is not the property of women but of men as the dominant group in a society or as the establishment. As a matter of fact, language has often been used to reduce the former to silence and to exile them from the world of signs, while forcing them to accept the terms that have been applied to them (*G*, 162).[34] Language must therefore undergo a kind of death, or submit to an "execution," before it can be reborn. It must descend to a state of fragmentation, anarchy, and silence (*G*, 164). Only after it has reached the zero degree, only after an interval or lacuna can it begin its ascent and be redefined or reinvented. A period of nothingness (muteness, the total refusal or absence of words) must follow, before a new language can be formed.

This formation begins with the lowest and simplest means of communication: signs (for example, a circle made with the thumb and index finger); signals (*G*, 176); inarticulate sounds, screams, and exclamations (*G*, 166–67); and secret gestures understood only by those who invented them (*G*, 175). Then, just as in a world revived after complete devastation, or after the Flood, the process of renaming begins. It is tantamount to a veritable genesis—an echo, but also a reversal, of Genesis. Woman now arises from annihilation as "une nouvelle espèce qui cherche un nouveau langage" (*G*, 189).[35] Thus, not only does she define herself as an entirely new species—to which the word *woman*, incidentally, no longer applies—but her central concern is that of a new language, freshly invented (*G*, 74). And since, as the text affirms, "il n'y a pas de réalité avant que les mots . . . lui ont donné forme" (*G*, 192),[36] if a new reality is to emerge, in the beginning will, once again, be the Word. Only this time, the Creation will be the prerogative of female creators.

This brings us directly to creation, through language, as the major undertaking of Wittig herself in *Les Guérillères*. In many ways, of course, the protagonists of that work are the author's avatars. Her work on language parallels theirs in general as well as in particular ways. In both instances, the first task is to combat language, the major cause of female oppression, but even more importantly, in order to destroy an edifice that is outmoded, atrophied, and incapable of transformation. Language is thus doubly contested and this at the site of language itself, the text. Words become active elements of auto-destruction, but also of auto-creation. In this they outdistance their role as "raw material" or "war machines" and assume the characteristics of the Phoenix, whose self-immolation leads to a self-determined rebirth.

The destruction of established traditions of language in *Les Guérillères* is extensive. In order to see it at work, it is best to begin with the simplest examples. This can be done by considering Wittig's treatment of common nouns that habitually appear in the masculine form (for example, "chasseur," "maçon," "soldat," and "parleur"). The dictionary gives solely these forms and can thus be considered as excluding women from the activities to which these nouns refer and as perpetuating the image of women as passive, weak, peace-loving, silent creatures. Wittig, on the other hand, feminizes these words in her text and, moreover, uses them in the plural (for example, "chasseuses," "maçonnes," "soldates," "parleuses"). By this simple expedient, she accomplishes a number of ends: a convention is destroyed; women take possession of domains from which they are usually excluded—they hunt, build, fight, speak (indeed, are speaking subjects); the solidarity of the women is indicated as well as the frequency with which they engage in these activities; and most important of all, new words are created that have both shock value and creative power. In some ways, Wittig's feminization of nouns parallels her treatment of male mythological figures, though on a less dramatic scale. But it also prefigures her much more extensive use of this device in her next work, *Le Corps lesbien*, where all nouns are used in the feminine form and where those that have a masculine gender in French, as well as their accompanying adjectives, are feminized.

Somewhat more complex is Wittig's reorganization of metaphors in *Les Guérillères*. This manifests itself, as has been pointed out, in a departure from what is often considered the central and absolute metaphor: the phallus.[37] This departure, or even total overthrow, has been amply illustrated by Wittig's use of metaphors describing the female sexual organ. Although these metaphors are at one point refused by the protagonists since they risk creating a partial or fragmented image of the female body, Wittig herself retains the two basic ones: the circle and the cycle (the first clearly visible, the second subtly inscribed into the structure of *Les Guérillères*). The circle remains as a sign of wholeness and the cycle as a sign of the fundamental (biological) organization of the female body— and thus its affirmation. This is in itself tantamount to the destruction of a male-oriented system of metaphors and to the creation of a completely new orientation. Most of all, it results in a strikingly innovative effect, a revolutionary foundation for an entire work of fiction.

Other important changes, this time in the area of grammar, concern a device that on the surface appears quite simple but that is actually rather involved: the use of verb tenses and forms. The verbs in *Les Guérillères* are all in the present (except in the last sequence where the imperfect and the *passé simple* appear), mostly transitive, and in the active voice. Some reasons for the use of the present tense have already been discussed. There are, however, others still to be explored. Here the present tense is temporal, which links it to utopic discourse, abolishes linear time, and creates a world free from the opposition that usually exists between past, present, and future, or between fantasy and reality. It also suggests the notion of eternal return,[38] and as a result, it creates parallels between ancient and contemporary civilizations or even eliminates all habitual distinctions of a chronological variety. Moreover, the concept of eternal return accentuates the mythic quality and eschatological pattern that are important components of *Les Guérillères*.

The use of transitive verbs, while very frequent in this work, is not as striking as Wittig's experimentation with intransitive verbs in *Le Corps lesbien*, but it does create an interesting relationship between subject and object. It is linked, in some ways, to her predominant use of the active voice. The latter translates the nature of Wittig's protagonists, who act and take possession in every respect—especially of words themselves, as is also indicated by the much repeated phrase, "elles disent." In the progression toward the status of speaking subject, after having been long deprived of it, nothing could be of greater importance than what is stated by that phrase. As a matter of fact, the passage from the passive voice to the active one indicates the entire trajectory of that evolution from object of (male) discourse—as exemplified in the "féminaires" or in women's "histoire" discussed earlier—to subject of their own discourse. It indicates autonomy in the realm of language by autonomous beings.

A similar progression is reflected in the lexicon of *Les Guérillères*. It is, as so many other aspects of this work, a total overthrow of stereotyped or constantly reiterated notions. One such notion, for example, is that of women (and women writers) as being reticent to use concrete terms for body functions—preferring euphemisms or circumlocutions; avoiding invectives, curses, and obscenities; and shying away from any direct references to sexuality and, especially, to sexual organs. All these stereotypes are destroyed by Wittig in this text. Concrete body functions, such as urination or vomiting, are described in direct fashion (*G*, 9, 11). Invectives, curses, and obscenities also occur, sometimes developed in detail and at great length (*G,* 140, 152, 153). Overt references to sexuality and to sexual organs (especially those of the female) are extremely numerous and totally explicit (*G,* 9, 24, 29, 41–42, 61, 152, for example).

The lexicon of *Les Guérillères* contradicts what is generally expected in the work of a woman writer in other ways as well. Rather than emphasizing words relating to "womanly" occupations and preoccupations, it contains a great deal of terminology that refers to the hunt, warfare, equestrian feats, strikes, demonstrations, political activities, diplomatic negotiations, and other types of action traditionally reserved for men (engineering, masonry, races, officiating at rituals, and so on). All of these terms indicate an expansion of the terminology found in *L'Opoponax* (terminology which was not particularly unexpected, except for the vocabulary dealing with the hunt and war games). And they also show a more pronounced trend toward innovation. Yet because she introduces these terms as though nothing were more natural than their appearance in her work, the subversion they imply is not instantly noticeable. It becomes clear only upon reflection that they constitute a type of undercover attack upon the establishment and that they are aimed at the dictatorial attitude that decrees what words can be used by whom.

Nevertheless, Wittig's lexicon in *Les Guérillères,* although it does not yet show the extreme audacity that characterizes *Le Corps lesbien,* is already an effective means of mining the ground of what is habitually considered the permitted—and very limited—range of the woman writer's vocabulary. The manner in which this can be accomplished is powerfully stated by the protagonists of *Les Guérillères:*

> Elles disent qu'en premier lieu le vocabulaire de toutes les langues est à examiner, à modifier, à bouleverser de fond en comble, que chaque mot doit être passé au crible.[39] (*G,* 192)

Of course, action as drastic as this does not yet occur in this particular text, but it is both a threat and a desired end. As such, it expresses the extremes to which the destruction of traditional limitations in the realm of vocabulary must be—and will be—taken.

A similar attack upon traditional notions occurs in another domain also: the scope of sense experiences that are expected (and permitted) to be related in a text by a woman writer. For example, while there are many descriptions of an olfactory nature that do not shock stereotyped notions, such as those involving pleasant odors—perfumes and the scent of flowers, herbs, or spices (*G,* 10, 18, 31)—there are others that are distinctly unexpected and unpleasant—the smell of vomit, the nauseous fumes of marshes, and the stench of carrion (*G,* 12, 19, 11). Visual experiences are equally full of contrasts. There are scenes of great beauty, filled with vivid colors, such as the one set in a cherry orchard (*G,* 23), or the one in which oil is pressed from various plants and flowers (*G,* 49–50). But there are also visions of horror or scenes filled with grotesque sights, such as the one in which a mummy is used for a rain-making ritual (*G,* 20), or that in which the dreadful carnage of war is described (*G,* 147–48). In this, as in other areas, Wittig shows that she refuses to be limited to a prescribed range of expression and that she claims the right to enter into domains that are usually considered unseemly or "unwomanly"—and even the right to totally overthrow all such stereotypes (*G,* 192).

The most fascinating overthrow of all, however, concerns literature itself. In *Les Guérillères,* this is suggested in the final portion of the text and is strangely enough put forward in a highly literary manner: by interweaving two poetic texts—the poem by Wittig that encircles the central *récit* and portions of a famous sonnet by Stéphane Mallarmé, "Le vierge, le vivace, et le bel aujourd'hui." A great deal can be noted from this final portion of text. Wittig has a predilection for using poetic texts to underscore her own text (already seen in *L'Opoponax* but accentuated by its repetition here). The appropriation of the other text is more complete here than in her earlier work, because the portions of the Mallarmé poem no longer appear within a prose passage but in a text that is of the same literary genre, that is, a poem. As in *L'Opoponax,* the two texts are not separated or distinguished from each other (by punctuation marks, spaces, or other methods of differentiation) but form a whole. Thus Wittig's text has "swallowed" Mallarmé's or at least incorporated it in the true sense of the word. Also, Wittig's poem (in capitals) overtakes that of Mallarmé or outsizes it. And finally, in each case, the author of the other text is male, and thus the appropriation of his work is a form of pillaging or conquest by a female writer, who in each instance is Wittig herself.

But it is necessary to look even more closely at what the author has done at this point in her work, for it is probably the most revealing portion of *Les Guérillères*. While the two main texts that are interwoven with Wittig's own in *L'Opoponax* come from love poems (by Baudelaire and Scève) and thus parallel the fundamental thematics of that novel, here she chooses lines from a sonnet by Mallarmé that deals, fundamentally, with the struggle against impotence and the yearning for creation. It is thus well suited for interweaving with Wittig's own poem, which speaks, essentially, of the same subject. However, the latter contains greater vehemence and more drastic action. It centers on a very unusual suggestion and a truly audacious one. Despite the intensive "word work" and the intense involvement with literature that distinguish *Les Guérillères*, Wittig now maintains that literature cannot be confined to the written text, and must itself die to be reborn or to undergo eschatological action. The struggle for creation must include a totally destructive phase.

This is expressed in the end/beginning (for the end is also a new beginning) of the poem encircling the central *récit:*

NON / SIGNES DÉCHIRANT
SURGIS VIOLENCE DU BLANC
DU VIVACE DU BEL AUJOURD'HUI
D'UN GRAND COUP D'AILE IVRE
TROUÉ DÉCHIRÉ LE CORPS
(INTOLÉRABLE)
ÉCRIT PAR DÉFAUTS

SURGIS NON / SIGNES ENSEMBLE
ÉVIDENTS / DESIGNÉ LE TEXTE
(PAR MYRIADES CONSTELLATIONS)
QUI MANQUE

LACUNES LACUNES LACUNES
CONTRE TEXTES
CONTRE SENS
CE QUI EST À ÉCRIRE VIOLENCE
HORS TEXTE
DANS UNE AUTRE ÉCRITURE
PRESSANT MENAÇANT
MARGES ESPACES INTERVALLES
SANS RELÂCHE
GESTE RENVERSEMENT.[40]
(G, 205)

The first clue to this difficult text is that it begins with the word "NON," thus indicating the predominant themes of negation, refusal, and zero. Almost instantly, the Mallarméan poem appears, by a play on words, through the use of *signes* (signs), a homonym of *cygne* (swan)—the bird of Mallarmé's poem. It resurfaces again in the phrases "VIVACE . . . BEL AUJOURD'HUI" and "UN . . . COUP D'AILE IVRE." However, Wittig has substituted the word *blanc* for Mallarmé's *vierge* and added *grand* to "un coup d'aile ivre." The action between Wittig's text and Mallarmé's includes a partial destruction of the latter by the changes made in the former, which begin by the substitution of *signes* for *cygne*. Moreover, the text of Wittig's poem (while allowing portions of Mallarmé's to show through in glimpses and fragments) appropriates the central image of the swan and alters it. While Mallarmé's metaphor concerns imprisonment, immobility, entrapment, sterility, and exile, and while his poem only suggests the possibility (represented by a question) that impotence in the domain of creation might be vanquished by the new ("vierge"), vital ("vivace") present ("bel aujourd'hui"), Wittig affirms several other notions. Her poem's central image is far more active, and its action is more violent. Her "SIGNES" tear asunder. The whiteness in her poem is aggressive and can pierce or dismember the intolerable body (of writing or of a certain kind of writing) with a great, wild, drunken wing-beat. And while Mallarmé only expresses the hope that his "cygne" might arise and shake off the deadly torpor that holds him fast,[41] Wittig announces (by her use of the future and in

66

an affirmation rather than a question) that this liberating action will indeed take place.

Wittig also describes the stages necessary in order for literature to become a truly creative act. It must, like the Phoenix—a rather different bird than the swan—risk its own annihilation if it is to arise anew from its ashes. Indeed, the Phoenix, who appeared in the first part of the poem (*G*, 7), has already announced this, and the mythical bird is also present here—both by implication, and because the poem's parts, although separated by hundreds of pages, form a whole. The cyclical notion of destruction/creation upon which, as we have seen, *Les Guérillères* is built, is thus now applied to the art of writing itself.

The first step of the cycle is summed up in these lines from Wittig's poem:

> TROUÉ DÉCHIRÉ LE CORPS
> (INTOLÉRABLE)
> ÉCRIT PAR DÉFAUTS.

"LE CORPS" suggests those tests (or that corpus of texts) that must be subjected to violent action (pierced or torn to shreds) because they were written by default. But it can also be interpreted as those texts that pierce or tear apart the (female) body, calling it faulty. And, of course, the very first word of this part of the poem ("NON") indicates the refusal or total negation that is the initial step in the cycle. "NON" is repeated in the first line of the second stanza, and is followed by references to the next stage—the descent into nothingness and silence:

> LE TEXTE
> ....
> QUI MANQUE
>
> LACUNES LACUNES LACUNES.

The threefold repetition of the term *lacunes* emphasizes this stage of the zero degree of writing or the momentary death of literature.

The third stage is especially interesting. It is the creation of new texts out of this silence, these lacunae, this interval.

This was already suggested in a short passage in *Les Guérillères*, where reference is made to a new form that can be sought in the interstices of the existing language, in the spaces of nonenunciation: "Cela se manifeste juste dans l'intervalle . . . cela peut se chercher dans la lacune . . . dans tout ce qui n'est pas la continuité de leurs discours, dans le zéro, le O, le cercle parfait que tu inventes" (*G*, 164).[42] The opposition between "leurs discours" (the language of the "others," here also defined as that of the "masters" or the dominant establishment) and that yet to be invented is significant, but even more so is the fact that this invention begins in the domain of nonlanguage, in those places that have not been contaminated by established discourse: intervals, lacunae, and spaces. And the privileged areas are those of nothingness ("zéro"), those designated by the sign that is allied to the zero as both turning point and new creation ("O"), and those that signal an autonomous invention ("le cercle parfait que tu inventes")—incidentally those which are prominently apparent in *Les Guérillères*.

There is, however, a more audacious notion put forward in the last portion of Wittig's poem. More drastic than the recreation of texts (such as the "féminaires") that is represented in Wittig's text, it states that the new writing envisaged necessitates the sacrifice not only of an existing form of literature, but of an existing text. This sacrificed text might even be *Les Guérillères*, for the concluding lines refer to a future writing, "CE QUI EST À ÉCRIRE"[43] that will take the form of:

VIOLENCE

HORS TEXTE
DANS UNE AUTRE ÉCRITURE.

It is thus apparent that the action of (violent) creation may occur not only in future texts, but even outside of texts, located in a space not yet in existence, in "MARGES ESPACES INTERVALLES." This empty space, this nonexistence, is, however, full of promise—even though that promise must be at the sacrifice of writing itself.

In the concluding lines of the poem, Wittig reiterates all of this:

SANS RELÂCHE
GESTE RENVERSEMENT.

These lines can be interpreted as meaning that the writer (this writer), and what she has written, can disappear (very much the way that the "opoponax" vanished at a certain point in *L'Opoponax*), after they have fulfilled their function—a function far greater than the writing of a particular book.

Other interpretations also suggest themselves. The statement can be considered an expression of humility (as has been mentioned, a trait Wittig deems necessary in a writer); the recognition of other forms of action, outside of writing, that destroy so that renewal can occur; and the conviction that annihilation is a necessary step toward rebirth.

The last of these interpretations affirms that the destruction of the work of art—the text before us—prepares the transformative phase that leads to a new and even greater creation—one that is characterized by a more total form of renversement. This is indeed borne out of Wittig's next work, *Le Corps lesbien*, her most audacious undertaking to date and one of the truly outstanding texts in recent French literature.

3

J/e est une autre

In order to realize that Wittig's next book is her most audacious to date, it is not even necessary to open it. Its title is far more daring than any of her preceding ones. And on the dust jacket of the first edition, the title *LE CORPS LESBIEN* (in bold capitals) is followed by a list of bodily secretions that begins with "LA CYPRINE."[1] This alone constitutes a defiant renversement of several traditional taboos: direct reference to exclusively female sexuality, reference to the sexual organ, and most of all, reference to the secretion that marks erotic pleasure in the female. Totally frontal in approach, the words on the cover are tantamount to an exposure of the female genitalia in a state of arousal, and thus flaunt every prohibition imposed by our society. Indeed, so great is their shock value that they serve to select those daring enough to open the book. Not every one will. The timorous or the prudish are discouraged from the outset. Those who continue, however, are rewarded by a work of rare power and beauty.

It should also be added, however, that the shock value mentioned is only one aspect of the initial impression created. Another facet is celebration, which, although less immediately evident, is of equal importance. In order to perceive it, it is necessary to step outside Western culture and remember that in Hindu mythology and ritual the exposed female genitalia (yoni) are objects of adoration and revered symbols of the creative forces of the universe.

But let us return to the title itself. In the "Author's Note" that prefaces the English translation, *The Lesbian Body*, Wittig explains that the title announces a "theme which cannot even be described as taboo, for it has no real existence in the history of literature." Thus it emphasizes the complete break she wishes to accomplish from existing forms. She goes on to say that the text constitutes a "total rupture" in that it falls into the category of works "written by women exclusively for women."[2] This obviously indicates a new path, a novel approach to the situation of writer and reader. But it is an innovation rather than a restriction, for it can be interpreted, primarily, as the creation of a different form and as a chosen pact between the author and her public, rather than as a bid of separatism.[3]

By emphasizing literary considerations, Wittig draws attention to one possible interpretation of the title. *Le Corps* could refer to a corpus of texts (different from or in opposition to the dominant body of literature), for she also expresses her "fascination for writing the never previously written" and "the desire to do violence by writing to the language."[4] A link is also established, however, between this corpus of texts, the body of the text, and the female body. As Wittig herself says:

'The body of the text subsumes all the words of the female body. *Le Corps lesbien* attempts to achieve the affirmation of its reality. The lists of names contribute to this activity. To recite one's own body, to recite the body of the other, is to recite the words of which the book is made up. . . . The desire to bring the body violently to life in the words of the book.'[5]

The title then refers to three important concerns: the break with traditional literature and the creation of a new body of texts; the body of the text, which, in its "word work" and through the power of the word, "brings to life" or creates the palpable reality of the female body; and a body thus far "unattained,"[6] the object of fascination and desire.

Another aspect of the title is that it not only "do[es] violence to language," but it also renews language by creating the impression that the words used are being heard for the first time. Also, as suggested before, it serves to sort out the book's public, eliminating those not daring enough to proceed, but inciting those who are. In this sense, it is an act of defiance, of provocation, and yet it is also an invitation.

And because it constitutes an aggression, it is intimately linked with desire and with the fundamental nature of the work of art as Wittig sees it. *L'Opoponax* already showed this, and *Les Guérillères* reaffirmed it. In *Le Corps lesbien*, however, this transgression is expressed from the very start, in the very title of the work, and thus it either attracts or repels the potential reader from the outset.[7]

The words that constitute the title are repeated again at the beginning and at the end of the list of words (which Wittig calls "names," but which are actually anatomical terms that encompass all parts and functions of the female body—its organs, secretions and excretions, activities, and characteristics). Emphasis is placed on the transgressive quality of this list by the fact that the initial mention of "LE CORPS LESBIEN" is followed by the term "CYPRINE" and by the fact that its final mention is preceded by the word "PUBIS." This obviously puts the female sexual organ and the secretion that marks the height of female erotic pleasure in a privileged position in the text and reinforces the effect of the title. This is further accentuated by a typographical device chosen by Wittig, for the entire list is in capitals and achieves prominence by virtue of this alone. And the use of this list (its beginning and end, that is, the parts that contain the most audacious terms) on the dust jacket of the first edition is yet another way of drawing attention to the work's challenge of traditional notions.[8]

Upon examining the list itself, a number of significant factors become evident. It contains terms designating (in this order) secretions and excretions of the (female) body; the body's outer and inner surface, with its organs and substances; the body's reactions and expressions, movements and actions; the body's encounters with another (female) body; and the various parts of this body, ending with the pubis. As Wittig herself says, "the text subsumes all the words of the female body."[9] In its minuteness and exhaustiveness, it might appear like a complete catalogue of all the female body's separate parts and activities, something resembling a vivisector's manual. Yet while the list has the effect of "creating a new version of the *écorché* and the skeleton which exist for study,"[10] and

72

while it might therefore serve as a dissecting device, Wittig, by the simple expedient of using the words "THE LESBIAN BODY" at the start and finish, reassembles all the disparate parts into a whole, reconstitutes it, and gives life to this body—indeed succeeds in "bring[ing] the real body violently to life."[11]

Other aspects concerning this list are not as immediately discernable: for example, Wittig's reference to it (cited earlier) as a list of "names." This might appear, at first, as an error on her part, a simple misnomer. However, remembering the groups of names in *L'Opoponax* or the long chain of names that wound its way through the text of *Les Guérillères* suggests that the list of terms that traverses the pages of *Le Corps lesbien*, although it no longer consists of names, might have similar functions. The list also serves to emphasize unity in multiplicity, plenitude through diversity, and totality despite disparity. Just as the names of women in *Les Guérillères* came from all times and from every part of the globe yet formed a unified whole, so do the most diverse parts and activities of the female body (identical from the beginning of time and in all places) constitute a living entity. And just as the use of names emphasized the act of naming as a form of creation, the use of terms relating to the female body is tantamount to the creation of that body. In both instances, what is basically affirmed is the power of the word for giving life.

Even less easily seen is the manner in which this list functions in the text of *Le Corps lesbien*. True, it both divides and unifies—(as did the list of names in *Les Guérillères*, and by the same methods)—and thus does not, at first glance, constitute an innovation in the work of Wittig. However, while in the former instance the list of names created a regular structure (by intersecting the central *récit* at intervals of six pages, except at the end of each of its three principal parts), in *Le Corps lesbien* these intervals vary somewhat and are therefore not as obvious as elements in the text's architecture. There are eleven parts to this list, and in the French original (something that is not respected in the English translation), each one covers two or two times one, which, in Arabic numerals, is 11 pages. Also, the central portion of the text consists of 111 poetic prose sequences. These numerical divisions provide

the key to the book's structure, but only if through an awareness of the importance of numbers in the work of Wittig, can
this key open the door of possible interpretations.

Thus, despite her statement that "our [female] symbols
deny the traditional symbols,"[12] it is helpful to consult the
symbolic meaning of the numbers 11 and 111 in order to
elucidate Wittig's choice of structure for *Le Corps lesbien*. Once
again, it is a question of symbols that have transhistoric and
transcultural meanings and that thus have universal applica-
tions that exceed the narrow boundaries of those "traditional"
symbols to which Wittig appears to refer in her pronouncement. And as was seen in the case of *Les Guérillères*, such
symbols were fully applicable to an interpretation of that text;
indeed, they were so closely allied to its central preoccupations
as to be impossible to have arisen accidentally. To begin with,
the number eleven has the following, widespread meaning:
"S'ajoutant [au] 10 qui symbolise un cycle complet, le 11 est
le signe de l'excès, de la démesure, du débordement . . .
incontinence, violence, outrance . . . début du renouvellement mais aussi désordre . . . rebellion . . . la transgression
de la loi."[13] It is clear then that this symbol is in perfect agreement with Wittig's aims and coincides with the major characteristics of *Le Corps lesbien* (excess, overflow, violence, and
outrage; and the start of renewal, rebellion, and the transgression of laws). The meaning of the number 111 provides further
clarification, for that number symbolizes "une partie qui forme
un tout dans le tout, un microcosme dans le macrocosme, qui
distingue et individualise . . . un groupe dans un ensemble."[14]
Since the number 111 applies to the sequences that constitute
the central text of *Le Corps lesbien*, it is evident that it characterizes them admirably. Indeed, each one of them constitutes a
part that forms a whole within a whole, a microcosmos within
the macrocosmos (of the body of the text as well as of the
female body), a group within a set, an assemblage (literary or
anatomical).

Symbolic also, in some respects, is the placement of the
words "LE CORPS LESBIEN"at the beginning and at the end
of the list that "subsumes all the words of the female body."
This placement creates a circular structure. The complex
meanings of the symbol of the circle in *Les Guérillères* suit its

application here as well. But to create a circle is also to loop the loop and to add a cyclical dimension to that of totality and unity. And of course, the cyclical nature of the female body is another of the physiological and psychological realities of that body that is suggested by the circle. From another viewpoint, the placement of those all-important words suggests the alpha-omega sequence (not reversed, this time, as it was in *Les Guérillères*), which refers to a whole, even a sacred dimension. This is reinforced by the possibility of an allusion to the *ouroboros*, the serpent that bites its tail and symbolizes cyclical evolution, autofecundation, and eternal return—all of which are applicable here.

The number of the short, poetic prose sequences that constitute the central portion of the text is also revealing in a variety of ways. Yet these sequences are not numbered in the text, and only by counting them does it become apparent that there are 111 of them. Perhaps the fact that they are not numbered is as indicative of their importance as was the fact that the significant figure of the beloved was not named at one point in *L'Opoponax*, and in every instance in *Le Corps lesbien*.

The symbolic meaning of 111 has been discussed. As in numerology however—a branch of knowledge that appears to interest Wittig—this number consists of three ones that, when added together, give the number three. Three was already a key symbol in *Les Guérillères* and it is therefore no surprise that it should reappear here with all the meanings that were discussed in the former instance. However, in *Le Corps lesbien* (which, incidentally, consists of three words), it is also clearly linked to the figure of the Triple Goddess, as the following passage shows:

> J/e suis celle qui mugit de ses trois cornes, j/e suis la triple, j/e suis la redoutable la bienveillante l'infernale, j/e suis la noire la rouge la blanche. . . . je tonne de mes trois voix la vociférante la sereine la stridente.[15] (*C*, 165)

This Triple Goddess, who appears in a number of mythologies, is the divine counterpart of the various aspects of the lesbian body (both of the text and of the human female), and the goddesses' three incarnations, as well as her three voices, are in accordance with the characteristics of the work. She and the number associated with her are opposed to the number two and its binary, male symbolism. Two is referred to in the same passage as "la stupide dualité " (*C*, 165), and this duality must be extended, or expanded, in order to reach the complexity and plenitude of the female, symbolized by the number three.

The same passage—as indeed the entire central portion of the book—contains a striking innovation: the first person pronoun is written in unorthodox fashion ("J/e"). The same is true for *m/a*, *m/on*, and *m/es* throughout the text. Once again, as in previously noted instances of typographical or grammatical inventions, this is not a case of novelty for novelty's sake nor a contrived device for attracting attention, but an example of simple means to accomplish complex ends. Indeed, the reasons for using this particular form for the first person voice (of the speaker, the speaking subject, the narrator) are multiple and of the greatest significance. Wittig herself has discussed them at some length and provided important insights:

> *J/e* is the symbol of the lived, rending experience
> which is m/y writing, of this cutting in two which
> throughout literature is the exercise of a language
> which does not constitute me as a subject.[16]

Thus, the first thing achieved by this new form of the first person pronoun is a representation of the schism Wittig describes, a representation of the tearing apart of the writer forced to write in a language that is not hers, is foreign to her, and is even hostile to her enterprise. So intense is this "rending experience" that to write *Je* is something which Wittig says she is "physically incapable" of doing.[17] The main reason for her choice, then, is not a cerebral but an emotional one— passionate because "lived," and almost visceral in nature.

The use of the *J/e*, however, does not only express the harsh fate of the woman writer that Wittig speaks of in the quote given above. It is also a type of "war machine." This is revealed in another statement in which she affirms "the desire to do violence by writing to the language which *I* [*j/e*] can only enter by force."[18] In this sense, the slash is a wedge driven into an existing convention, a type of military tactic by which an enemy can be vanquished. And because it is something resembling a neologism (or at least a new form), it destroys a time-honored tradition, literally cuts it in two, and after annihilation, recreates it. This is by now a familiar practice of Wittig, yet nowhere in her previous work has it been applied to something as deeply ingrained, as firmly established, as the form taken by the first person singular pronoun. The audacious suggestion arising from this deathblow and resurrection is that the *I* is not immutable, nor (by implication) predominantly masculine, as is generally assumed, but that a female speaker can appropriate it, alter it, and thus express her presence, authority, autonomy, and originality as a writer. This becomes evident in one of Wittig's statements:

> The *j/e* in *The Lesbian Body* is not an *I* destroyed. It is an *I* so powerful that it can . . . assault. . . . This *I* can be destroyed in the attempt and resuscitated. Nothing resists this *I* . . . which spreads itself in the whole book, like a lava flow that nothing can resist.[19]

Nevertheless, this powerful, resistant *I* has arisen only after a fierce combat, after an experience of fragmentation or dismemberment. It is the result of a transformation that has its origins in a painful schism. Wittig herself has spoken of this in the following terms:

> L'expérience . . . d'une femme écrivain est complète-ment schizophrénique. Il faut toujours faire coupure entre les deux: d'une part, employer un langage qui n'est pas le nôtre . . . et la lutte qu'on mène sur un autre plan, qui tend à casser tout ça, à essayer de faire à travers et dans le langage autre chose.[20]

From this quote it can be seen that, although the rendering both of the schism experienced by the woman writer and of her struggles to destroy this state of affairs is important to Wittig, one of her major aims is innovation and metamorphosis ("de faire . . . autre chose") in the domain of language.

So strong is this penchant that Wittig would probably agree with Rimbaud, who (in his famous "Lettre du voyant") expressed his willingness to face illness, torment, indeed the disintegration of his psyche, in order to achieve the transformation that would allow him to say, "Je est un autre" ("I am another"). In Wittig's case, a similar risk is run, a parallel transformation (with all its inherent dangers) is accepted. However, the result is an even more drastic alteration—one which could allow her to proclaim, "J/e est une autre."

This risk, this danger to the self, might also explain the use of the first person singular everywhere in the body of the text. It differs radically from the *on* of *L'Opoponax* or the *elles* of *Les Guérillères,* for all the former impersonality has vanished and the distance has been discarded. The self is there in all its vulnerability, torment, and fragmentation, but also in all its power, jubilation, and creative affirmation. In other words, the change from *on* to *elles* to *j/e* is a progression from the objective to the subjective, the impersonal to the intensely personal, the descriptive to the emotive, and from surface to core, from the collective to the broken, divided, yet triumphant self. However, this *j/e,* as subjective, personal, even singular as it at first might seem, also attains a universality that is astonishing.

It has been shown that universalization is one of Wittig's major aims in her works of literature, and the manner in which it is achieved in *Le Corps lesbien* is of great interest. Among the first contributing elements is, of course, her choice of subject matter. *Le Corps lesbien* is, without a doubt, one of the greatest love poems ever written—and this irrespective of what might, at first, appear to be a restriction to a certain kind of love (indicated in the title of the work). Taken on the most fundamental level, it is the most intense, and the most complete, exploration of every possible aspect and of every imaginable facet of the emotional and physical experiences that constitute love—everywhere, at all times, and between all possible individuals. In spite of Wittig's statement that the book falls into the category of works "written by women exclusively for women,"[21] its power does not, essentially, come from this at all. It resides in the singularly passionate and astonishingly complex poetic renderings of acts and feelings that all living beings can experience and share. Wittig is quite right in saying that she is here "writing the never previously written," but it is not so much a question of an innovative kind of literature as of the degree to which she has intensified and exceeded previous forms of that literature.

It can easily be seen that *Le Corps lesbien* might be compared to the Song of Songs, one of the greatest love poems of all time. This, of course, leads to several observations. It shows that Wittig has once more abandoned genres she had previously explored and moved on to other domains. This time, it is not the bildungsroman nor the epic that she appropriates (and subverts) but a work that almost constitutes a genre by itself: the Bible. What is more, she has chosen the Old Testament (a vital part of the male-dominated Judeo-Christian tradition). This makes it the perfect target, another bastion to be stormed, a territory to be conquered and claimed for her own. However, the Song of Songs is also the ideal challenge for her poetic and combative talents. Not only is it known for the magnificence of its writing, but it is considered among the finest expressions of love in which a male subject addresses a female object of desire. What could constitute greater defiance than to attempt to equal this love poem's magnificence and yet to totally subvert the poem's aims by making both lovers female? There is no doubt that Wittig succeeds on both counts with *Le Corps lesbien.*

However, Wittig's work also distinguishes itself from the Song of Songs by its predominant tone. While the latter is characterized by tenderness and by lyrical descriptions of the beloved, *Le Corps lesbien* has been aptly called "un chant passionnel et sauvage" accompanying "un combat impitoyable" in which "violences, déchirements . . . vont jusqu' à la destruction et la décomposition du corps aimé."[22] In its vehemence, indeed in its totally relentless destruction of the traditional tone of love poetry, it differentiates itself not only from this biblical love poem, but also from other examples of such poetry. Some of these were indeed written by women—such as the works of Sappho, the *Letters of a Portuguese Nun,* or the great songs of mystical love—and have been compared by critics to this work of Wittig.[23] (A comparison which seems more appropriate but has, to my knowledge, not been made, is with the sonnets of Louise Labé, to whom there is a subtle reference via a brief quote from her poetry [C, 153]—a reference not easily detected unless the reader is thoroughly familiar with Labé's work). Yet in all these cases, whether the author is a man or a woman and whether the love poetry in question is of a heterosexual or a homosexual nature, there is no example of violent passion that can equal that which appears everywhere in *Le Corps lesbien* and which is maintained with almost unbearable intensity. In this sense, it is indeed something "never previously written," for its tone attains a paroxystic quality that does not appear in any of the most famous works in this genre.

The only comparisons that seem possible are with portions of Wittig's earlier works: the most passionate passages of *L'Opoponax* relating to the love relationship between Catherine Legrand and Valerie Borge, and certain intensely lyrical sequences of *Les Guérillères*. But these were isolated instances, while *Le Corps lesbien* consists almost entirely of prose poems written in that vein. The only contrast (or relief) provided is the tone that characterizes the list of anatomical terms that winds its way through the text—a tone reminiscent of the one that pervaded *L'Opoponax*. The tone is objective, and almost cold, by virtue of the list's scientific provenance. And yet, because the list also serves to "recite one's body, to recite the body of the other,"[24] it functions as a litany or a hymn celebrating the body, and celebrating the love of one's own body and of the body of the beloved. As in the lyrical passages of *L'Opoponax* (only in reverse this time), the contrast of tones heightens the effect of the predominant one in each work. Thus, in *Le Corps lesbien*, the neutral tone achieved by the use of scientific vocabulary increases the intensity of the poetic sequences that constitute the body of the work and increases, by extension, the poetic vision of the body of love.

This litany of all parts of the body also functions as a way of dismembering it. In this way, it underlines the traditional fragmentation of women's bodies (already treated in *Les Guérillères*). But here the body is also reconstituted and recreated (through love), and all its disparate parts are reassembled and enhanced. Just as the use of the *j/e* served to both deconstruct and reconstruct the self, so does the list of separate elements of the (female) body serve to emphasize the power of reunification that results in a reborn whole.

It is not by accident that the myth of Isis and Osiris (who

is female here) is central to *Le Corps lesbien*. It will be treated in detail in the pages that follow, but even at first glance provides an important clue to the understanding of the list in question. In simplest terms, this myth speaks of the disparate and dispersed parts of the beloved (Osiris), reassembled by the lover (Isis)—of a triumphant rebirth after dismemberment and annihilation.

Furthermore, this list, in its completeness, establishes the integrity and totality of the body. Already affirmed in *Les Guérillères*, where "elles disent qu'elles appréhendent leurs corps dans leurs totalité" (*G*, 43),[25] this taking possession by women of their own bodies is carried out in *Le Corps lesbien*. They have become subjects rather than objects, active rather than passive, creators instead of creations. And this implies the reconquest of the body as well as of its various activities, both physiological and emotional. The list (anatomical in nature) implies the former, while the prose poems that constitute the central text express all the facets of the latter. This reconquest is also accentuated by the two sorts of typography used (large capitals for the list, small type for the prose poems), which can be compared to two kinds of flux—another suggestion of an important aspect of the female body and of the vast flow of emotions that pervades the text.

The interaction between the list and the poetic sequences further establishes a thematics of discontinuity continuity, and of fragmentation–unification. The former interrupts the latter at intervals of approximately fourteen pages. This—as has been the case for other numbers—is highly significant. Several observations suggest themselves. The intervals correspond to the fourteen parts of Osiris' body, dispersed and reassembled by Isis.[26] Fourteen, however, is also one-half of twenty-eight, the midpoint of the lunar and menstrual cycle, and thus has sacred as well as profane, cosmological as well as biological, implications. Also, while the number fourteen is usually associated with the moment in the middle of the menstrual cycle when ovulation takes place (and therefore when the possibility of reproduction exists), the number twenty-eight is associated with the occurrence of the menstrual flow (which indicates the destruction of the ovum and the elimination of the virtuality of reproduction). Therefore, the traditional interpretation of ovulation and menstruation is subjected to renversement. Creation in the form of reproduction is destructive and its opposite is celebrated.

Also, the ritual festival of menstruation (which takes place on the twenty-eighth of the month, thus doubling and reinforcing the number fourteen or the completion of the cycle) glorifies the female cycle, and is another example of the various types of reversals practiced by Wittig (C, 60–61, 90). It overthrows the secretive, often shameful attitude of women in many societies regarding this physiological occurrence and the taboos associated with it (attitudes and taboos that make women "impure," "unclean," and "cursed"). In place of such attitudes, Wittig substitutes the celebration of this specifically female attribute—not in terms of the potential of pregnancy, but as a phenomenon pertaining exclusively to the female body. Moreover, Wittig not only glorifies menstruation, but she also uses it for its shock value—at least for a squeamish or prudish reader. This is strikingly illustrated in one of the poetic sequences in which the lover imbibes the menstrual blood of the beloved in a ritual imitating and subverting that of the Eucharist (C, 61).

Indeed, such treatment of various aspects of the Christian Mass is evident not only in details such as this but in the entire structure of the book. The various parts of Le Corps lesbien can be seen as an appropriation and recreation of the Holy Mass: Introit, Gloria, Invocation, Passion, Ascension, and Assumption. This is reinforced by well-known phrases from liturgy that appear in Wittig's text, such as "siécle des siécles" (C, 91, 96, 109, 114), "ainsi soit-il" (C, 131), and "ad Vitam aeternam, Amen" (C, 164).[27] And of course in the central portion of the Mass, Communion, the phrase "this is my body" (echoing the "Corps" of Le Corps lesbien) figures prominently. This treatment of the Mass accomplishes a number of things: it constitutes a transgression amounting to heresy; it appropriates a male-dominated ritual; and it reinforces the high point of the Mass (Communion) but redefines it, for the communion here is not with a male god but with a female beloved. Also, because references in the work are predominantly to pagan divinities (and specifically to female ones), the subversion is total and sacrilegious on a number of counts.

Christ himself, the central figure in the Mass, is subject to such action. In this work he is feminized—that is, renamed, becoming "Christa" (*C*, 30, 138), and he is surpassed by Osiris, who has also undergone a sex change and become female (*C*, 78, 87, 130). The Virgin Mary as well has been removed from center stage and has been replaced by Isis, another divine mother according to the traditional Egyptian view, but here portrayed not as her son's lover but as another woman's. Interestingly, the two myths (that of Christ and that of Osiris) involve annihilation and resurrection. They are thus fitting illustrations, or incarnations, of the central thematics of Wittig's text. Both myths themselves have also been destroyed and recreated and therefore further fit her central aim of renversement.

Other well-known mythological figures subjected to reversal (by feminization) include Achilles, Atreus, Ganymedes, Icarus, Ulysses, and Zeus (*C*, 101, 118, 39, 185, 16, 39). The figure of Ganymedes is particularly interesting, because Wittig has not only made Zeus' male lover female, but she has changed his name by a fusion that results in a new being that is androgynous in nature (thus confusing or unifying genders) and that bears a name that is actually a neologism with all that it implies—"Ganymédéa" (*C*, 39). By choosing to join the name of Medea to that of Ganymedes, or (in another instance) to Archimedes, Wittig accomplishes a variety of ends. She attributes importance to Medea, who, as has been pointed out, is a figure from a prepatriarchal myth,[28] but who is also there depicted as a sorceress, a ferocious, antimaternal woman who destroys her offspring. Moreover, by inserting the female name into masculine ones Wittig achieves a "mélange de signes" and "se situe, comme elle situe son texte . . . en dehors du système masculin-féminin"[29]—an extremely important concern, as has been mentioned (which also determined the term *lesbian* in order to move beyond the traditional confines of the designations *man* and *woman*). Besides, it shows how many complex ends the author achieves by a device that is deceptively simple when first seen, or that even seems lusory on the surface.

While numerous male mythological figures appear in altered form and even their actions are recreated—for example,

Icarus does not fall into the sea alone but accompanied by her beloved, and Orpheus does not lose Eurydice as a result of a backward glance but triumphantly resuscitates her (*C*, 185–86, 11–13)—female divinities and mythological heroines abound in the text. They include Latona and Niobe, the Sphinx (which, in French, has a doubly feminine form, *sphyngesse*), Isis, Ishtar, Astarte, Persephone, the Gorgon, and others (*C*, 26, 45, 87, 102, 103, 124, 138, 166). In certain sequences, they are grouped together—for example, Ishtar Astarte (*C*, 102 – 3). In others, a large number of them constitute a newly created conglomerate or even an exclusively female pantheon whose members come from a variety of mythologies—for example, Artemis, Aphrodite, Persephone, Ishtar, Albina, Epona, Leucippa, Isis, Hecate, Pomona and Flora, Andromeda, Cybele, Io, Niobe and Latona, Sappho, Gurinno, Ceres, Leucothea, Rhamnusia, Minerva (here the daughter of "Zeyna," not of Zeus) and Demeter (*C*, 73–74).

Sappho appears in this assembly, raised to the stature of a divinity. Indeed, she is treated as such during the entire series of prose poems—invoked, celebrated, implored, solicited, glorified, feared, propitiated, and prayed to as if a goddess (*C*, 58, 107, 108, 130–31, 143, 165). Such divinization of the greatest woman poet of all time seems natural in a work by a woman poet, which is written—one might say—under her aegis. More than a muse, she has become a numinous figure and can be compared to Isis, who, according to the Egyptian *Book of the Dead*, "possédait le pouvoir du Verbe vivant, [un] pouvoir plus grand que celui de Ra divin roi-soleil . . . le pouvoir de nommer grâce auquel nous pouvons symboliquement fragmenter et unifier le monde"[30] (a power akin to the aims of *Le Corps lesbien* and its author). But there is also something that differentiates Isis from Sappho and makes the latter an even more apt choice for Wittig's purpose. First of all, Isis is an accepted (and in that sense traditional) divinity, while Sappho's divine status is invented by Wittig and is thus a new creation. Then also, Isis is habitually associated with a male lover, Osiris (who, although feminized in *Le Corps lesbien*, is nevertheless generally remembered in his masculine form), while Sappho's lovers are reputed to have been female. Moreover, Sappho was a poet the glory of whose works has endured for centuries but some of whose writing may have been destroyed as a result of the hostility of the male literary establishment. All these considerations certainly enter into Wittig's sense of relatedness with Sappho, and her glorification and divinization of this denizen of Lesbos.

Perhaps it is even the association with the Isle of Lesbos—from which the term *lesbian* is derived—that explains Wittig's predilection for this term and the importance accorded to it by the title of her work. She has, of course, explained this choice in other ways (mainly as a means of moving beyond the usual designations of gender or as a term signifying an autonomous human being). But the question arises whether it is not primarily the link with Sappho that is most significant, for the "lesbian" viewpoint (or the one Wittig refers to as "gay" in "The Trojan Horse") is of no more import for the greatness of Sappho's poetry than the question of whether the Dark Lady of Shakespeare's sonnets was a man or a woman. And this is equally true for *Le Corps lesbien*, where Wittig's poetic gifts are at their zenith.

The Isle of Lesbos, and indeed islands in general, constitute privileged settings in this work. Whether they are "les vertes Cythères" or "les Lesbos noires et dorées" (C, 30)[31] or unnamed islands that appear in numerous sequences (C, 16, 41, 47, 84, 89, 90, 106, 130, 153, for example), they share certain important characteristics. Symbolically, and in almost every culture, islands are figurations of paradise, the abode of the blessed or chosen, even the realm of the immortals where the woes of the world cease, and where earthly or heavenly delights abound.[32] But islands are also places of refuge, of shelter, of voluntary exile. And by their very position, they are set apart, distinctive, opposed to the surrounding elements or to landbound spaces. Moreover, they are surrounded by the sea and in constant contact with the watery element. Also, the very form of islands (an oval or a circle) links them to the symbolic shapes that occupy an important place in Wittig's work, as well as to the letter O, its homonym "eau," the female genitalia, and even the vaginal secretion often compared to seawater. It is easy to see why islands figure so prominently in Wittig's text.

Islands, moreover, are here contrasted with a different

setting: the city. It can even be said that these two sites are opposite poles and that the major tension—the combat concerning the beloved—involves the movement between them. The city is alternately described as Hell ("cette géhenne"), a somber abode ("la ville de nuit"), and a place surrounded by a labyrinth (*C*, 7, 53, 83). And—most importantly— it is described as the site of the lover's exclusion, her separation from the beloved. The last of these is shown in the lover's lament, repeated in several sequences: "J/e suis frappée d'interdit dans la cité où tu vis. Là j/e n'ai pas le droit d'aller" (*C*, 34); and "J/e n'ai droit de cité dans le lieu où tu vis" (*C*, 149).[33] But the city is also a negative setting contrasted with that of the island, because it is linked to civilization, to tradition, to limitation, to all that is landlocked. It is a closed place or an enclosure, a circular trap (the circle with pernicious connotations). Associated with torment and death, it is diametrically opposed to joy and life, as the following statement shows: "Adieu continent noir tu mets le cap pour l'île des vivantes" (*C*, 89)[34]

An opposition is also established in terms of elements: on the one hand, those that are hard, rigid, and static—metal, stone, ice, and glass; and on the other, those that are fluid, mobile, and capable of transformation—the sea, waves, tides, rivers, and winds (also literature, the body of the text, and the body of woman). In this respect, stasis is contrasted with flux, tradition with innovation, and perhaps even the male erotic experience—the erect city—with the moving sea, flowing river, or deep lake. Moreover, cities are *man*-made, while natural surroundings are the work of nature—invariably associated with women. And even though there are no men in the cities of *Le Corps lesbien* (or indeed anywhere in the text, having been eliminated or simply discarded) the symbol of the city itself remains, a site against which its opposite is pitted—a threatening image, but also one against which battle is waged. The island, on the other hand, emerges as the homeland of women, a place of subversion and of the reversal of standard values. This probably also accounts for the island names frequently mentioned in the text: Lesbos and Cyprus (the birthplace of Aphrodite and linked to the term *cyprine*[35]), symbols of art and desire.

Colors also play an important role in *Le Corps lesbien*, much more so than in Wittig's former works. This results in a text that is more vivid, more sensual (that is, more appealing to the senses), thus decreasing emotional distance and involving the reader directly. Also noteworthy, however, is a predilection for certain colors. This was already true in Wittig's first two novels, but nowhere is the meaning of colors as vital for the interpretation of the text as in *Le Corps lesbien*. Here, as could be expected, the colors linked to the figure of the beloved are the most prominent and the most significant. They are golden and black, appearing either separately or in conjunction (*C*, 7, 14, 20, 32, 33, 47, 119, 126), and they are in some instances joined by violet (*C*, 92–93). It is relatively easy to see that golden and black suggest brilliance (or light) and darkness, the diurnal and the nocturnal, the sun and the moon—opposites united into a whole. But it is the last of these colors (violet) that appears with extraordinary frequency (both as colors and as flowers) and in a variety of shades: mauve, purple, parma, lilac, violet, and lavender. True there was already evidence of this predilection in *L'Opoponax* and again (even more noticeably) in *Les Guérillères*, but it is in *Le Corps lesbien* that this color becomes so prominent that it constitutes something resembling a leitmotif. It appears forty-two times in this text,[36] sometimes in as many as three instances on the same page (*C*, 179). The most arresting example of its use is the sequence in which it is mentioned fifteen times and associated with Sappho, rain, rounded hills, light, the body of the beloved, beach sand, flowers, and perfumes—obviously, all female symbols (*C*, 130–32).

The prominent and purposeful use of violet raises questions about the meaning of this color, for it is evidently more than a preference such as that a painter might have for a certain palette. It is obviously there for certain reasons. One of these is that it is a color used by "initiates," a sign chosen by the members of a "countergroup." This becomes clear through the choice of violet for the cover of a publication such as *Vlasta*, which describes itself as a "revue des fictions amazoniennes" and states that it is devoted to "lesbian" publications. The same color is prominently used on the dust jacket of the first edition of *Le Corps lesbien* for the list of anatomical terms that appears there. However, while these choices could be linked to a desire to affirm one's opposition to the male literary establishment, Wittig's use of that color (and its multiple variants) seems to be primarily poetic, as is easily proven when it is seen in context. It is also a reference to Sappho, whose predilection for that color is evident in her poetry. As in so many other instances, provocation or subversion are but a part of Wittig's purpose, the main intent always being literary—that is, poetic.

And, perhaps because any such consistent emphasis on one color—even though that color flaunts traditional attitudes and has poetic value—might suggest rigidity or an incapacity for transformation (both of which Wittig clearly opposes in "The Trojan Horse" and in her fictions), she juggles colors with total freedom and even insists on her right to do so. This can best be seen in the following passage:

> A un geste d'Aphrodite la bienheureuse, toutes . . .
> échangent leurs couleurs. Leucothéa devient la noire,
> Déméter la blanche, Isis la blonde, Io la rouge, Ar-
> témis la verte, Sapho la dorée, Perséphone la violette,
> les transformations les gagnent de proche en proche,
> l'arc-en-ciel du prisme leur passe sur la figure.[37]
> (C, 74)

Thus, we see that even goddesses' attributes are not fixed. At the incitation of Aphrodite, they proceed to change in kaleidoscopic fashion, resembling the play of colors in a prism or rainbow. The latter, a wondrous natural phenomenon, is the result of the interaction of sun and rain, but it is also the symbol of a covenant. In this instance, however, the covenant is not with the one, terrible (male) God of the Old Testament, but with a series of (female) pagan divinities.

The same kind of freedom, or capacity for transformation, is evident in Wittig's treatment of other elements in *Le Corps lesbien*—for example, her handling of time. Here, as in previous works, she shows a predilection for the use of verbs in the present tense. This establishes a strong sense of presence as well as a utopian quality (which was already quite evident in *Les Guérillères*). But it is primarily the creation of a feeling of timelessness that seems to motivate the choice of the author in this text. The fundamental experience portrayed—that of love in all its aspects—is not limited to a particular epoch, but has existed from time immemorial and can even be projected into the far future. This is expressed in the work by sequences that appear to be located in the ancient past (somewhere in antiquity—which also suggests prepatriarchal cultures), as well as in those very striking sequences that are futuristic and tend to resemble science fiction (for example, C, 179–80). It is reinforced by the nonchronological order of sequences in the text. This, as in *Les Guérillères*, creates an impression of atemporality or of experiences that take place totally outside of time. The last of these is probably the most significant, since it expresses the intensity of the love experience, which is such that time seems either to stand still or not to exist at all. It is allied to what has been said to characterize the encounter with the numinous, but also with creation (especially literature).[38] In that sense, time, or Time ("le Grand Temps," as Mircea Eliade calls it), is a concept that links love, the numinous, and creation—a triad to which Wittig certainly subscribes in this work. A fourth element, however, might be added to the three mentioned above: that of transgression—which is common to them all and which she uses, in her free handling, indeed her renversement, of temporal notions.

Wittig's treatment of space in *Le Corps lesbien* is equally fascinating. While the settings of various sequences seem to be characterized by polarity—the island against the city, as has been noted—the privileged space is essentially that of the body (or the body of the text) itself, as the title already indicated and as the list of anatomical terms reiterated. This is important on a number of counts. It emphasizes that, in this work, corporality is foremost, that it is indeed an *écriture du corps*,[39] a celebration of love's body. But it is also the creation of a specific space (differentiated from space in general), an action that connotes the establishment of a sacred place.[40] Thus, what might on the surface appear as delimitation is also sacralization—sacralization of a space (the female body, in this instance) that has formally been subject to vilification. It is therefore another form of renversement as well as a vindication.

It is within this space, which is indeed a whole world,

that all the action in *Le Corps lesbien* takes place. It seems as if this microcosmos were an entire cosmos, so complex are its structures and so complete the experiences depicted there. The list that reiterates all its parts, its activities, and even its origins (as the striking mention of exclusively female chromosomes that combine to form a female embryo shows[41]) is proof of this. And the 111 sequences that form the central text are a total exploration of all emotions imaginable—and some that only Wittig has imagined. The latter range from the greatest possible tenderness to the fiercest savagery, from the most profound sorrow to the most intense joy, from the height of pleasure to excruciating pain, from despair to triumph, from the desire for destruction to that of resurrection, and so on. And in this world, moreover, all forms of life exist: vegetal, animal, human, and superhuman; real and imagined; microscopic and astronomic; and everything ranging from chromosomes to constellations. It is as though the body (of the text and of woman) were a model or a replica of the universe[42]—a universe newly created, never before seen in all its complexity.

And this universe comes into being, achieves reality, by an act of creation: that of recitation. As Wittig herself has said, "To recite one's own body, to recite the body of the other is to recite all the words of which the book is made up."[43] Recitation is a term that elicits numerous reflections. Initially it suggests the "orality" of the text and puts an emphasis on a form of delivery often considered the province of women.[44] It is also linked to myth, ritual, and poetry. Moreover, it seems to indicate the manner in which the author has meant her text to be read—as poetry, where sounds are of the utmost importance, and where the tonality and sonority of words constitute their distinguishing element (that which separates them from prose). Recitation is thus a key term for the interpretation of *Le Corps lesbien,* one that opens the door (partially obscured by more obvious, but also misleading, readings of the work) to an understanding of its fundamental character.

The poetry of *Le Corps lesbien* is indeed what determines its greatness, for the audacity of the subject matter, the innovative approach to numerous literary conventions, even the singularity of Wittig's inventions alone, would not have made it the masterpiece it undoubtedly is. It is her poetic gift above all, seen here in all its magnitude, that ranks her with the finest of her predecessors and contemporaries: among others, Sappho and Virgil, Labé and Scève, Baudelaire and Mallarmé, and Saint-John Perse and Ponge. Some of them (as we have seen) have been integrated into her texts. Others are only silently present or can be invoked for comparison. But it is clear that poetry forms a vital part of Wittig's world—a world in which she herself occupies an important place.

A look at some of the greatest passages in *Le Corps lesbien* shows to what poetic intensity the text can soar. Not that it is easy to choose these. The entire work attains such a level of saturation (known as one of the hallmarks of poetry) and such density of imagery, that any isolated passage is insufficient for demonstrating Wittig's artistry, and it is tempting to refer to them all. Nor is it possible to give examples of only one type of poetry. She excels in the use of a variety of poetic modes, and as a result, it is difficult to select one mode as an illustration of the predominant one in the work. Lyrical, elegiac, liturgical, visionary, dithyrambic, scientific, surrealistic, as well as a number of other (formerly nonexistant or subverted) forms of poetry occur in *Le Corps lesbien*.[45]

This array of forms might, at first glance, seem to be tantamount to inconsistency, fragmentation, and dispersion. In actuality, however, it is reminiscent of the exploration and enumeration of all aspects and facets of the body (in the list of anatomical terms) that, although disparate, form a living whole. It is also a way of demonstrating the vast variety of emotions that are, each and every one, an indispensible part of the experience of love. Most remarkable in this work of Wittig, is that she includes emotions (and forms of poetry) that are usually excluded from poems dealing with love. Traditionally, love poems express feelings of tenderness, longing, and melancholy or they contain a celebration of the superior attributes of the beloved, a glorification of an ideal. Although some of these characteristics appear in Wittig's work, they are so intensified as to seem of a different order, or they are found side by side with such violent forms of expression that many readers are astounded, shocked, or horrified.

It seems that most critics have dwelled on the latter. They speak mainly of the fury, crudeness, and harshness that appears in this work;[46] the obsession expressed there;[47] the desire for provocation;[48] the delirium, carnage, and ferocity;[49] and its "combat impitoyable," which results in the "destruction et décomposition du corps aimé . . . son sacrifice."[50] They also note that it constitutes an aggression, an "attouchement pervers qui vous renverse et vous tord," and they point out that it is "une oeuvre audacieuse . . . viscérale," which is "radicalement subversive."[51] By doing so, they recognize the unusual qualities of *Le Corps lesbien*. However, it is probably an exaggeration to emphasize, to such an extent, the violent aspect of Wittig's poetry. And yet it is vital to speak of it, for it has a number of important purposes. It makes a work of art, even though it is a love poem, into a "war machine" that destroys existing forms. It pits a new approach against traditional models. But most of all, it explores the experience of love at depths, and in ways, never before attempted.[52] The last of these aims distinguishes this work by Wittig from most love poetry and makes it outstanding in this realm.

Once again though, it is not the singular point of view that gives the work its greatness, but the universalization (this time not only in breadth but also in depth) and the completeness of the author's enterprise. In this sense, it is impossible to agree with those critics who see Wittig's major accomplishment in *Le Corps lesbien* solely as the celebration of lesbian love and the destruction of the phallocentric approach.[53] Instead, it seems to be the best illustration of what she herself states as her aim (and as the aim of avant-garde literature) in the concluding paragraph of "The Trojan Horse." There is an interesting paradox between this pronouncement on the importance of universalization and that which is found in the "Author's Note" in the American edition of *The Lesbian Body*, where Wittig appears to place the emphasis on separatism and the singular point of view. It is tempting to discount the latter or at least to suggest that, given her fundamental and persistent penchant for renversement, the statement made (more recently) in "The Trojan Horse" is both a reversal and a broadening of her earlier point of view. And it is the latter that most significantly determines the complexity, the completeness, indeed the universality of the poetry found in

Le Corps lesbien, for the power of that work would be equally great, and its audacity hardly diminished, if it spoke of any other kind of love—between male and female, two males, parent and child, two siblings, a human being and an animal, and so on—with the same passion, the same profundity.

A comparison with two other great contemporary French writers might prove the validity of this affirmation. Considering the work of Marcel Proust and Jean Genet, it becomes clear that both their studies of love (or love-hate) relationships owe their depth and intensity, not to the fact that, in the case of Proust, all the male-female liaisons might be homosexual ones in disguise, nor to the fact that Genet speaks of maids, Blacks, and criminals yet, fundamentally, always of homosexual relations, but to the universal quality of the two authors' insights and to their artistry as writers. Both these attributes are also present in the work of Wittig. This very quality makes her writing outstanding and will undoubtedly make it last as both these writers' works have lasted.

In the case of Wittig, Proust, and Genet, it is essentially the quality of the writing itself that distinguishes their work from lesser literature of the same epoch and kind, for neither audacity nor universalization alone suffice to explain their greatness. In the final analysis, it is the stylistic element that determines the stature, uniqueness, and import of their work for present and future readers. It is this all-important aspect of the writer's craft that demands the closest attention (as Wittig herself has suggested in "The Trojan Horse").

Thus it is clear that it is the "word work" in *Le Corps lesbien* that is at the core of Wittig's entire enterprise. It is to this that she has obviously directed the greatest effort, and there her gifts are at their most evident. Even more than in any of her former texts, her innovative use of language, her inventions in the realm of grammar and syntax, and her overthrow of conventions that are considered immutable, are noticeable in this work. Some of these are outgrowths or developments of past techniques. Others are entirely novel and have no precedent in her fictions. Some even stand in total opposition to what has gone before. This shows, once more, that both continuity and discontinuity characterize her writing, in specific as well as in general terms. And it also shows that the body of her work is something vitally alive, subject to change, transformation, and destruction and recreation.

The most obvious elements of Wittig's work with language in this text instantly show that it is here a question of two main types of language: one totally objective (that is, scientific); the other its very opposite (highly emotional, subjective, and poetic). The first is reminiscent, yet also a further development, of the language that characterized *L'Opoponax*. The second, although it appeared in small doses both in *L'Opoponax* and in *Les Guérillères*, is new because of its frequency and sustained intensity. These two types of languages create two poles, two diametrically opposed zones between which a tension exists that contributes to the text's vitality. As a matter of fact, so striking is the contrast between these zones, that the reader is constantly transported from one register to another and is forced to shuttle between intensely emotive and cooly impersonal domains of language, and between the feelings evoked by each. This produces something akin to a series of shocks by which the reader is kept continually alert, never allowed to settle into one form of expression or one type of emotion. Rather than producing something similar to comic relief, or a reprieve from too great intensity, this interim use of neutral language seems to function in a manner not unlike that of black humor, which allows a writer to subject his/her reader to a series of otherwise unbearable experiences.[54] Moreover, each sort of language sets off and heightens the effect of the other. And the language contrast also draws attention to the importance of language itself, if only by the variety of emotions it inevitably evokes.

Paradoxical as it may initially appear, however, while the two language poles established in *Le Corps lesbien* seem, at first, entirely distinct (indeed opposed), the fact that the objective, impersonal, scientific list—contrasted with the emotionally charged central sequences by the variation in typography—can also be read in a recitative, incantatory fashion, breaks down the barrier between the two and destroys what might otherwise appear to be entirely different categories. This could be interpreted as another instance of renversement, an overthrow of traditional distinctions, or an innovative treatment of language registers. As a matter of fact, to suggest that scientific terms can be "recited" (as Wittig does in the "Author's Note"), or that they can become an incantation, attributes an entirely new function to them: one that denies the usual association with objective discourse and, instead, links the scientific to magical, poetical, nonrational forms of expression. This is indeed a novel suggestion and a form of attack on a certain type of establishment. In addition, considering the stereotypical belief that the rational, and, especially, the scientific, domain is the exclusive property of males, its appropriation and subversion by a female writer is, of course, another instance of conquest—this time, of language itself.

This is certainly also quite evident in the takeover that Wittig accomplishes in an area instantly evident in *Le Corps lesbien:* that of the gender of nouns (and of their accompanying adjectives). While this, of course, does not strike the English-speaking reader and is, indeed, impossible to render in translation, it is arresting or even quite shocking for the francophone. All nouns in the text (relating to living beings, human or animal) are either feminine or feminized. The examples in *Le Corps lesbien* are too numerous to cite, but some are so striking as to invite quoting: "bourreleuse" (*C*, 8), "inquisitrice" (*C*, 21), "sphyngesse" (*C*, 45), "ravisseuse" (*C*, 85), "voyeuse" (*C*, 152), "enfourrurée" (*C*, 88), "taure génisse" (*C*, 117), "agnelles nouvelles-nées" (*C*, 8), and so on. In some instances, these are archaic forms ("agnelle"). In others, they are the result of a feminine form based on a masculine one (for example, "inquisitrice" is based on *inquisiteur* "ravisseuse" on *ravisseur*, and "voyeuse" on *voyeur*). In still others, they are true neologisms ("enfourrurée"). In many cases, the new words contain an echo of those that originally had a masculine gender, but that were appropriated—subjected to a sex-change operation—and thus emerge in a recreated (feminine) form. By the use of archaic forms, words that were forgotten or have fallen into disuse are resuscitated and function almost as neologisms. In the case of actual neologisms, the words are indeed heard for the first time, since they constitute an entirely new creation. In all instances, the power of transforming language is achieved, and the process of freeing words from their everyday meanings (emphasized by Wittig in "The Trojan

Horse") is accomplished. Thus, while the feminization of language is an important process in this work, its poeticization seems of even greater significance. In fact, the first is part of the second. But the second is an even more fundamental concern to the author.

In this text, the same is true for Wittig's experimentation with verb forms. The first step is her overthrow of the traditional use of intransitive verbs—that is those that express an action but adhere to the subject, remain attached to it, and are incapable of passing over to an object.[55] Wittig, on the contrary, uses intransitive verbs in a way that makes the action pass immediately from subject to object (of desire). This does more than just express the liaison or relationships between the self, the other, and the world. It creates a new syntax. The result can be seen in such arresting phrases as: "J/e te suis j/e te viens" (*C*, 100) or "j/e te suis tu m/ /es" (*C*, 135). [56] Once again, the destructive and recreative qualities of Wittig's use of pronouns are impossible to translate into English and are thus often overlooked by a reader who cannot appreciate the startling innovation these phrases constitute in French or the shock they create for the ear of a francophone.

Another nontraditional or antitraditional aspect of the verb forms used by Wittig in *Le Corps lesbien* is her preference for the passive voice. This is in total opposition to the rules of the official French language, where the active voice is always preferred because the subject of the verb is perceived as an active being, akin to a conqueror, or at least in a dominant position. Wittig's predilection for the passive voice is thus a challenge to the establishment. More importantly, however, it is the sign of a new relationship between the self and the other, and between one's body and that of the other, as well as of a change in the narrative point of view. It has been suggested that, in *Le Corps lesbien*, the passive voice expresses the effacement of the individual subject and the affirmation of a communal experience; the interaction between the "j/e" and the "tu" (lover and beloved), which demands a passivity of the senses, a receptivity toward the other, or a consent to allow oneself to be invaded by the other; and total union.[57] While this interpretation seems highly pertinent, the change in the accepted use of verb forms, so striking in this work, is also there for the sake of transformation—for the sake of newness that has as its major function to awaken the reader and shock him into awareness, or into greater sensitivity to language.

Much more evident than the changes in verb forms (especially for the anglophone reader) is Wittig's lexicon in *Le Corps lesbien*. This lexicon is profoundly revolutionary, especially because it is primarily a vocabulary dealing with eroticism— a domain which, itself, is still somewhat taboo for women to speak or write about with complete freedom. Daring to use erotic vocabulary thus constitutes an aggression, or the claim to a birthright not often recognized. Besides, the particular kind of vocabulary used by Wittig in this text challenges several other existing traditions of the dominant society: on the one hand, an idealistic treatment of the female body and the erotic experience that denatures the reality of that body; on the other, a vulgar or obscene representation that makes it solely into a sex object. Her lexicon has nothing in common with the language of either of these conventional approaches to sexuality. It is visceral, carnal, direct, concrete, and anatomical in the truest sense of the word—that is, a language describing the body in *all* its aspects (internal and external, from entrails to skin, from bones to flesh, and from the hidden recesses of the brain to the most evident secretions). It leaves nothing unsaid, even those parts and activities of the body— menstruation, for example—that are considered unmentionable in the very works that invade the female body in the most ruthless fashion (such as hard-core pornography). So complete is the vocabulary relating to the physical reality of the female body/bodies (vocabulary most evident in the long list of anatomical terms that traverses the text) that it evokes the creation myths in which the human being/beings achieve form and life through an act of naming. The body of words becomes a body that lives—moves, secretes, excretes, acquires autonomy and sexuality, and loves.

The last of these activities is given the greatest prominence in *Le Corps lesbien*. The body language of this work creates what has quite rightly been called a "poetic anatomy of the female body,"[58] but what could perhaps be even better described as an anatomy of love, for eroticism is here inextrica-

bly linked to love. In contrast to the traditional division between the two—which often results in the former's descent
into pornography and in the latter's appearance in idealized
portrayals—Witting insists on their complete unification. She
also destroys the usual characteristics associated with each of
them when seen as separate experiences—such as the tenderness, euphemism, and circumlocution of love poetry, and the
directness, ferocity, and concrete imagery of erotic writing.
Such categories are no longer applicable and are, indeed,
totally overthrown. Furthermore, such labels as sadism, mas-
ochism, perversion, cannibalism, even necrophilia, have lost
all their meaning. Emotions of the most varied kind (and the
vocabulary to express them) are all part of, and incorporated
into, Wittig's portrayal of this experience, which knows no
boundaries or categories.

Indeed so total is the exploration and expression of every
aspect of erotic love, that this in itself constitutes the greatest
form of audaciousness found in this text. Nothing is left unsaid
(or unwritten). The most secret, or forbidden desires come to
light. Nothing that might usually be considered shocking or
revolting is discarded. Taboos no longer have any power, and
transgression of all established norms is natural here. Thus
the text contains startling sequences that depict the flaying of
the body of the beloved, the beloved's dismemberment in the
most bloody fashion, cannibalism, vivisection, and the tearing
apart of the lover by the beloved (C, 9, 13–14, 17, 27, 33–34).
All these cases, and many others not cited, express the violent
desire for a total exploration of the beloved—which includes
the most hidden aspects of the body (the entrails, the skeleton,
the brain, the optic center, the lungs, the heart, and so on)
and the source of life itself. It is a mutual invasion, an interpen-
etration by which lover and beloved are more than naked
before each other but actually enter into the furthest recesses
of each other's being in order to know, to feel, and finally to
achieve, total union.

The last of these, expressed either with great ferocity (C,
53, 123) or with utmost tenderness (C, 141), is the ultimate
aim of what might, at first glance, appear shocking or violent
for violence's sake. Absorption (C, 138), devoration (C, 99,
137), and incorporation (C, 43, 101) are all part of this passion-

ate desire for union of the most fundamental kind. Variations on this theme are manifold in the text. They include sequences that depict not only the joining and merging of human bodies but also their unification with animals (from whales to protozoa, from sharks to swans, from wolverines to lambs). The latter can be interpreted as demonstrating the animal nature of passion (in positive terms) as well as the myriad forms that the desire for union takes. This is also evident in the sequences that show the transmutations of the lovers, which allow them to become rain, storms, the sea, tears, trees, flowers, and so on.

As much as the union of lover and beloved pervades the text, its opposite also occupies an important place. Loss, separation, yearning, and exile are depicted with equal intensity and frequency. Although such thematics are part of the traditional material of love poetry (as is the desire for union), it is the manner in which Wittig expresses them that constitutes their singularity. In this respect as well, the vividness of imagery and the originality—indeed the total lack of banality or stereotypes—distinguish her treatment of these emotions. The torment of the lover far from the beloved, is expressed in terms rarely, if ever, seen. For example, the beloved becomes a statue, as hard and indifferent as stone; an empty space, a void, blind to the lover, walled up; a paralyzing, immobilizing force; invisible, negation personified; inert and unresponsive as a corpse; and the forbidden one (*C*, 25, 31, 35, 39, 66, 68–69, 95).

It is the last of these portrayals that is the most striking and the most prevalent in the work. The beloved, addressed as "m/a plus interdite" (*C*, 95)[59] and very frequently surrounded by a series of obstacles and prohibitions, is a figure that dominates numerous sequences in *Le Corps lesbien* and that demands analysis of this representation. Many interpretations suggest themselves. It reiterates the forbidden form of love, announced in the title and explored in the text. It underscores the transgression that is central to Wittig's literary enterprise in general. It echoes the association of love, transgression, and art (already established in *L'Opoponax*). It emphasizes the importance of that which is taboo, and also sacred. It is intimately linked with what is not named, must not be named, or is unnamable or ineffable. Most significantly, it has to do with the name of the beloved—she whose name must not be uttered. This interdiction (or nonenunciation) was already noteworthy in *L'Opoponax*, where the name of Valerie Borge was the only one not pronounced by Catherine Legrand, and where the term that described the emotion of love, *l'opoponax*, was a cryptonym.

In *Le Corps lesbien* all these forms of prohibition apply. The beloved is surrounded by various obstacles: distance; figures antagonistic to the lover; forces that separate, remove, and exile; and the very greatness of the loved one that elevates her beyond the reach of the lover. But she is also, and most especially, she who must not be named. Thus nowhere in the text is her name pronounced, or inscribed. Instead, however, she is addressed by an extraordinary number of epithets, whose function seems somewhat similar to that of the cryptonym. These range from "m/a très délectable" to "folle execrable," from "m/a plus sombre" to "m/a plus solestre m/a celestre" (*C*, 17, 25, 46, 103), and they sometimes combine the most unusual attributes, for example "m/on beau protozoaire m/a verte infusoire m/a vorticelle violente" (*C*, 43).[60] In fact, hundreds of these epithets appear in the text, matching the vast number of the transmutations of the beloved's figure. It can also be seen that the use of the possessive pronoun, the epithets, and the various representations of the beloved in an unusual diversity of forms are a way of attempting closeness or posession—always, however, without naming her.

Thus the name of the beloved and the act of naming derive their greatest power from their very absence. This absence increases the sense of tension, of an almost unbearable desire that longs to be satisfied yet is maintained at the highest peak precisely because it is not. Also, because of the interdiction associated with this absence, it is raised to the level of a taboo and becomes affiliated with the sacred. This becomes evident from a variety of indications in the text: phrases such as "ainsi soit-il" (*C*, 11), the "so be it" pronounced by the sacrificial divinity in the Christian religion and the terms applied to the beloved—such as "ineffable" and "innomable innomée" (*C*, 100, 44), traditionally reserved for divinities whose names either may not be taken in vain or may never be uttered, since to do so would constitute profanation in a number of religions. And yet the lover claims to be one of the chosen, or the initiated, the only one who knows the name of the divinity— or of the beloved. She chooses to keep this name a secret (*C*, 147) and therefore reveals herself as the keeper of the cryptonym—which she refuses to reveal, even under threat of torture by the uninitiated (*C*, 66). She menaces those who dare to utter it (*C*, 8) and is herself cruelly punished if she pronounces it, even when alone with her who must remain unnamed and unnamable (*C*, 44).

It can be seen that the possession of the name is of paramount importance and gives great power to the lover, yet the name must remain unspoken. As a result, the relationship between lover and beloved is something comparable to that of acolyte and divinity. And the beloved, in this work, is indeed the greatest of all divinities, precisely because she is "[l]a plus innomable." Her divination is also suggested by the fact that the numerous goddesses who appear in the text are named (Aphrodite, Artemis, Demeter, Ishtar, Isis, Minerva, and so on), while not even a letter or syllable of the beloved's name ever appears. This causes her to remain shrouded in mystery and silence, which adds to her numinous quality and elevates her above all lesser divinities.

In related fashion, the very first sequence of *Le Corps lesbien* contains the announcement that "ce qui a cours ici . . . n'a pas de nom" (*C*, 7)[61]—in other words, that what will take place, in the text, is something unnamable, a voyage into realms that are totally "other," that is to say, unbearable for the uninitiated, so terrifying or awesome are they. Indeed, in these realms, sacrificial rites are practiced and the great mysteries of death and resurrection take place (*C*, 8, 13–14, 99–100, 134–35, 141–42, 171, 184–85).

The latter constitute the core of the fragmentation and reunification, dimemberment and reassemblage, and destruction and recreation that is so important in *Le Corps lesbien*. While this fragmentation and reunification was indeed evident in Wittig's previous works, it is not until this particular text that it is present in all its magnitude. It is, of course, already apparent in the list of anatomical terms that catalogues all parts of the body—a list which divides yet achieves unification by virtue of its completeness or totality, and in which Wittig also establishes unification by the simple but effective device of eliminating commas.[62]

Dismemberment and reassemblage is reinforced by the numerous sequences in the text where the body of the lover and/or of the beloved is destroyed and recreated. It reaches its climax, however, in those sequences that contain representations of the dying and resurrected, or sacrificed and resuscitated, god/goddess. Among these divinities, it is naturally the figures of Christ and Osiris that instantly come to mind. And as might be expected, Wittig has resorted to the characteristic action of renversement in her treatment of them. Christ becomes "Christa" (C, 30) and the famous last words uttered by "her" are equally feminized: "mère mère pourquoi m//as-tu abandonnée."[63] To accentuate the echo effect, however, the last words are repeated three times, as in the biblical version (C, 138–39). Osiris, as has been shown, is also represented as female in this work. Yet greater importance is given to the Isis-Osiris myth than to that of Christ. This is evident by the far greater number of sequences in which the former appears, thus effecting another renversement by the emphasis of a pagan myth over a Christian one.

In the sequences devoted to Isis and Osiris (C, 127, 130, and especially 86–87), the dispersion of the parts of the body (of the divine beloved) and their reconstitution, or resurrection, are both celebrated. In the first instance, the gathering and reanimation are an act of love, and the miracle of resurrection occurs because of it. It is the intense desire of the lover (the "j/e" that speaks but is as fragmented as the beloved) that reanimates the loved one and breathes life into her formerly dismembered, now reassembled, body. And this miracle of recreation is accompanied by a shower of cherry blossoms, in a tableau that has all the hallmarks of a myth (C, 130). In the second instance, a well-known myth is, itself, destroyed and resurrected in a new form. Here the Isis/Osiris myth no longer portrays the divine couple as male and female, but as two female lovers. And instead of the phallus, which in the original myth occupies such a central place, it is the various parts of the female genital organ ("ta vulve tes nymphes ton clitoris," C, 127) that are emphasized. Not only does Isis reconstitute the body of her beloved (Osiris), but she breathes life into the latter, sings and dances in order to drive away the goddesses of death, and decrees that, from the union of the two lovers, little girls will be born (*C*, 87). This recreation transforms the original Egyptian model in many ways: Isis resurrects Osiris as Christ resuscitated Lazarus, breathes life into her as did the Old Testament creator when he formed the first man, dances as did Shiva to create the world, and in a final renversement, affirms that the result of Osiris' resurrection and the divine union of the couple will be the birth not of a male divinity but of human females ("petites filles"). The latter, of course, suggests a miraculous birth. This links it to the virgin birth of the Christian myth and the mother/son relationship also evident there, yet subverts both by substituting two female parents and multiple female offspring. It also serves as a link (and a clue) to a very unusual item in the list of anatomical terms: "$XX + XX = XX$" (*C*, 144). Once this is deciphered, it becomes clear that it refers to the joining of two pairs of female chromosomes that will result in a female embryo. It is striking that this physiologically impossible phenomenon is included in a list of physiological terms that are quite scientific, and also, that such a miraculous birth is placed among otherwise totally profane (physical) elements. As a result of all this intricate weaving and of the various cross-references established, the Virgin Mary, the two female lovers, and the redefined couple of Isis and Osiris are combined into an entirely new whole.

But there are also many other aspects of the Isis-Osiris myth that are of major significance in *Le Corps lesbien*. One critic, for example, quite rightly points out that Wittig's new version of the Egyptian myth contains an important metaphor that clarifies both the structure and the thematics of the work. To paraphrase, the body/text is fragmented, just as is the dismembered body of Osiris, because the group of narrative poems without apparent links portrays beings who act upon one another in hundreds of different ways, and because the list that enumerates and commemorates the various parts of the (lesbian) body interrupts the flow of the prose poems at intervals of approximately fourteen pages, corresponding to the fourteen parts of the body of Osiris that are dispersed and reassembled by Isis.[64] Another critic adds further insights by reminding us that, according to the Egyptian *Book of the Dead*, Isis possessed "[le] pouvoir du Verbe vivant" and that this power was greater than that of Ra, the divine sun god. Thus, Isis incarnates the power of discourse and naming, thanks to which one can symbolically fragment and reunify the world.[65] In addition, the power of naming (accentuated by the frequent use of the word *nom*), as well as that of not naming, are powers conferred by the act of speech or by silence, both of which are in the possession of the writer—this writer.

And yet writing itself is not directly referred to in *Le Corps lesbien* (as it was, to some extent, in *L'Opoponax* and, in much greater measure, in *Les Guèrilléres*). There are no texts produced by the protagonists, nor does the written word function as a means either of communicating or of redefining their bodies and their world. Instead, it is the spoken (and the unspoken) word that is of major import. In this sense, *Le Corps lesbien* is a much more oral work, more direct and more physical as a result, and in keeping with its subject matter. Also, as has been mentioned, the entire text is to be "recited" according to Wittig. This, on the one hand, allies it more closely to poetry and, on the other, links it to that type of communication referred to in the concluding lines of the poem at the end of *Les Guérillères*, which speak of something outside of, or beyond, texts.

However, although the act of writing is not represented in the work, language itself is emphasized. This is evident from the important portion of the list of physical activities relating to the various organs involved with language (the ear, the vocal cords, and the mouth) and to the sounds produced (ranging from cries to laughter, from moans to whispers, from weeping to songs, and from silences to words) (*C*, 144–45). Even more significant is the sequence where language is destroyed and recreated (*C*, 116–17). It takes place, significantly, in a circular square, a reminder of the circle and the mandala that were of such importance in *Les Guérillères*. The news of what has happened to language is announced by the beloved, and therefore she is the harbinger of its annihilation and rebirth—an important role. The new language has a guttural sound consisting solely of consonants (all vowels having disappeared) and produces grunts, harsh noises, and a scraping of the vocal cords that are comical and cause uproarious laughter in the listener (the lover). Long, incomprehensible phrases are repeated by a crowd of women and joined by the beat of a tom-tom, which resembles a death kneel suggesting the burial of the old language. This is followed, by the "résonances insolites de la langue transformée", that is the formerly unknown, unheard of, and metamorphosed language, repeated by thousands of voices. A violent storm then occurs, which brings down torrents of rain (a fecundating phenomenon), and everything ends in a song of celebration.

Clearly the text of *Le Corps lesbien* does not submit language to such dramatic destruction and recreation. But while it uses much of the language of its culture, the transmutations that Wittig effects—although of a more subtle kind—are nevertheless of the same order. This has already been seen in her treatment of the first person singular and possessive pronouns, her choice of passive and intransitive verb forms and her nontraditional use of the latter, her orthographical changes and her feminization of nouns, her elimination of traditional punctuation (especially the elimination of commas), her invention of neologisms, and so on. But probably the most striking transformation is one of degree rather than of kind, for it is the density of the language in *Le Corps lesbien* that produces the most powerful effect—the almost unheard-of accumulation of highly charged words, unusual images, and torrential rhythms. These create a verbal flow that has the power of a tide, so violent and accelerated that it sweeps over the reader with irresistible force. It attacks and carries away all debris—everything that is old, static, or stereotyped (in this domain as in every other)—and ends in a triumphant, musical celebration of language and its newfound possibilities.

It can even be argued that the central subject of *Le Corps lesbien* is the annihilation and resurrection of language and that the most profound love relationship of which it speaks is that between the writer and the word. Indeed, the fundamental *corps à corps* that takes place here is that which involves words. The pleasure of the text outstrips all others. It is an orgasmic experience of the most intense kind. If this is grasped, many other details in the work can be reinterpreted and can assume a different meaning. For example, Isis (she who possesses the power of the "living verb"), through her union with Osiris, produces offspring that are neither male gods nor human females but living words. And the various types of dismemberment and reassemblage performed on the body of the beloved by the lover are symbolic of the acts of the writer upon the body of language.

Perhaps this also explains the prominent place that Sappho occupies in *Le Corps lesbien,* and even her elevation to the stature of a divinity (*C,* 58, 74, 107, 130, 165), for she is celebrated, primarily, not for her preference for female lovers but for the magnificence of her poetry—the literary genre in which language and the writer's work with language attain their greatest intensity. This is the love relationship glorified by Wittig, and it is in this sense that she can be considered the true heir of Sappho.

Moreover, Wittig assumes a function in regard to Sappho that is not unlike that of Isis in regard to Osiris in the Egyptian myth. Sappho's body (of texts) was also fragmented—incidentally, by the actions of male and Christian power figures (such as the Byzantine emperors who, in 380 A.D., burned her works and replaced them by the Christian poetry of Gregory of Nazianzus; or Pope Gregory VII, who publicly burned her lyrical masterpieces in Constantinople and Rome in 1073 A.D.)[66] It was only partially reassembled, thanks to recent findings in Egypt, in the bands of mummies and in sacrophagi.[67] But it is resurrected in Wittig's text—at least in the form of celebration and divinization.

And yet, despite Sappho's place in *Le Corps lesbien*—her role as ancestress, muse, and immortal goddess—it is interesting to note that not a line of her poetry is cited in the work— as is the case for other poets, such as Du Bellay or Labé (*C,* 16, 153). This can be interpreted either as another case of not uttering (or writing) what is sacred and thus as the highest form of tribute, or as a sign of the independence of the writer (Wittig), who must distinguish herself even from the greatest and most venerated of her predecessors in order to achieve total freedom in her own creation.

Freedom seems indeed one of the major preoccupations,

even a key notion, apparent in the entire course of Wittig's literary career. This notion is obvious in her refusal of traditional elements in every domain of her writing, in her inventiveness and originality, in her constant exploration of new paths, and even in her rejection of past accomplishments (though they be her own). All of these are forms of liberation. But perhaps the greatest of all is Wittig's growing predilection for laughter. The development of this predilection is evident in the more and more frequent use of humor that is noticeable in proceeding from *L'Opoponax* to *Les Guérillères*, and in the almost constant presence of humor in *Le Corps lesbien*. It is all the more striking because the subject matter of the last two works is far from humorous. In *Le Corps lesbien*, contrasting it with most love poetry where laughter very seldom appears, the verb *rire* and the noun *le rire* appear in dozens of instances. And the context in which they are found is almost always that of joy, fullfillment, triumph, and plenitude. The bitter side of laughter (self-mockery and macabre humor), which appeared in *Les Guérillères*, seems to be entirely lacking here. At most, laughter in this text balances the torment or despair that predominates in certain sequences, but even there it frequently indicates a turning point where painful emotions are dissolved, or resolved, by laughter. It thus serves as an antidote to suffering, a way of destroying and transmuting pain. Most of all, however, laughter in this work seems a more visceral form of expression, something that arises from the body's core (as well as from the core of the text) and, as a result, has the most profound meaning.

This is perhaps most clearly shown by the ending of *Le Corps lesbien*, which closes on a joyous note (in contrast to *Les Guérillères*), among jugglers and acrobats, and amidst festive sounds, pleasing odors, happy shouts, and bursts of laughter (C, 188). The last image of the beloved is equally filled with this sense of felicity, for she is addressed as "m//a rayonnante" (C, 188), shining with such brilliance that, surely, her countenance is illuminated by radiant laughter.

Felicity is also represented in other ways in the final sequence of *Le Corps lesbien*. For example, the number seven appears prominently here. It designates the group of female jugglers ("bateleuses"—a feminization of *bateleur* or *le Bateleur*, who incidentally is an important figure in the Tarot, where he symbolizes the artist) surrounded by a circle of "spectatrices," among whom the beloved is found playing a musical instrument and gazing at the sea. A song arises from group number seven and a chorus of female voices takes up the melody in unison. A joyous exchange then occurs in which the "bateleuses" of that same group lend the balls they have been juggling to others in the assembly who wish to practice their artistry. Acrobatic feats then follow and a general atmosphere of harmony, plenitude, well-being, and joy prevails.

The number seven, as can be seen, is intimately linked to this felicitous ambience and it is significant that it appears in the ultimate sequence of the work. Its meaning must be sought, considering Wittig's interest in the symbolism of numbers, which has been apparent in many instances. Such investigation reveals that—universally[68]—this number indicates "un cycle accompli . . . un renouvellement positif."[69] It is thus an apt choice for designating the accomplishment of a cycle (the text in question) and a positive renewal, both of the portrayal of love and of a literary genre. But the number seven also symbolizes totality (of space and time), as well as life and movement, power and perfection.[70] This further coincides with many important aspects of the thematics of *Le Corps lesbien*. However, the Talmudic symbolism of that number is probably most closely linked to the central concerns of this work, for there, it denotes the totality of the human being (male and female at the same time, or beyond the categories of gender). Moreover, the seven is an integral part of the lunar cycle, and therefore closely allied to that specifically female event that is part of the "blood mysteries"[71] or the mysteries of transformation.

In all these ways then, besides its relationship to the number fourteen (discussed above in relation to the parts of the body of Osiris and also to ovulation and nonfertilization), the number seven is certainly the most important of the examples of Wittig's use of numerology. It is also relevant that it should appear in the final sequence of the text, at the moment of reaching completion. Significantly, it was nowhere apparent before in *Le Corps lesbien*. It seems to have been reserved for the moment that marks the accomplishment of a cycle and the climax of the work.

The cyclical nature of the text, already established by the repetition of the words "LE CORPS LESBIEN" at the beginning and the end of the list of anatomical terms, is further accentuated by the very last sentence of the work: "J/e te cherche m//a rayonnante à travers l'assemblée" (*C*, 188).[72] It is clear that the search for the beloved continues, that passion is unending, and that the quest goes on. Thus *Le Corps lesbien*, despite the seemingly exhaustive nature of its exploration, is an open-ended work. Nothing could be more fitting, for it speaks of life and movement, positive renewal that is constantly sought, and desire without end.

All these qualities evidently extend beyond the confines of the text, beyond the body of the beloved, and suggest the most vital of Wittig's concerns: the continuity of the quest for creation.

4

The Living Word

Only three years went by before Wittig's next work, *Brouillon pour un dictionnaire des amantes*, written in collaboration with Sande Zeig, followed *Le Corps lesbien*. The English translation of the title (*Lesbian Peoples' Material for a Dictionary*) may make it seem as though this text is a sequel to the previous one, but this in an erroneous impression. Actually, various misleading nuances exist in this translation. First of all, *brouillon* indicates a rough draft and thus suggests a work that is flexible, and subject to change, or transformation. This meaning, which does not come across clearly in the translation, is much more in line with, and continues to affirm, what Wittig has repeatedly emphasized in her writing. Also, the term translated as *lesbian* was originally *amantes*, that is, lovers (feminine gender), which has a different shade of meaning and could indicate a change of direction that has occurred since her previous work. Although the term *amantes* does not reveal all its complexity until the text itself is explored, its presence in the title already suggests a new point of view.

The literary genre that Wittig has chosen for this work is, of course, entirely different than that of her earlier works. This time, as the title announces, she has decided to create a dictionary. She has thus, as in past instances, appropriated a genre that is known to be the province, and the property, of the male establishment. This alone is another example of her continuing renversement of traditional notions and habitual actions, and it is worthwhile noting on that account alone. However, Wittig's overthrow is much more subtle than that. It involves both adhesion and subversion at the same time, an almost playful juggling with various characteristics of that genre. By calling her work a dictionary she creates certain expectations (some of which are fullfilled, while others are unexpectedly frustrated). Thus, simply consulting the title and the author(s) reveals nothing unusal except that this is a special type of dictionary ("des amantes") and that its authors are both female. The dual authorship is not startling since dictionaries are written by teams or have several contributors traditionally. Only the fact that the authors are both female is a striking innovation and an attack on established notions.

The fact that this is a particular kind of dictionary elicits reflection. The phrase "des amantes" can be read in two ways (in French) and suggests that this is a work not only *for* lovers but *by* lovers. Thus the phrase either implies a relationship between the contributors and the readers that is closer than usual in such a work, or it implies that this is a text "by women for women" as Wittig called *Le Corps lesbien*.

On the other hand, since a dictionary deals directly with language (with the meaning of words), Wittig adheres to the traditional definition of the genre. And the choice of this genre is not in itself unexpected, considering her profound involvement with language and her continuing interest in "word work." What instantly distinguishes her "dictionnaire" from others is that it only superficially bears any resemblance to them. True, entries are arranged according to an alphabetical order, cross-references are present, and definitions for all the words are included. In actuality, however, *Brouillon pour un dictionnaire des amantes* is a work of fiction. This immediately establishes several important notions: the overthrow of a long-established tradition in which a dictionary is not fiction; the recreation of a well-known genre; and the strong suggestion that existing dictionaries are not a body of facts or a series of immutable meanings and rules, but fictions created by the establishment, and that they are therefore not fixed, but subject to challenge, redefinition, and metamorphosis.

In this work as in her previous ones, the last of these notions is fundamental for an understanding of Wittig's purpose. Language (which takes its most rigid form in dictionaries), and words that are defined in dictionaries according to accepted meanings (that indeed cause certain attitudes as a result of these meanings) and that resist change, must be severely attacked, undermined, and destroyed if these attitudes are to change and a new reality come into existence. The power of the word is thus recognized, both in its negative results and in its positive virtuality. Wittig is certainly not alone in realizing this. Socio-linguists have studied the role of language in determining reactions and in forming the outlook of a society, and they have noted that (concerning women and other underpriviledged or dominated groups) it can have a subtle, but extremely dangerous influence. But they have also expressed the hope that changing the language and the definitions given to highly charged words can have a salutory effect upon attitudes.[1] Of course languages change slowly in general, and many societies (France being foremost among them)[2] are resistant to such change. It is only by a frontal attack on the instrument of word definition—that is, the dictionary—that a writer can attempt to destroy the very source of atrophy and negative attitudes and can begin to arrive at a positive transformation.

It can certainly be suggested that this is Wittig's fundamental aim in *Brouillon pour un dictionnaire des amantes,* which functions both as a "war machine" and as an agent of metamorphosis. However, the work does not do this by taking on the form of a treatise, a pamphlet, or a *roman à thèse.* Instead, it is a highly imaginative, and even frequently lusory, work of fiction, which in most instances consists of entries that are "ciselés comme des poèmes en prose"[3] and that actually resemble poetry. Therefore, while the traditional form of the dictionary is decried as fiction (in the negative sense), a new type of fiction (this time in the positive sense of the word) takes its place. And opposed to the scholarly, serious, authoritative tone of the former (which implies a type of tyranny over words or at least a value judgment without appeal), the tone of Wittig's new "dictionary" has been described as a "mélange insolite d'érudition, de lyrisme et de malice,"[4] an innovative blend of the informative, the poetic, and the ironic. There, the real and the imaginary, the factual and the invented, merge to the point where they are, at times, even difficult to distinguish.

Indeed, one look at the bibliography that appears at the

end of the work confirms the last of these affirmations. There, among the sources cited, are such authors as Louise Labé, an actual literary figure, but there is also someone named Pascale, obviously an invention (*Pascal* feminized). Moreover, the places and/or dates of publication are also invented by Wittig. For example: "LABÉ, Louise, *Elégies*, Gaule, âge de fer"; "BRONTÉ, Emily, *Poèmes*, Grande-Bretange, âge de la vapeur" (*D*, 250, 249). Similar indications appear in other instances also, for example: "Grand pays, Premier continent, âge de gloire"; "Palestine, âge de bronze"; "Albion, âge de la vapeur"; "Germanie, âge de fer"; "Celtie, âge de gloire" (*D*, 251, 250, 249).

It becomes quickly apparent that these changes in definitions of place and time—important categories, usually considered immutable—are a way of refusing to accept time-honored conventions of various types: spatial and temporal notions; names of countries and ways of indicating dates; and bibliographical notation. But they are also inventions that substitute a novel way of naming and indicating space and time, and that have nothing to do with convention. Moreover, this defiance of space and time has a lusory effect, something resembling the art of the juggler (a figure who already appeared— in female form—in *Les Guérillères*, gained in prominence at the end of *Le Corps lesbien*, and acquires even greater importance in this work) or acrobatics (an activity also glorified in *Brouillon pour un dictionnaire des amantes*). Similar treatment of a playful nature characterizes names of authors and works attributed to them. Thus, there are such bibliographical entries as: "*Ainsi parlait Frédérica*, conte pour enfants, âge de l'acier rapide" (*D*, 249), obviously an ironic reference to Friedrich Nietzsche's *Thus spake Zarathustra*, here described as a tale for children; or the sly jibe at Stendhal's famous work, *De l'amour*, by a change in authorship that attributes it to "XENVILLE, Marie-Thérèse, Gaule, âge de gloire" (*D*, 252). Thus, complex ends are once again achieved by what appear to be simple means, and serious ones are achieved through humorous techniques.

Other evident changes concern authorship and readership. It is, of course, common knowledge that dictionaries are habitually written by men, fundamentally address themselves to men, and are meant to be consulted by men. They are frequently considered to be "above the heads" of women, excluding them, yet also assuming the right to define them. In that sense, they are not very different from the "féminaries" described in *Les Guérillères*. Wittig's "dictionnaire," as has already been noted, reverses the traditional gender of both authors and readers, as well as the relationship between them. Since both are female here, a bond exists between them rather than an interaction of dominator-dominated or subject-object. Moreover, since both are designated as "amantes," these antagonistic categories no longer exist at all. The interchange has its parallels in love, which (as was shown in the previous work) consists of a continual interchange, or a union, between lovers. The term *amantes* is, of course, far more complex in its meanings, as will shortly be seen, but it already provides a key from the very start that helps to measure the distance of Wittig's text from the type of work that was begun in France by the Académie Francaise—a bastion of conservatism and rigid decrees, a haven of male "immortals" to which only recently, and probably somewhat reluctantly, the first woman, Marguerite Yourcenar, was admitted. To storm such a bastion, to invade such a haven, is indeed a challenge, and Wittig rises to it with evident enjoyment and great imagination.

As a matter of fact, though, more than the dictionary is challenged from the very start. The text begins with an epigraph that can be considered a subversion of the first words of Genesis: "Au commencement, s'il y a jamais eu un commencement."[5] It seems less important that this pronouncement is credited to Phyllis Chesler (an American feminist) than that, in an immediate defiance of the Bible, it implicitly attacks the original verse that follows, that is, "In the beginning was the Word." In this verse, "the Word" signals the creation of the world by a male God and the beginning of a tradition that Wittig wishes to undermine—indeed immediately refuses.

This is instantly shown by the very first entry in the text: "ÂGE." It is a retelling or recreation of Genesis, or at least of the section dealing with Paradise and the Fall. The importance of this is underlined by a second entry in the work, dealing with Eve, and with the Garden of Eden, which itself is renamed, becoming "le jardin terrestre" and thus losing its sacred dimension as a divine creation (*D*, 49). It is a place of strictly earthly delights, chief among them being the harmony that reigns there until the place is destroyed and the original golden age comes to an end. It is followed by the silver age, the bronze age, and the iron age (as in many pagan mythologies). Then comes "the soft stone age," "the steam age," "the cement age" or "the rapid steel age," and finally, "the glorious age" (all Wittig's own inventions). Nowhere in this entry is there the mention of a divine Creator, of Adam as the first human being, of Eve as temptress and sinner, or of the Fall. Paradise is an earthly garden, and the loss of paradise is not due to having eaten the forbidden fruit of the Tree of Knowledge. In fact, one of the last entries in the text, "VIE," states that the two trees in the middle of the garden were the tree of opposites and the tree of life (*D*, 241 – 42), and all the women (for this garden is filled, exclusively, with female inhabitants) have eaten of the tree of life there. The result is the exact opposite of that described in the Bible. The flowers and fruit of this tree, rather than ushering in the reign of death and suffering (including childbearing in pain), confer immorality upon those who have partaken of them. Thus, the entire concept of original sin and its consequences is destroyed, undermining the fundamental notion that underlies the Old and the New Testament, as well as the entire edifice upon which Judeo-Christian doctrine is built. It can therefore immediately be seen that Wittig is concerned not with issues that deal with a specific written document (the dictionary in this instance) but with those that have to do with an entire civilization and a quasi-universal belief, or at least a belief that is very wide-spread in the Occident. Once again, it becomes evident that a particular concern or point of view gives way to much vaster perspectives and that this new "war machine," her "dictionnaire," aims at universalization.

In recreating the various ages that follow each other, a similar action comes into play. By insisting that the original golden age is followed by a series of periods that are characterized by progressive decline but will finally be succeeded by the reestablishment of the original harmony, splendor, or glory, Wittig negates the notion of the end of the world (another concept of Christian doctrine). Instead, she seems to subscribe to a number of other mythologies and religions in which a belief in an eternal return and a cyclical view of time prevail. Thus, rather than a linear progression of history (characteristic not only of Christian belief but of scientific thought), a circular vision is established. Implicit in this is the refusal of a narrow, but (in our society) predominant, concept and the substitution or restitution of a wider point of view, having its origins in a greater variety of cultures and beliefs.[6]

It has become evident that even a glance at the most obvious elements of *Brouillon pour un dictionnaire des amantes* reveals a great number of important notions suggested by disarmingly, and deceptively, simple means. The same is true of the structure of this text. Although upon a cursory examination it resembles a traditional dictionary, it soon becomes clear that this resemblance is only superficial, first of all because the entries in Wittig's work are fewer as well as highly selective in nature. A great many words are not found there. This is, of course, suggested in the title, for the work is called a "brouillon," meaning a first (rough) draft or only a beginning. Thus, from the very start, it announces its partial character or unfinished state, subject to change and development. It is therefore also open-ended and extends beyond the confines of the text before us. The fact that the collection of entries is selective, and not complete, suggests another series of important notions. It is proposed as a work that is fragmented, or filled with lacunae. Consideration of the entry, "DICTION-NAIRE" in Wittig's dictionary (*D*, 77–78) provides a most interesting explanation of this structure (as well as another example of a *mise en abyme*—a discussion of the dictionary within the dictionary). The entry in question reads:

> La disposition du dictionnaire permet de faire disparaître les éléments qui ont distordu notre histoire. . . . C'est ce qu'on pourrait appeler une disposition lacunaire. Elle permet également d'utiliser les lacunes à la facon d'une litote . . . où il s'agit de dire le moins pour dire le plus.[7] (*D*, 77)

As can be seen, the first reason given for the structure of Wittig's "dictionnaire" is that it permits the elimination of terms that have been harmful to women because they have distorted their "histoire" (meaning both history and story, as was already seen in *Les Guérillères*). This falsification and distortion, also perpetrated by the authors of dictionaries, is here implied, while in *Les Guérillères*, "elles" accused men in general of having twisted literary and historical representations of women. In order to combat this practice in the present text, these terms are reduced to nonexistence, to mere blanks, condemned to silence, wiped out so to speak. They are not even thought worthy of accusation, but are simply absent from the work. This treatment parallels that to which women were subjected, that is, condemnation to muteness, exile from language, dispossession and reduction to zeros.

But there is another explanation given for this lacunar structure of the text. The blanks (or nonexistent entries) can function in the same way as understatements do, that is, "to say the least in order to say the most." (*D*, 77) This is a very important notion that not only illuminates the purpose of selectivity (in this or any other literary text), increasing the value of each entry, but that also explains the use of various forms of understatement in Wittig's former works: the "objective language" of *L'Opoponax*, which prevailed even in intensely emotional sequences; the lacunae referred to at the end of the poem in *Les Guérillères*; and the nonenunciation of the name of the beloved that was found in *L'Opoponax* and, especially, in *Le Corps lesbien*. In fact, the entire text of *Brouillon pour un dictionnaire des amantes* is also an understatement—a way of saying the least to say the most—since it is much shorter and much less complete than traditional dictionaries. Yet it is implied that Wittig's "dictionnaire" says much more than the traditional ones do, or at least things of far greater import to its authors and readers.

It also says a great deal more than expected to the reader who has thoroughly explored Wittig's former texts. Careful consideration of a number of the entries in *Brouillon pour un dictionnaire des amantes* reveals that it is also a kind of concordance to her previous work, and that it provides insights (or hindsights) vital to their understanding. As a matter of fact, some notions expressed there become clear for the first time upon reading this text, almost as though it were necessary for their comprehension and they were written expressly for this purpose. Although this is not an avowed aim, it certainly seems a necessary one, hidden from view as are many important things in the fictions of Wittig. At any rate, it is of great value for anyone wishing to delve deeply into the literary corpus of the author. It also shows that this corpus is an intricate network in which all of her texts participate, and that the links that join them are sometimes only uncovered after a great deal of exploration, which requires consulting not any one isolated text alone but the entire body of her work. The further this corpus that forms an organic whole is probed, the clearer certain key concepts and underlying themes become, but the more its complexity also comes into view.

It is probably this complexity that has led certain critics, if not to abandon the search, to oversimplify Wittig's undertaking in *Brouillon pour un dictionnaire des amantes*. Thus, one critic states, for example, that "l'étude thématique . . . est rendue difficile par la complexité du texte" and therefore chooses to concentrate primarily on the structural unity that is based on the relationship between three prominent groups in the work: "les amazones, les amantes, et les mères."[8] Another critic sees the central theme predominantly as an ideological one—that is, relating to the internecine struggle in the women's liberation movement—and sees Wittig's major concern as an attempt at a resolution between the two opposing factions and of the conflict centering on the terms *femme* and *mère*.[9] Although these issues are certainly of interest, it seems reductive to treat *Brouillon pour un dictionnaire des amantes* solely in this manner. It leaves out or ignores some of the most fascinating insights that can be gained by studying the complexity of this text and its relationship to all of Wittig's previous fictions.

One of the first ways in which this can be done is to look at the work in the context of everything that has gone before. It then becomes apparent that the existence of this text was already planned or prepared long ago. This is hinted at by the refusal of the dictionary definition of the term *opoponax* and its recreation in *L'Opoponax*. It is again alluded to in *Les Guérillères*, where the "féminaires" (resembling traditional dictionaries) were destroyed, and where a new work, created by a joint effort, was written. It is subtly but powerfully suggested in *Le Corps lesbien*, where all past definitions of erotic love were overthrown and given entirely new interpretations. Not only was the destruction and recreation of existing terminology a constant in the former works of Wittig, but the lacunar structure of *Brouillon pour un dictionnaire des amantes* was already present there in what was not said (or named), in the purposeful fragmentation that occurred in those texts—achieved through typographical variation, spacing, and the break in the first person singular pronoun—and in the importance attributed to lacunae at the end of the poem that appears in *Les Guérillères*. It is, however, only directly commented on in this "dictionnaire," where Wittig explains the aims she wishes to accomplish by the use of this technique.

The same kind of explicitness is also present when it comes to other matters. The chief among them is, of course, language. In Wittig's "dictionnaire," there are several extremely interesting entries under this heading. The first of these introduces a new female divinity of Indonesian provenance (different from Isis who in *Le Corps lesbien* possessed the power of the "living verb"). She is "l'ancienne déesse Vac . . . qui incarne le langage,"[10] and she expresses herself through sounds that resemble those of the roaring wind (*D*, 113–14). In this entry, the origins of language are described as preverbal utterances akin to the noises produced by the elements and comparable to the cries and calls of animals. They are are described as "modulations . . . stridulations de la voix" that have a force that equals, or perhaps even exceeds, that of articulate speech (*D*, 113). This is reminiscent of the beginnings of the new language that ushered in a new world in *Les Guérillères*, and that started with a series of gestures and signs, as well as other preverbal forms of expression. Indeed, it is allied to the primordial nature of communication, when language had not yet become a necessity.

This is evident from another entry, under the heading "HISTOIRE," which depicts the earthly paradise (or the "jardin terrestre") that originally existed. In that paradise, communication was so perfect that the inhabitants "n'avaient pas besoin d'utiliser le language" (*D*, 123–24). It is only later in this reinvention of the biblical story of the Tower of Babel, when discord arose and the golden age came to an end, that languages came into existence, became diversified, and resulted in incomprehension as well as in the start of "des exégèses infinies et . . . des déchiffrements de sens" (D, 128).[11] In other words, the loss of the primitive, Eden-like state brought about the end of wordless understanding and harmony, and the Fall is here a descent into dissension, intellectual bickering, and endless discourse upon language. Thus the natural form of communication was destroyed, and in its stead an artificial science of language was created.

Wittig continues to elucidate this "original" state and also the first known language. Under the heading "LANGUE" (D, 150–51), many other clarifications are found. This language, now lost, was also known as "la langue 'des lettres et des chiffres' " (a reminder of the use Wittig herself made of letters and numbers in past texts), and it was "une langue à la fois plus simple et beaucoup plus compliquée que celles qu'on a connues par la suite" (D, 151).[12] It was also a language that had enormous power, both of destruction and creation, for it "était capable de créer la vie ou au contraire de 'frapper' à mort" (D, 151).[13] In other words, it did exactly what Wittig herself does with language in her work. Moreover, the entry goes on to state, "on ne peut pas imaginer que cette langue était composée avec une construction et une syntaxe aussi rigides, rigoureuses, représsives que celles que nous connaissons" (D, 151).[14] This is a precise description of the rigid, repressive structures that Wittig refuses to use in her fictions. Finally, this entry shows that the role that sound played there, even though open to conjecture, was probably extremely important in creating the poetic quality of that language. Once again, this quality is something Wittig herself emphasizes in her writing.

An even more perfect parallelism can be found in the entry "VOYELLES"—incidentally, the last entry in *Brouillon pour un dictionnaire des amantes*—where the rebirth of language is described (D, 247–48). It takes place on a Polynesian island (a new sort of "jardin terrestre" or paradise) and consists of an entirely new language totally devoid of consonants (a renversement of the language described in *Le Corps lesbien* in which all vowels had disappeared. This language resembles a song and approximates that of the white whale. Often this song involves "la voix tenue sur . . . un o . . . ce n'est pas une phrase, c'est une modulation" (*D*, 248).[15] This last description almost exactly duplicates the important image found at the beginning of *Les Guérillères* (the siren whose song was "un O continu"), and it thus shows, once again, the continuity that exists in Wittig's texts as well as the importance of this particular work for understanding the links that join it to former ones.

In all the above instances, the emphasis is placed upon spoken language and, thus, on oral communication. This is certainly in accordance with the impression of orality, recitation, incantation, and chant (in the sense of both song and chant) that Wittig wishes to create in her fictions. However, written language and the role of the writer(s) also have an important place in *Brouillon pour un dictionnaire des amantes*— just as they did in *L'Opoponax*, where Catherine Legrand emerged as a budding writer and in *Les Guérillères*, where "elles" created a joint text. In Wittig's "dictionnaire," the beginnings of written language are attributed to Thetis, Carmenta, and Kali, all of whom were instrumental in the creation of the alphabet (*D*, 14). According to the text, the first of these three, Thetis, had a preference for vowels (*D*, 228), and the inhabitants of the Polynesian island involved in the rebirth of language shared this preference (*D*, 248). This similarity establishes a circle that leads from birth to rebirth, or from written to oral communication—or vice versa—and even merges the two. A similar type of merging also characterizes the roles of those who communicate by means of language, for they are alternately referred to as "conteuses," "récitantes," "poétesses," "musiciennes qui récitaient," and "narratrices" (*D*, 206). The most important term applied to them, however, is "porteuses de fables"—as can be seen from the numerous repetitions of this term in the text (*D*, 64, 91, 206, for example).

The term itself is of great interest and significance. It defines the role of those that deal in literature—in its creation and transmission—in a variety of innovative ways. For example, they are female (as is evident from the feminine form of the word—not *porteur* but "porteuse"), but they refuse and redefine their primary function in life, for they are not bearers of children (who, in French slang, are referred to as "pon-deuses," that is, creatures who lay eggs) but bearers of works of literature, or "fables." In designating literature as "fables," its fictional aspect is emphasized in contrast to such forms of writing as treatises, ideological pronouncements, or "litter-ature engagée" in general. Certainly, the word *fables* is not used here in any prejorative sense. Instead, it indicates works in which the imagination plays a predominant role (just as it does in Wittig's own fictions). Indirectly then, the appellation "porteuses de fables" reveals Wittig's definition of the writer's role and affirms her predilections in that domain. As a matter of fact, she insists that in the utopian era that is frequently referred to in the work ("l'âge de gloire"), such writers (in the plural) will indeed exist and will confirm, by a full display of their powers, this image, obscured or distorted by a long history of repression and dissension.

Even more revealing than the term applying to writers, are the descriptions in this text that relate to the tool used by them, the "raw material" of which Wittig speaks in "The Trojan Horse": words. The entry "MOTS" contains a great deal of significant material—so much so that it warrants being quoted almost in its entirety:

> A cause de tous les déplacements de sens, glisse-ments de sens, pertes de sens que les mots ont ten-dance à subir, il arrive un moment où ils n'agissent plus sur la ou les réalites. Il faut alors les réactiver. Ce n'est pas une opération simple et elle peut prendre toutes sortes de formes. La plus répandue est celle que pratiquent les porteuses de fables. . . . elles ra-content . . . les métamorphoses des mots. Elles-mêmes changent les versions de ces métamorphoses, non pas pour rendre les choses plus confuses mais parce qu'elles ont enregistré ces changements. Ils ont pour conséquence d'éviter pour les mots une fixation de sens.[16] (*D*, 172–73)

This passage shows, first of all, that words lose their strength, or meaning, with use, and must be "reactivated." Having undergone a slow death—from wear and as a result of habit—they need to be reborn. This new birth takes the form of a metamorphosis or a number of metamorphoses and—in Wittig's texts—that of neologisms, of an unusual lexicon (archaic, seldom used, or taken from specialized fields), or of poeticization of commonly employed terms. However, and here Wittig seems to reveal her own penchants most clearly, the versions of these metamorphoses also undergo change; not, as she explains in this entry, for the sake of creating confusion, but because these changes are necessary. Their most important aim is to avoid "pour les mots une fixation de sens,"[17] that is, fixity, rigidity, even rigor mortis.

One of the best examples of this metamorphosis of words is *Brouillon pour un dictionnaire des amantes* itself. As has already been pointed out, its title indicates that it is a first (or rough) draft, which means that it can be changed, expanded or otherwise transformed and is not a rigid, fixed construct. Moreover, words that have lost their meaning and vitality through overuse or misuse are here "reactivated," that is, totally redefined. The examples of such action are extremely numerous. Readers need only consult the definitions of "ARBRE," "AVOIR," "BAGUE," "BOUCHE," "CADAVRES," "DORMIR," "FAIRE," "FEMME," "MACHINE," "MOURIR," "NOIR," "OEUF," "PLUIE," "VOLER," and so on, to see what metamorphoses of meaning these words have undergone. But there are also examples of words newly born, neologisms: "donastère" (*D*, 79), for instance, which is built on "monastère", but which has nothing in common with a monastery, and indeed refers to an exchange of gifts ("dons")—in this case those of two female lovers; "héraine" (*D*, 121), which suggests an alteration of heroine but also contains a reference to Hera—here redefined as a goddess of war and relieved of her role as the wife of Zeus and patroness of childbearing; and "prédécessrices" (*D*, 226), which is a feminization of the French word for predecessors and has the additional advantage of producing a word whose sound is unpleasant to the ear of a francophone, thus creating a shock effect that is, according to Wittig, salutory.

As interesting as these examples of the transformation of words are, it is not until the much more audacious changes that occur in this text are recognized that Wittig's fundamental concern with renversement becomes clear. As she has said (when speaking of her work with words), transformation is not a simple operation (*T*, 47–48). And indeed, it is not easy to detect the most arresting of these changes. A slight hint as to their nature can be found in the "bibliography" at the end of *Brouillon pour un dictionnaire des amantes*, which, as has already been noted, contains both real and imaginary or reinvented authors and innovative designations of places and times of publication. The latter include "Celtie" for Ireland and "Gaule" for France, as well as eras such as "âge de beton" and "aĝe de vapeur". This leads to the supposition that there might be similar transformations, or inventions, within the body of the work itself. But it is not until an entry such as "CIRQUE" that the extent to which surreptitious changes in the habitual character of a dictionary (a work that is considered to be a repository of facts and unquestionably reliable) is revealed (*D*, 60). First of all, the word "cirque" (circus) is given a new meaning and is thus, itself, redefined. Also, in the definition given, a quote is attributed to a source that, at an initial glance, seems in keeping with those that are mentioned in the bibliography at the end of the text ("Théophano, *Hippolyte*, Grèce, âge de gloire"). Upon closer examination, however, this quote is recognized as an almost exact replica of a passage from *Le Corps lesbien* (*C*, 187), and therefore not by the author cited or published at the place and time indicated in the bibliography. This discovery is revealing on a number of counts. It shows that Wittig feels free to invent an imaginary author (whose name, significantly ends in *o* to whom she then attributes her own (real) work; that this work, or part thereof, is altered (but only slightly); that this change demands alertness on the part of the reader and the critic, and an intimate acquaintance with her previous texts; that there is a link between all the works that form the corpus of her fictions; that she is capable of a playful attitude even toward her own work; and that what appears to be fact can, indeed, be questioned or reveal itself as fiction.

This discovery leads, in turn, to a variety of questions that must be asked about this text, for it might be a key to much that has gone before and that has often remained unclear or not fully realized. It may be possible to consult *Brouillon pour un dictionnaire des amantes*, not at all as a dictionary (or even as the renversement of one) but as a guide book to the entire body of Wittig's fictions and perhaps as the most valuable tool she has furnished her readers (or her critics) for the understanding of her work. And this consultation, it seems, is best undertaken in a manner that she herself had indicated in *Les Guérillères* (*G*, 74): not in the usual, alphabetical order, but almost anywhere, at random. However, since habits of some sort of hierarchy are hard to break, there is a tendency to be drawn to entries that appear to shed the most light on questions either unresolved or still somewhat shrouded in mystery. But now much more wariness or some degree of caution is indicated, for even the answers that are found, will not necessarily be conclusive, as past experience has shown.

The first such entry, given the importance of this figure in the text that immediately preceeds *Brouillon pour un dictionnaire des amantes*, is that which defines Sappho (raised to the level of a divinity in *Le Corps lesbien*, but never present there through quotes from her poetry). But the entry under the heading "SAPHO" initially evokes surprise and/or frustration, for it is a completely blank page (*D*, 213). This silence is, of course, highly eloquent, given the importance of lacunae (of what remains unsaid or unwritten) and the statement made elsewhere that "to say the least is to say the most" (*D*, 77). Therefore, this empty space is the greatest form of tribute and constitutes another example, as well as a further illustration, of similar occurrences in previous texts.

On the other hand, further probing of this work reveals a number of quotes from Sappho's poetry (*D*, 19, 20, 29, 41, 109, 121–22, 152, 172, 201, 231). This is a direct reversal of what Wittig did in *Le Corps lesbien*, where Sappho herself appeared but none of her poetry was quoted. Consulting all the known works of Sappho (including those fragments that were discovered fairly recently and were available at the time when Wittig's "dictionnaire" was written)[18] and comparing them with the quotes that Wittig has used, reveals some very interesting inconsistencies. Sometimes an entire poem by Sappho is cited (for example, *D*, 19, 152), and sometimes only part of a poem is used (for example, *D*, 41, 231). Sometimes lines from diverse poems and fragments have been assembled (for example, *D*, 29), while in some rare instances lines that cannot even be found in Sappho's known works are cited (for example, *D*, 109, 172). Most striking, perhaps, is the fact that Sappho's best-known poem, "Ode à une aimée"[19] is not used by Wittig at all.

This handling of quotations from the work of Sappho invites commentary and raises several intriguing questions. For example, it seems paradoxical that Wittig turned Sappho into a divinity in *Le Corps lesbien*, placing her above the state attributed to her by Plato when he called her the "tenth muse," and yet, in this work, has felt totally at liberty, when quoting her, to subject her poetry to deletion, addition, and interpolation. Indeed, it seems at first difficult to reconcile these two attitudes. Perhaps the answer lies in that same fundamental penchant for renversement that we have seen in operation in so many areas of Wittig's fictions. Perhaps this leads her to overthrow, or at least to transform or recreate, even what she herself holds in the highest esteem—in this case, the poetry of Sappho. Thus, rather than treat the latter's work with the kind of adulation that resembles the worshipful (but rigid) attitude of the literary establishment, she "reactivates" or revitalizes it through transformation. Some might call this heresy. But it comes closer to the kind of transgression that (for Wittig) is intimately connected with the work of art. In this sense, it can be considered yet another form of tribute paid to the art of one of the greatest of all poets, Sappho.

Quotes from Sappho, moreover, are only part of the texts by other writers that appear in *Brouillon pour un dictionnaire des amantes*. Others are taken from the (real and imaginary) works of various female writers who come from all parts of the globe and many different periods of time. This, of course, is a reminder of Wittig's concern with universalization—evident, for example, in the lists of women's names in *Les Guérillères*. Only in this instance the emphasis is placed on the names of *writers*. Among them, Wittig herself appears—as has been shown—but under a pseudonym ("Théophano," *D*, 60), and the text quoted from her work is a slightly changed version of a passage from *Le Corps lesbien*, but is said to come from a work entitled *Hippolyte*, published in ancient Greece. Thus, to the pseudonym is added a pseudotext as well as a pseudoplace and pseudotime. Another source of quotes that frequently appear in the work is even more freely invented: "*Bibliothèque, ensemble des livres et des fragments du passé sauvés par les amantes pendant la dernière période du chaos*" (*D*, 22, 43, 58, 69, 83, 101, 147, 191, and so on).[20] This is clearly a collection of texts imagined by Wittig and attributed to the positive action of the "amantes" (referred to in the title of this work), who saved these texts and prevented their destruction during a chaotic era. Nothing is revealed about this "période du chaos," but the inference is that it concerns a time or times of persecution—such as those when Sappho's works were burned, or when texts by women writers were subject to mutilation, suppression, or appropriation by male writers. By means of her invention, Wittig rescues, from destruction or obscurity, texts that—she would have us believe—would otherwise have been irremediably lost. She thus symbolically resurrects or reconstitutes what has been fragmented, disjointed, or dismembered. Moreover, she reassembles a body of texts in an action very similar to that which concerned the body of the beloved in *Le Corps lesbien*. And since it is here the lovers ("amantes") who are credited with this action, the parallels between the two works become especially clear and pronounced.

The term "amantes" is also clarified by this association, for they are shown to be lovers in the double sense of the word—that is, those whose beloved is both a human being and literature. Further proof of this is the entry "AMANTES," which reads as follows:

> Les amantes sont celles qui, éprouvant un violent désir les unes pour les autres, vivent/aiment dans les peuples, suivant les vers de Sappho, "en beauté je chanterai mes amantes." Le peuple d'amantes des amantes rassemblent toute la culture, le passé, les inventions, les chants et les modes de vie.[21] (*D*, 15)

It can thus be seen that the lovers of whom Wittig speaks in this work are those that had appeared in *Le Corps lesbien* and whose violent desire was explored in all its myriad aspects in that text. They are also the followers of Sappho, concerned not only with love but with beauty and song (poetry), and they are those who preserve a cultural heritage, all that is most precious throughout the ages (especially inventions and songs). Implicit in their last function is, of course, the notion that the treasures of the past are those that have to do with creation. The "amantes" are thus instrumental in saving works of art from chaos (as the reference, "*Bibliothèque*" indicated) and in perpetuating creation. It becomes clear, then, that their attributes are much more complex than is initially suspected, or than those noted by the critics who consider them only as variants upon "lesbians" (a term that, as we have seen, also has innovative meanings when used by Wittig).

Moreover, the term "amantes" itself applies to a utopian representation, for it is associated with "l'âge de gloire" prophesied in the text, when all that was lost will be recovered, and when, the cycle having come full circle, the bliss that reigned in the "jardin terrestre" will be regained. As can easily be seen, this is a renversement and recreation of the Judeo-Christian myth of the end of the world and the second coming. However, it comes even closer to various pagan myths of an eschatological nature, for they speak of the destruction of an existing world in order for a new one to arise, or else of a return to the Origins, which constitutes both the highest form of felicity and the passage from chaos to cosmos.

The Time of Origins in *Brouillon pour un dictionnaire des amantes* (aside from being a reversal and redefinition of Paradise) is closely linked to those who lived "in the beginning": the "amazones." In this text (in contrast to *Les Guérillères* where the Amazon myth appeared only in the background), amazons are very frequently represented. Long passages—emphasized by repetition and thus functioning both in a descriptive and an incantatory manner[22]—deal with their attributes. In some ways, these coincide with the Amazon myth as it is generally known. Wittig's "amazones" also live in exclusively female communities, perform the ablation of their right breast by burning, ride horses, hunt, engage in battle, and live in natural surroundings far from civilization. But there adhesion to the myth stops, the text states that these amazons were the original inhabitants of earthly paradise, where they lived in total harmony, and loved and celebrated each other. A more unusual characteristic, however, is that they also liked to play (as did the "guérillères"). At a certain moment, a secularized version of the Fall occurred. This took place when the first cities were established (cities which, as in *Le Corps lesbien*, constitute the opposite pole of a natural setting—the island or the garden). It was then that harmony was destroyed and a schism occurred, splitting the occupants of paradise into two groups: "amazones" and "mères." The "mothers" considered the "amazons" immature and labeled them eternal children, or "those-who-do-not-assume-their-destiny" (*D*, 15). The last of these appellations is, incidentally, a side-swipe at the famous Freudian formula, "Anatomy is destiny." When the "amazons" were banished from the cities of the "mothers," they became war-like and violent, fighting to preserve the former harmony, and changing the meaning of their name to signify that aim. They consequently spread to every continent on earth, to islands, and even to ice floes. And it is thanks to them—the entry "AMAZONES" states in conclusion—that the advent of the glorious age, which reinstitutes a state resembling that of the original "jardin terrestre," was made possible (*D*, 15–16).

Various elements in this description of the "Amazones" are broadened and deepened in other entries that are found in the work. For example, the schism and banishment that followed the golden age of harmony resulted in the dispersion of the "Amazones" all over the globe and in their transformation into beings designated by other names (which once again illustrates Wittig's interest in fragmentation, metamorphosis, and universalization). The text mentions the names and lands of various "amazones" after their exile from earthly paradise: Albina of Lydia, Anahita of Anatolia, Atalanta of Greece, Bedjas of Africa, Diana of Etruria, Eurypyla of Nubia, Harpalyca of Thrace, Holda of Scandinavia, Laodamia of Crete, and so on (*D*, 12, 19, 26, 39, 77, 87, 119, 129, 151). But the "amazones" are also reported to have existed under other forms and with different names: witches, the Furies, Medusa, the Harpies, and so on (*D*, 36, 101, 109, 120). In other words, they were both transformed and accused of all sorts of misdeeds or attributed negative traits.

Those who were instrumental in the destruction of the original state of felicity—the "mères"—are described in terms that depict them as the evil ones in this struggle, which echoes and subverts the biblical combat between God and Satan or the forces of light and darkness in a variety of mythologies. Such a portrayal is, of course, also a renversement of another traditional concept: the celebration of woman as a fertility goddess, the Magna Mater, the mother of God, the genitrix, or the central object of a cult known as "Momism." In this text, the "mothers" are disdainfully referred to as those who "regardaient pousser leur ventre" (in a narcissistic contemplation of their fruitfulness). They themselves invent other epithets to describe them, such as "mère-la plénière, mère-celle-qui-engendre," well suited to the function of reproduction that defines them.[23] They are also called "mères statiques," in contrast to the nomadic "amazones" who value a vagabond existence, discovery, exploration, and movement. Soon also, these "mères" began to call themselves "femmes." They then established a variety of categories into which they divided the "amazones," while they themselves chose only this single appellation. The "amazones," on the other hand, refused all such distinctions and categories, as well as the terms "femme" and "mère" (*D*, 171–72)—as could be expected from the heroines in a text by Wittig. As the empire of the "mothers" gained in power, it created an absolute or totalitarian value system that made procreation the highest good (*D*, 64). Its adherents called themselves "femmes" in order to designate their specific (even exclusive) function: "celles-qui-engendrent-d'abord-et-avant-tout."[24] Those who had once been called "amazones," on the other hand, were excluded from this category, exiled, and forced to dissemble their movements in order to protect their freedom. Even their name was no longer used (*D*, 94). As all traces of them became vague, they existed only in fables or underwent a series of transformations.

The text of *Brouillon pour un dictionnaire des amantes* states that the heirs of the "amazones"—not in the biological sense, of course—are those who are called "amantes." They are already present in the work's title, both as those who have created the text and as those for whom it is created (if subscribing to the dual meaning of "des amantes"). Numerous passages in the text are devoted to their genesis, their history, and their attributes and activities. From the very start, they are distinguished from those who are engendered in habitual (biological) fashion, since theirs resembles a miraculous birth or parthenogenesis. The text says that they created themselves. Also, they appeared everywhere in the world at once, springing up as in spontaneous (universal) generation. At the very same instant, all language barriers magically also disappeared. This is in exact opposition to the moment when the language of the "jardin terrestre" became diversified and the barriers between languages arose. This original language—understood and shared by all the "lovers"—is now recovered (*D*, 39). Thus, in opposition to the occurrences in the biblical book of Genesis, genesis and the recovery of the word go hand in hand in this text. Moreover, creation and the power of the verb are now the prerogatives of female beings.

It is not only the birth of the "amantes" that is represented in a fabulous manner however. Their attributes and activities are described in similar fashion. They live in tropical regions and prefer trees for their habitat. They have animal companions, "bed animals," and even speak the language of animals. They can modify their body secretions and odors as will. They eat the dead bodies of their lovers and sleep in spherical shelters resembling beehives. They rediscover America. They transform themselves into various animals (as they had already done in *Le Corps lesbien*). They refuse the verb "to have" or "to possess." They anoint themselves with the secretions of plants (including "cyprine," used in another sense than in *Le Corps lesbien* but also reverting to the meaning given there) (*D*, 45, 201). And they celebrate indolence. They are able to change color. They use hoops to express desire that they dare not declare openly (which is reminiscent of *L'Opoponax* and *Les Guérillères*). They practice ornamental scarification. They transmit heat and electricity from body to body and emit energy as well as colors. They have a predilection for pantomime, acrobatics and juggling. They use mushrooms to produce hallucinatory states and enter into a state of delirium or amorous ecstasy during which their eyes, arms, legs, and clitoris, detach themselves from the body. They refuse spatial and temporal distinctions, expanding and merging time and space, and gliding from one dimension to another. They practice the embalming of the living in order to regnerate the body. And they rewrite Genesis. They are also said to live in outer space; to sing "songs of transformation" and play "games of transformation" during "love wars" (where cruelty and tenderness are part of the "tension inherent to the state of love"—an exact description of the range of feelings and experiences described in *Le Corps lesbien*); to celebrate the "récitantes" and the "porteuses de fables"; and to refuse the accumulation of lies that is termed science. They are said to live on smoke; to see visions in which appear "les Irréelles" (note the word "elles" in this term), who resemble divine guides and indicate the way to promised lands (an obvious subversion of Moses' function in the Old Testament). They are said to be carried in the pockets of kangaroos when young. They are said to have disdained and abolished written law. And they are said to celebrate menstruation, which they refer to as "the tears of the moon," and to eat the ovules as a rare delicacy. They refuse the notion of death and have reactivated the Elizabethan meaning of the verb "to die" (that is, to achieve orgasm), they celebrate the clitoris and oppose the "myth" of vaginal orgasm (another mocking reference to one of Freud's famous theories). They cultivate snapdragons because they resemble the female genitals. They reproduce by way of the ear (a sacrilegious allusion to the Virgin Birth) and find erotic stimulation in rain. They have resolved the problem of overpopulation. They know, from early childhood on, how to fly. They have created new sounds and a new musical scale and speak a language that resembles song. And they excel at visions of the past, present, and future—the last always joyful.

As can be seen from this vast array of attributes and activities, Wittig's amazing range of invention is at its zenith when it comes to the beings who assume prominence from the very beginning of this work (indeed, from its title). They obviously elicit the full display of her powers of imagination and innovation. Even more than the "amazones," who in themselves were a variation and enlargement upon a well-known myth, they stand out as the central figures to emerge from this text. In their representation fact and fiction mingle, good humor and malice alternate, reality and fantasy appear side by side, tenderness and violence coexist, and opposites are inextricably joined. Many of their attributes parallel those of figures who appeared in earlier texts or incarnate attitudes expressed there: for example, the predilection for nature and animals; the opposition to established laws; the celebration of specifically female sexuality; the refusal of spatial and temporal distinctions; the redefinition of words; the subversion and recreation of various myths; the predilection for transformation; and the formulation of a new language. Some attributes, however, are new in this text: for example, the active role of the "amantes" in the preservation, transmission, and gathering of literary texts; their visionary powers; their colonization of new lands on a universal scale; and their founding of a new kingdom in a new age of glory, which, it is affirmed, has already arrived.

Probably most important of all, however—and suggested by the prominent place that the "amantes" occupy in *Brouillon pour un dictionnaire des amantes*—they can also serve as guides for the interpretation of all of Wittig's fictions. A backward look confirms this, for they are at once the "petites filles" of *L'Opoponax*, the "elles" of *Les Guérillères*, and the female lovers of *Le Corps lesbien*. Indeed, as is confirmed in *Virgile, non*, they are also the avatars of the characters who follow in her later work. In their complexity and vivacity, and in the kaleidoscopic nature of their portrayal, they are representations par excellence of the beings whom Wittig chooses to designate by a variety of terms (or not name at all) and whose possibilities are endless.

Something else also emerges from this particular portrayal. It has many of the characteristics of a fable. This in itself is quite in keeping with a work by an author who designates female writers as "porteuses de fables," and who is, herself, one of that tribe. It can easily be seen that many traits of the entire text, and especially those of the passages dealing with the "amantes," resemble those of fables: for example, the element of fantasy; the unusual, even "miraculous" attributes of the main characters; the natural way in which more-than-natural or supernatural events are related; and the comments on current issues that are made in an indirect or seemingly ingenuous manner. On the other hand, however, the use of this literary genre (the fable) has traditionally been the prerogative of male writers—Aesop and La Fontaine being the most famous examples—and its appropriation is therefore as important as her appropriation of the dictionary. But it is also striking that Wittig has chosen to use this particular literary genre (the fable) in a text designated as a dictionary, since the latter is habitually a work in which factual material is presented in objective fashion. This unusual mixture provides an unexpected overthrow of habitual categories. But it also creates a hybrid text comparable to an androgynous creature, and thus moves beyond genres and genders. This creation of a hybrid text shows how far Wittig's fictional works can go—far beyond any ideological pronouncements on the same subject—and with what artistry she can treat themes that others might present in prosaic ways.

The prominent use of fable elements might tempt one to see the entire text as a fable if not for the factual material that suddenly intrudes (or is incorporated into) *Brouillon pour un dictionnaire des amantes*. As a matter of fact, so inextricably are the two joined that it is frequently most impossible to distinguish them. This technique also serves a variety of ends. It keeps the reader active, constantly on the *qui vive*. It makes what is generally termed "reality" difficult to dissociate from fiction. It suggests that truths can be communicated by imaginary material, and that fables can convey hard facts. By juggling such various elements, Wittig overthrows a number of traditional notions. But she also shows that it is an activity that appeals to her on a number of counts, not the least being its lusory character.

Indeed, perhaps most striking in this work is its playfulness. This is especially so because it often deals with painful matters—the schism between various female fractions, the fate of women writers, the persecution of the "amazones" and the "amantes", and so on. All of these are, for the most part, treated in a manner that might seen unexpected: that is, devoid of the dramatic or tragic overtones that frequently characterize works dealing with such subjects. In Wittig's text, fantasy, humor, and a play of the imagination prevail. Only now and then a harsh note is heard. This is the case for the entry "MARIE-ANTOINETTE ET MARIE-LAURE DE LAMBALLE" (*D*, 168), which shocks the reader into the realization that hatred exists and manifests itself in physical (and verbal) violence. But this sudden eruption of a very different tone only highlights the predominant one in the work, which itself differs from what is habitually found in texts with similar preoccupations, or even from Wittig's own previous work. It must be remembered that *Brouillon pour un dictionnaire des amantes* immediately follows *Le Corps lesbien*, which despite a few playful passages and an emphasis on laughter, was one of the most striking examples of highly dramatic, deeply passionate writing. In this respect, the present text suggests a renversement of the previous one or at least a refusal to remain fixed in any literary approach.

Such a tendency is evident even in small details found in *Brouillon pour un dictionnaire des amantes:* for example, the reversal of meanings Wittig attributes to words that, in themselves, reverse the traditional meaning. This can be observed very clearly in the case of the word *opoponax*. This term was not used in *L'Opoponax* in accordance with the dictionary defintion but was given a series of quite different meanings. In the present text, it reappears on a number of occasions, and in each and every case it is used according to the dictionary definition (*D*, 36, 96, 189, 195). This shows, once again, that Wittig's penchant for renversement is so strong that it even applies to renversement itself, both in minute ways and in larger terms. A similar, but more complex action of this type concerns the Baudelairian quotes that play such an important role in the last section of *L'Opoponax*. As was noted, a significant portion of Baudelaire's poem, "L'Invitation au voyage," was omitted, specifically the refrain "Là, tout n'est qu'ordre et beauté / luxe, calme, et volupté." Surprisingly, this very refrain appears in *Brouillon pour un dictionnaire des amantes*, in the entry entitled "ORGASME" (*D*, 191). But now it is said to come from one of the group of books saved by the "amantes" during the last era of chaos (the *"Bibliothèque"*), and there is no mention of Baudelaire at all. This shows that Wittig is capable not only of reversing her own omissions but also of attributing works by known authors to unknown (or imaginary) sources. And by attributing a line from a poem as well known as this particular one by Baudelaire to an author who is obviously imaginary, she calls attention to her engagement in reversal or appropriation. However even such a practice is at times reversed, for in another instance Wittig does exactly the opposite. Under the entry "LABÉ (LOUISE)" is a quote from an actual work by this real poet. However this quote has been altered to include words that do not exist in the original (*D*, 149).

So continual are such transformations, that any conclusions that are drawn must remain questionable—that is, open to further transformation. That is why, at this point, the kaleidoscope suggests itself as a fitting image. It is obviously the perfect instrument for effecting a change of view, a metamorphosis of given elements, or a series of visions that are never the same. As might be expected, it is given a prominent place in this text. Significantly, however, even this agent of transformation is transformed by the author. The entry "KALÉIDOSCOPE" reveals this (*D*, 145–46). First of all, it is referred to in the plural as "sacs à images," thus changing its habitual form and multiplying its possibilities. Then we are told that "les kaléidoscopes qui contiennent les matériaux les plus disparates sont ceux qui permettent les meilleures compositions,"[25] thus emphasizing the value of disparate elements for the production of superior compositions, and showing their relatedness to the work of art as Wittig sees it. Furthermore, the entry goes on to mention kaleidoscopes that are reported by the "porteuses de fables," to exist on a Polynesian island. These kaleidoscopes produce sighs, whispers, songs, moans, and other sounds of unknown origin. They thus combine visual and auditory elements into creations that appear closely allied to literature.

From this and other indications, the realization emerges that this work—which poses as a "dictionary," has been considered primarily as an ideological pronouncement,[26] and could be described as a fable or a modern legend—is actually a subtle statement about the nature of art. But even the term *statement* must be instantly qualified, for nothing is directly stated here. It is something that only emerges (as do words on a palimpsest) after a very close look at the text itself, because there is a tendency to be dazzled by the glowing colors and vivid forms that appear on the surface and somewhat obscure the underlying concerns. These concerns must be sought in the shadows—for example, in the small entry under "OMBRE." Under this heading is the statement "les amantes de l'âge de gloire traîtent leurs ombres comme des personnes vivantes" (*D*, 188)[27]. This statement suggests that shadows ideally have as much reality as that which is tangible and has firm, substantial outlines. Perhaps it also implies that here less is more (as was the case for understatement, ellipsis, and lack of enunciation), and that what remains hidden, partially obscure, or difficult to find is of the greatest significance.

This leads to the conclusion—despite the fact that any conclusion is probably also suspect—that this text (as well as all of Wittig's previous ones) deals, on the deepest level, with the work of art: literature first and foremost, but also music and painting, as well as the "lesser" arts, such as pantomine, juggling, and acrobatics. Reflections on art were discernible in all her past works: in a number of passages in *L'Opoponax*, especially those involving Catherine Legrand and Valerie Borge; in the sequences of *Les Guérillères* concerning language; and in the intensified "word work" of *Le Corps lesbien*. They are equally important in *Brouillon pour un dictionnaire des amantes* and will continue to be present in the works that follow. To reflect on the nature of art within a work of art itself is, of course, not unique to Wittig. Examples of such reflections abound, especially in contemporary literature.[28] Unique to her, however, is the manner in which this is done, the prodigiously imaginative way in which she has dealt with this subject and the subtle treatment she has given it—so subtle, that her work is often misread, and surface elements have been taken for the core.

Perhaps this is due primarily to the fact that Wittig's fictions are individually so absorbing that they each elicit and foster appreciation separately. Yet they should ideally be read as a whole or as a corpus of inextricably linked texts, for only when they are combined do they illuminate each other and reveal their deepest concerns. Perhaps Wittig even indicates this approach herself, for it resembles the action that appeared in emblematic fashion in *Le Corps lesbien* and that can be discerned again in *Brouillon pour un dictionnaire des amantes:* the reassembling of separate parts (of the human body and of the body in literature) in order for a recreated whole to appear. This is an important clue and should be heeded as such.

But the application of this notion is also, first and foremost, a labor of love, indeed an act of love in keeping with Wittig's fundamental approach to literature. And in this text, the importance of lovingly reassembling further enlarges and deepens the meaning of the term "amantes" to designate those who reassemble texts and give them new life. It seems to define not only the writer and the reader but also the critic— in other words, all those whose relationship to literature is akin to that amorous rapport and revitalizing experience that has been so well described by one of the finest critics of our time as "le plaisir du texte."[29]

5

Dante, No

A long interval—a decade to be exact—separates the publication of Wittig's next work, *Virgile, non,* from that of her previous one.[1] It is as though an extended moment of silence intervened. Knowing the significance of not saying (or not writing) from a study of her past texts, there is a tendency to interpret this lacuna as a period of great importance—a time for reflection, for the gathering of fresh forces, or for what one poet described as "se lover pour mieux créer."[2] This indeed seems to have been the case for *Virgile, non* strikes out in new directions, adds a number of formerly untapped resources, and reveals unprecedented facets that distance it from Wittig's former fictions.

This is immediately evident in the work's title. Virgil, who appeared briefly in *L'Opoponax* (via his poetry), resurfaces here, but only to be instantly negated, refuted, and excluded by the word *non* that follows his name. At first glance, this seems primarily a rejection either of a famous male writer or of a literary figure from the past, both of which are in accordance with Wittig's previous attacks on a dominant establishment and on outmoded forms of writing. But this work's title is a more direct statement of refusal than any of her former titles. The *non* is an up-front, head-on assault that states opposition much more explicitly than did even the most audacious titles of her previous texts (such as *Le Corps lesbien,* which created a shock effect but affirmed rather than negated). But it also refers to a known figure, Virgil, rather than inventing a neologism (which was the case for *L'Opoponax,* for *Les Guérillères,* and even, to some extent, for the dictionary *des amantes*).

In doing so, it both evokes Virgil and the works created by him, and negates him as well as his works by the addition of the word *non*.

Although on the surface the title seems simple, it is actually quite complicated. It immediately calls up more than Virgil himself, but also his presence in Dante's *Divine Comedy*. Thus, what is attacked or refuted in the title is the figure and the work of both the former and the latter. This is indeed a major challenge, to the male as well as to the literary establishment. It makes Wittig's new "war machine" a double juggernaut that indeed merited a ten-year period of preparation. In one sweep, and even before the opening of the book, she has negated not only one but two of the Western world's most celebrated writers, and she has assaulted literary monuments that are considered eternal.

From the very first page of *Virgile, non,* Dante is the primary object of Wittig's destruction and recreation, and his most famous work is the object of her renversement. Just as in *The Divine Comedy,* a guide appears to lead the narrator on his journey. This, of course, already indicates several instances of subversion and transformation: the appropriation of one of the literary masterpieces of Western culture; the claiming and recreation of the work of a male writer by a female one; and the use of a text celebrating Christian doctrine for quite different ends. Most striking of all is the metamorphosis of Dante's famous male guide, Virgil, into a female one who leads a female narrator. Moreover, Virgil is renamed here. He has become Manastabal (*V, 7*). The one she guides (soon named also) is called Wittig (*V, 9*).

Also instantly noticeable is the fact that this new text is written in the first person. This is, of course, an innovation for Wittig and establishes the distance of this work from *L'Opoponax* and *Les Guérillères* (where *on* and *elles* were used). True the first person pronoun appeared in *Le Corps lesbien,* but in fragmented form (*j/e*). In *Virgile, non, je* and all possessive pronouns are intact. This might be interpreted either as a renversement of *j/e* and its vulnerability or as a way of stating a new attitude toward the self, which now appears to be reassembled, reintegrated and reborn. Such a state of wholeness is another way too of indicating a position of power, struggles won, or autonomy, or is perhaps a strong protective armor worn in the battle against opposing forces.

In addition, the narrator is named here for the first time in Wittig's fictions, and the name she bears is the author's own. Of course this practice is not unique to Wittig—as famous examples by Proust, Céline, and the writers of the recent new wave of autobiographies show—but in her case it has a special purpose and probably involves greater risk. With the exception of Céline, none of the above authors are primarily concerned with provocation and attack, and thus the use of their own names is not quite as dangerous. In Wittig's case, however, it can be interpreted as a move that brings her into the forefront, the firing line so to speak. It causes her to shed anonymity, to drop all protective disguises (which include even the facetious pseudonym noted in *Brouillon pour un dictionnaire des amantes*). And it reveals her personally, or at least in an active role (both as narrator and protagonist) in her work.

While the other principal character of *Virgile, non* has been given a name that appears fictional, there are several indications that Manastabal, as she is called, is closely linked to Wittig. First of all, as guide she also functions as a double and can therefore be seen as an alter-ego of the narrator. Then also, her name begins with an *M*, the first letter of Monique, and is thus another way of indicating the same close relationship. Moreover, *M* and *W* (incidentally the monogram of Monique Wittig) are reversals of each other and thus coincide very well with Wittig's fundamental and persistent penchant for renversement. Also, the fact that the name Manastabal contains the word *man* (and even an allusion to *ball*) yet refers to a female figure, provides another example of reversal or of the breakdown of marks of gender that is advocated by Wittig.

While all this is already evident in the first two pages of the text, other important elements only appear further into the work. For example, its structure is quite different from that of Wittig's previous fictions. It has been likened to that of "un grand poème en 42 chants comparable à la 'Vita Nuova,' "[3] and in some ways this description is a very fitting one. But while the evocation of this particular work of Dante has its merits, it needs to be supplemented. Given the importance of numbers in Wittig's previous texts, there is a need to conjecture about the forty-two sequences that constitute *Virgile, non*. Of course the meaning of and emphasis on the numbers six and seven in *Les Guérillères* and *Les Corps lesbien* leads to the assumption that similar considerations determine their use in this particular text. Very pertinent also is the fact that the number forty-two resulting from the multiplication of six and seven, determines the number of "chants" (in its double meaning of chant and song) in the work entitled "Vita Nuova." Indeed, *Virgile, non* speaks of a new life in a number of new ways: a new work, a new approach, and a new setting.

The last of these is probably the most striking. The entire book is set in San Francisco, as various place names indicate, such as "Le Pont Doré" (Golden Gate Bridge), "avenue Dolores," and "Castro [Street]. This is an innovation in Wittig's work, since all earlier texts had no precise location, but were, on the contrary, situated only in the countryside, on islands, in cities or gardens, or simultaneously in various parts of the globe. Here on the other hand, while San Francisco is only once named directly (*V*, 43), many indications are given that point to an exact place. Several interpretations suggest themselves from this. San Francisco is symbolic of a new world, located at the furthest point of the New World. And it is sufficiently distant from the Old World (and from the tradition not only of Virgil and Dante but of Wittig herself) to echo the distance of the author—who, incidentally, is living north of San Francisco at the time of the composition of *Virgile, non* (thus adding an autobiographical dimension to the text that reinforces the use of the first person singular narrative)—and to echo the distance of this work from "old," or former texts she has written.

Aside from the division into forty-two chants comparable to those of the *Vita Nuova*, *Virgile, non* is divided into three zones that echo those of *The Divine Comedy*. They resemble the "Inferno," "Purgatorio," and "Paradiso" present in Dante's work. This is important on various counts. It places emphasis on numbers that have great significance for both Dante and Wittig (three and its multiples). These numbers, however, have an entirely different, indeed opposite, meaning in both instances. Dante's Christian symbolism is contradicted by the pagan symbolism preferred by Wittig. Thus, here echo does not mean agreement, but rather appropriation and even obvious reversal to come.

This can be seen by the fact that this work depicts a profane voyage, as instantly stated (*V*,7), and involves living beings rather than the souls of the dead (although many of them are called "âmes damnées" or lost souls). Redemption here has nothing to do with Christian salvation, nor has damnation, which is not the result of divine wrath but of human viciousness. And the dimension of the sacred, indicated by the very titles of the three parts of *The Divine Comedy*, is nonexistent in Wittig's work, as is instantly evident by the renaming of the three major zones and/or the profane settings they refer to. This already indicates divergence from Dante's immortal work. As a matter of fact, the parallels between the two texts appear to underline the audacity of the decision to rewrite *The Divine Comedy* in modern terms, and to do so, as will be seen, with irreverence, ferocity, and humor—in other words, to profane it, and with it, the vast edifice of Christian doctrine upon which it is based and which is glorifies. In this, Wittig's *Virgile, non* resembles *Le Corps lesbien*, which profaned the "Song of Songs," and *Brouillon pour un dictionnaire des amantes*, which did the same to Genesis and thus to the Old Testament.

Heretical as a result of this alone, *Virgile, non* is also sacrilegious in strictly literary terms, for it dares to touch a work that is of such stature and renown as to constitute almost a genre in itself. Moreover, to change *The Divine Comedy's* high tone, lofty form of expression, and uplifting aim by substituting fierce irony, ribald humor, slangy expressions and "street talk," as well as profane and even what (in religious terms) would be called "sinful" aims is audacious indeed. Yet these characteristics are not constant in Wittig's work either, for *Virgile, non* can—and does—also rise to poetic heights, and it is capable of contradicting even itself (a quality known to those who have explored her previous texts). By its inconsistency, it overthrows the parallelism with *The Divine Comedy* as effectively as it does by the various other means discussed, but also with its own renversement. Alternatively noble and down-to-earth, poetic and quotidian, tragic and comic, a soliloquy and a dialogue, *Virgile, non* obeys no rules of genre and cannot even be defined in those terms.

And yet parallelism with *The Divine Comedy* is not entirely refused either, for there is a direct reference in *Virgile, non* that suggests a comparison. The text states that it has "un heureux déroulement . . . comme dans le poème que Dante a appelé 'comédie' parce qu'il finit bien" (*V*, 47).[4] Moreover, as has already been mentioned, Wittig's settings echo those of Dante in that they are divided into three zones. However some transformations in Dante's topography are immediately evident. In Wittig's text, the term *inferno* never appears. Instead, the sequences obviously situated in hell have profane settings and realistic titles (such as "La laverie automatique," "La gare centrale," and "Les stands de tir").[5] The term *purgatorio* is also absent and only *limbo* (the abode of pagans in Dante's poem) is mentioned here and has as its setting either a bar or a billiard room. *Paradiso* is retained (both as the term *paradis* and in its supernatural character) but, as might be expected, even that zone differs significantly from the Dantesque one.

Most important of all is the divergence that can be noted in the general architecture of the two works. This architecture, so significant in Dante's poem and so perfectly ordered (implying the perfect order of God's universe), is entirely demolished in Wittig's text. This can instantly be seen by the table of contents at the end of the work (incidentally another new element, since none of Wittig's previous texts contained such a listing). It shows that the various sites in hell, limbo, and paradise are visited in no predictable order and follow, instead, in total disorder. This is discussed and elucidated in a dialogue between Wittig and Manastabal:

> J'addresse la parole à Manastabal, mon guide, et je lui demande si la laverie automatique est le premier cercle de l' enfer. Elle dit: (J'ignore, Wittig, si les cercles de l'enfer ont été dénombrés. Mais qu'à cela ne tienne, je n'ai pas l' intention de te les faire visiter dans l' ordre.)
> Il me faut beaucoup d'entrain pour dire alors:
> (Allons-y dans le désordre, donc.)[6] (*V*, 20)

From this conversation it is obvious that the elaborate architecture established by Dante (in which the circles of hell and the various heavens are numbered) is questioned and/or negated.

Also, even if Dante's architecture were accepted, the voyage undertaken by Wittig and her guide would still take place in a disorderly, random, or chaotic fashion. This is not only an overthrow of Dante's system, of divine order, or of established categories, but a refusal of all order (as an absolute or totalitarian system). This is, of course, familiar by now, for it has been seen in numerous instances in Wittig's previous texts (especially in *Les Guérillères* and *Brouillon pour un dictionnaire des amantes*).

However, lest even disorder become systematic, Wittig has created a hybrid structure in which opposites are joined. For example, as can be seen from the table of contents—which incidentally has no such title—the "chants" are numbered from I-XLIII (*V*,139). They begin with an "ouverture" and end (or almost, for here again Wittig's predilection for a penultimate sequence of extreme importance prevails) with "L'arrivée." Initially, hell, limbo, and paradise follow each other (IV, V, VI), but this order is changed on several occasions and becomes limbo, paradise, hell (XXI, XXII, XXIII) or hell, hell, hell (XVI, XVII, XVIII). Besides, even though the names of some of these sequences suggest partial adhesion to Dante's format, other terms are introduced that come from an entirely different (not Christian but pagan) mythology. Suddenly, sequences entitled "Achéron: 1, 2, 3" appear among them. Thus, the river that must be crossed in order to enter hell, but also to proceed on the voyage toward paradise, is the one that, in Greek mythology, divides the world of the living from Hades, the abode of the dead. In addition, in the sequences devoted to it, Acheron is actually closer in comparison to the river Lethe, which bestows forgetfulness (*V*, 40, 99); and it finally becomes the stream of tears that are shed for the dead and that will free the living. The last of these is an entirely new creation.

A similar mixture of elements that contributes to the hybrid nature of this work is based on allusions to various works of art—not only from the realm of literature, but even (and this is also new in Wittig's work) from film. A fusion of literature and cinema can be seen, for example, in the description of the departure of Wittig and Manastabal (*V*, 7). It takes place not in the middle of life (as in Dante's poem) but in a desert at the middle of the earth (*V*, 133). It begins in a setting that is both desolate and pure: a beach, a zone devoid of all ornamentation, windswept, and unidentifiable. A comparison is instantly made with a silent film. And the way in which Manastabal and Wittig proceed on their journey recalls a sequence in Jean Cocteau's (not silent) film, *Orphée*, in which Heurtebise guides Orphée on his voyage to the underworld— a film that is, itself, a recreation of the Orpheus myth. This, in turn, is a reminder of Wittig's own recreation of the Orpheus and Eurydice story in both *L'Opoponax* and *Le Corps lesbien*.

Other literary allusions include some to *Alice in Wonderland*. One of these combines an evocation of paradise in the manner of Dante (complete with angels playing musical instruments, archangels and seraphim, and the figure of the beloved who resembles Dante's Beatrice with one in the form of a quote from the text of Lewis Carroll, the song "Soup, beautiful soup of evening" (*V*, 136). Although this fusion of *The Divine Comedy* and *Alice in Wonderland* is probably the most arresting combination of allusions, there are others that are equally original—for example, the outrage that is shown by Manastabal when Wittig decides to acquire a horse (as might a hero in a "Western" movie) in a sequence that is a variation on one of the circles of hell depicted by Dante:

> (Que feras-tu d'un cheval en enfer, Wittig? Souviens-toi qu'on n'est pas dans un western. Parfois ta confusion des genres a véritablement quelque chose de barbare.)[7] (*V*, 63)

But this "confusion of genres," mocked by Manastabal and qualified as "barbaric," does not always have to do with the works of others or with different genres. Wittig is also capable of creating confusion (or fusion) by suddenly including a quote from her own previous works without alluding to this borrowing. Thus, for example, the phrase "elles disent" that was so prominently used in *Les Guérillères* suddenly reappears in *Virgile, non* (*V*, 128–29). But here, in direct opposition to the previous work, it applies to the inhabitants of hell, "les âmes damnées," who are totally passive, accept male domination, and "do [not] say" or "speak."

Further "confusions" or fusions can be found in the temporal domain. Although this is not new in Wittig's fictions, only a few of her past techniques are retained and many unprecedented ones are added. All verbs in *Virgile, non* (as in previous instances) are in the present tense. A chronological or linear progression is overthrown (as in the refusal of past, present, and future in *Les Guérillères*, for example). In *Virgile, non*, however, anachronism is rampant and pushed to extremes. For instance, it is stated on the very first page that the voyage represented in this work is "tout ensemble classique et profane" (*V, 7*)—profane here meaning modern or present-day—thus wiping out all habitual distinctions between past and present. This is reinforced by the attire of Manastabal and Wittig. Although they contain echoes of Orpheus and Eurydice, Dante and Virgil, and Christ and St. Christopher (*V, 8*), they wear blue jeans, carry rifles, and are shod with sneakers. They speak street slang (*V,* 9, 19, 42, 49, 72, for example), ride motorcycles, jog, play billiards, and so on. But there are also sequences not only presented in antichronological fashion, but located somewhere entirely outside of time. These include the sequences dealing with the three crossings of the river Acheron, the struggle with the angel (XI.), and the scenes set in paradise (which, numbered only from one through six, significantly refuse the traditional notion of a seventh heaven). The use of the present tense of verbs in all these instances adds to the "confusion" or "disorder" that already arose from a mixture of genres and from the acceptance/rejection of Dante's structural scheme. Also, this present tense is antitraditional since it can designate past, present, future, and future perfect, as well as that which is atemporal or even eternal.

The same is true for spatial considerations. Although in this text a specific location is indicated (San Francisco) and various sequences take place in recognizable settings, the fact that these (real) sites are also literary or religious inventions gives them a hybrid character that overthrows or outdistances any of the categories into which they might be put. Thus, an automatic laundry is, at the same time, both a place that is very much part of our modern world (and the New World in particular) and one of the circles of hell; a California bar where patrons drink tequila and play billiards is, at once, recognizable and easily located and limbo; and an orchard full of flowers, fruit, and delicious edibles is both a picnic ground and paradise.

The dual protagonists of *Virgile, non* are equally hybrid constructs. As has been shown, they echo various figures from myth and literature and even from film. Moreover, they are both ancient and modern, "classical and profane," as is their voyage. But also, when considered as doubles they have their counterparts in a long line of such figures (the Dioscuri, the twins of Greek and Roman mythology; Gilgamesh and Enkidu; Poe's William Wilson; Céline's Bardamu and Robinson; and so on) and in the anima and animus of Jungian psychology. Moreover, they can also be considered alter egos, or two parts of the same personality (something like the "Lui" and the "Moi" of Diderot's *Le Neveu de Rameau*, except that *Lui* would have to become *Elle*, given the fact that both components are female). Gender confusion (or fusion) is also evident in the protagonists, as has been mentioned. This is further accentuated both by their description as "lesbiennes" (also pejoratively as "gouines" by their enemies) who refuse the traditional role of "femme" or "mère" (very much as did the "amazones" and the "amantes" in the work that preceded *Virgile, non*, as well as by the restrictions that make certain actions (such as heroic deeds, epic adventures, cowboy ventures, or mystical journeys) the sole prerogatives of males. As a matter of fact, the Manastabal-Wittig couple could best be designated by the term that appeared in *Brouillon pour un dictionnaire des amantes:* "héraïnes." However, even there hybrid characteristics are evident. In the case of Wittig (the fictional character) especially, heroic elements mingle with antiheroic ones. She is both courageous and cowardly, wise and foolish, resourceful and overcome with confusion, streetsmart and naive. And although Manastabal seems more experienced, more circumspect, and alternately chides, mocks, praises, restrains, or encourages Wittig, if considered an alter ego she is another part of the same self and thus adds to its composite nature.

Nowhere, however, is the mixture of opposites clearer than in the language (or languages) found in *Virgile, non*. This language has come a long way from the almost uniformly objective one of *L'Opoponax* and the intensely emotional one of much of *Le Corps lesbien*. In this text not only do the two merge but several new additions occur: the appearance of slang (a very up-to-date and low form too), which is arresting, especially in the context of the basic allusion to a lofty, poetic, even sacred journey; and the use of phrases in English, which, although rare, occur here for the first time (*V*,50,51). It is quite clear that these innovations in the realm of language are not used by Wittig for local color or to suggest a particular situation as were the Latin phrases in *L'Opoponax* for example). Both argot and English phrases seem to have as their purpose to break the link with an Old World literary tradition and also with an old world in terms of language.[8]

However, *Virgile, non,* is not written entirely in slang. On the contrary, lofty style and poetic passages (or even entire poetic sequences) appear there (mostly in connection with evocations of the beloved, who, incidentally, is a very palpable, down-to-earth Beatrice). Thus, registers of language alternate, and sometimes noble or poetic utterances are challenged or even mocked by Wittig's guide, Manastabal. For example, after a particularly lyrical passage addressed to the beloved (*V*, 64), Manastabal chides Wittig with the following words:

> Wittig, il n'est pas temps encore. . . . je te dis, ne te laisse pas emporter par les mots. . . . Je t'assure bien, Wittig, qu'ici ce n'est pas à coups de figures de style que tu t'enverras en l'air.[9] (*V*, 65)

Several insights can be gained from this angry utterance. Poetry is out of place in a context of misery (in the hell depicted here). To allow oneself to "be carried away by words" is to lose touch with what is concrete or real (suffering in this instance). "Figures of style" will not accomplish lofty flights or, since the phrase "s'envoyer en l'air" has a second, argotique meaning (to achieve orgasm and, in this case, by masturbation) will not procure someone solitary pleasure by an act of obviously literary nature. Poetry will have a place, but only when significant actions have prepared the way (in this instance after one has journeyed to the lowest reaches of hell, saved those "lost souls" whom it is possible to rescue and mourned those who have been doomed as a result of a destiny determined by their gender).

Moreover, from this passage and many others of a similar kind in *Virgile, non,* an entirely new tone emerges: that of self-mockery. This is something only rarely seen before in the fictions of Wittig (for example, *C,* 64, 112). While there have been many instances in which ferocious laughter, subtle irony, gentle quips, and other forms of humor have appeared, frequent use of this type of self-mockery is novel. It can be linked to the first person narrative, to the name of the author (given both to the narrator and to one of the protagonists or doubles), and even to the city in which the action of the novel takes place (not far from which Wittig, the writer of the text, lives). In all these cases, and by all these means, the self has been exposed, brought out into the open—has declared itself so to speak. This can be interpreted as evidence of self-assurance, strength, and courage. Self-mockery is thus possible, even in the domain closest to a writer, that is, writing, for it implies that one has attained that most difficult (and rare) of attributes: the ability to laugh at oneself. It is a salutory sign, a symptom of wholeness and suppleness, and the opposite of a narcissistic, overly serious contemplation of oneself and one's activities—even of those activities that are a vital part of one's life (such as literature for Wittig).

Of course, by extension Manastabal's admonition is addressed to all writers guilty of the same kind of overindulgence in high-flown utterance or of narcissistic attitudes manifested in an inordinate seriousness concerning their creations. And it is probably a reminder that what is most meaningful can happen "outside of texts" (as the last part of the poem in *Les Guérillères* already stated) rather than by means of literature.

This is perhaps also one of the meanings of the voyage undertaken by Wittig and Manastabal in *Virgile, non.* This voyage leads them through the various recesses of suffering or ends of night (explored with as much harsh realism, humor, and imagination as those to which Bardamu and Robinson journeyed in Céline's *Voyage au bout de la nuit*) in order to arrive at a state of understanding, compassion, and "passion active." The last of these, as explained by Manastabal, is the only remedy for hell, the only dawn that can follow the darkest ends of night. The description she gives of this state is highly significant:

> (Seule la passion active, Wittig conduit à ce lieu bien que les mots pour la dire n'existent pas. On en parle généralement sous le nom de compassion. Mais pour la sorte dont je parle le mot n'est pas de mise. Car elle bouillonne, fermente, explose, exalte, embrase, agite, transporte, entraîne tout comme celle qui fait qu'on est embrassé à sa pareille. La même violence y est et la tension. La passion qui conduit à ce lieu tout comme l'autre coupe les bras et les jambes, noue le plexus, affaiblit les jarrets, donne la nausée, tord et vide les intestins, fait voir trouble et brouille l'ouïe. Mais aussi tout comme l'autre elle donne des bras pour frapper, des jambes pour courir, des bouches pour parler.[10] (*V*, 107–8).

From this passage, it is evident that the "passion active" of which Manastabal speaks so eloquently yet so simply is a key notion for understanding not only this text but Wittig's entire work. All her writing seems to come from this core, and this emotion is at the root of most of her literary practices. These practices are, evidently, much more than "figures de style," but they are not always clearly comprehended in terms of their motivation. That is why the above statement is so valuable and offers so many insights.

First, for a feeling as profound as "passion active" no words exist or all words fall short. This is a reminder of the many instances in Wittig's fictions where what was most deeply felt (whether for a human being or a work of art) remained nameless, unnamable, and ineffable. Second, a word generally used (and/or abused), such as *compassion*, is too banal, too weak, and too worn to express something as vital as "passion active" or that wordless feeling that can only be described by another, parallel experience: passion in its quintessence. Here, the latter is not an abstraction but takes the form of concrete reactions (almost all of which have been explored, in depth and breadth, in *Le Corps lesbien*). These reactions are so powerful, so violent that they overwhelm a person in their throes. But they also provide new forces that allow a person to act, to battle, and to speak.

The last of these acts seems of the greatest significance, not only here but everywhere in Wittig's work. To speak is a key function. It is no accident that the phrase itself appears in various forms in a number of her fictions "on dit" in *L'Opoponax* and "elles disent" in *Les Guérillères;* that Isis, who appears at the very center of *Le Corps lesbien,* is thought to have the power of the "living Verb"; that *Brouillon pour un dictionnaire des amantes* celebrates the "conteuses," or the "porteuses de fables"; and that finally, in *Virgile, non,* the fundamental function of speaking is revealed. As can be seen from the important pronouncement cited above, to speak is not only to take possession of the word (a right long denied) but to bear witness and, most of all, to express "passion active." And considering the word *passion* in both of its meanings, this emotion consists of suffering, torment, and sacrifice, as well as intense love. Indeed, both meanings are inextricably linked, and both must be accepted if salvation and paradise (used here in their profane meaning) are to be attained.

Since it is this "passion active" alone that "donne . . . des bouches pour parler," Wittig's characters gain the right to speak only if they have earned it by a descend into hell or have spent "a season in hell." The latter, as a matter of fact, suggests parallels between *Virgile, non* and Arthur Rimbaud's *Une Saison en enfer* on a number of counts. And although no direct references to that work can be found in Wittig's text (except for the subtle appearance of several phrases from Rimbaud's poem, *V,* 20), many comparisons can be made between the two works: the exploration of all forms of suffering, malediction, and sacrifice, alternating with brief glimpses of beauty, wonder, and felicity; the grotesque and/or hallucinatory quality of many of these explorations; the fierce humor; the self-mockery; the abrupt changes in tone and the intrusion of low language; and also the hope that there are luminous visions (as in Rimbaud's *Les Illuminations*) that coexist with those of hell.

Another parallel (already briefly mentioned) is with Céline's *Voyage au bout de la nuit.* This work is nowhere mentioned in *Virgile, non,* but that should not be a deterrant since for a figure as important as Sappho *Brouillon pour un dictionnaire des amantes* showed a blank page. The resemblances between the two novels are more meaningful than any direct reference or even than the presence of quotes. For example, the Wittig-Manastabal couple resembles that of Bardamu-Robinson in a number of ways (except that the former are both female). Robinson as well as Manastabal seems to be a larger double of his companion. He precedes and guides Bardamu in his voyage through all the circles of a profane hell and to every corner of a world where suffering exists. The function of this journey to the end of night is to speak of what Céline calls "la vacherie des hommes"[11] and to bear witness to it. On the literary level, this is done through a series of scenes in which hallucination or delirium reigns but which have a basis in reality, and by means of a language that opposes the traditional one, creates the impression of oral delivery and everyday speech, and makes use of slang for its vitality, ferocity, and ability to shock and attack. These attributes coincide with many of those found in *Virgile, non.*

There, however, is where any resemblance to Céline's work stops. Indeed, many of its characteristics are subverted or entirely reversed. Thus, "la vacherie des hommes" of which Céline speaks (and which applies to all human beings) is to be taken literally in Wittig's text, since all the viciousness portrayed is perpetrated by "les hommes," that is, by men. And the victims, who are principally children (and animals) in *Voyage au bout de la nuit*, are, in *Virgile, non*, exclusively women. Most important though, while Céline's novel ends in failure, despair, apathy, and silence—the last sentence being "Qu'on n'en parle plus"[12]—indicating that the voyage undertaken here leads from compassion to indifference and from the need to speak to the weary wish to speak no more, Wittig's work ends in triumph, joy, and music, and the voyage there traces a trajectory that leads from night to dawn, from darkness to brilliant light, from compassion to passion, and from mute despair to powerful expression. And while Céline's protagonists discover that "la vérité de la vie c'est la mort,"[13] Wittig's affirm life, intensified and even with some intimations of immortality.

Some of the most fundamental aspects of the voyage that

constitutes the central thematics of *Virgile, non* promote the conclusion that more than any of these parallels this voyage most closely resembles the mythical hero journey that appears in every part of the world from ancient to modern times (which, incidentally, is certainly also in accordance with Wittig's interest in universalization and in the unification of space-time concepts). The characteristics of this mythical journey— so brilliantly analyzed by Joseph Campbell in *The Hero with a Thousand Faces*[14]—reveal many comparisons that can be made in this respect with Wittig's work. These characteristics include a night voyage among monsters and other hostile forces; a descent into hell or the underworld; trials, torments, and even symbolic death; final illumination or revelation; and triumph of the hero and the accomplishment of his quest. Except for the substitution of *heroine* (or *héraïne*) for *hero*, such a pattern appears to fit this particular work of Wittig admirably.

Nevertheless, some noteworthy renversements have taken place there. For example, while the monsters and other hostile forces in the prototype of the mythical hero journey often take the form of animals, demons, or fantastical creatures of whom some are female, in *Virgile, non* they are exclusively male. It is also striking that the animals who appear there, such as the "ulliphant" (*V*, VII), the giant butterfly (*V*, XXI), or the "bourlababu" (*V*, XV)—who, incidentally, speaks slang as well as English—are totally benign, charming creatures,[15] who help rather than combat the protagonist. Added to these changes or reversals is the fact that Wittig's heroines have both a heroic and an anti-heroic nature, making them hybrid creatures rather than uniformly grandiose beings such as those traditionally found in sagas or myths that conform to the archetype (or stereotype) of the hero.

By combining such a great variety of night journeys of pagan or nonreligious origin with the one described in Dante's *Divine Comedy*, Wittig has achieved a highly original union— one that, as in many previous instances, breaks down traditional categories. It refuses the distinction between Christianity and paganism, the sacred and the profane, the ancient and the modern, the beyond and the here-and-now, and the lofty and the low. In broadest terms, *Virgile, non* also tends to subvert mythological patterns of a universal nature, literary genres, particular works of literature, ancient and modern hero figures, language distinctions, and even her own previous creations and recreations. The last of these subversions, although not surprising, is the most interesting. Here, as elsewhere, *Virgile non* shows its distance from Wittig's earlier works. Its structure is new. Although it has some similarities with that of her previous works (such as the emphasis on disorder and nonchronological aspects), it does show a definite progression—that is, a trajectory that goes from the point of departure and the beginning of a quest to the point of arrival and the accomplishment of this quest. This is quite different from the circular structure of past works and from the open-endedness sometimes found there (as in *Le Corps lesbien*, for example). In this text, although descent and ascent alternate—the plunges into the various circles of hell or corners of darkness versus the glimpses of paradise, with some moments of rest or reprieve in limbo—the main trajectory is an upward one. This movement is also clearly shown by the depiction of a desolate landscape in sequence I and of a fecund, joyous, luminous one in sequence XLII. Despite the tortuous nature of the journey, the somber detours, and the difficulty of the road, the movement is an ascending one. The zigzags and dead ends are necessary stages and make the final victory all the more valuable. An overly simple, straightforward vertical motion would be both uninteresting and unfitting to the subject of the work.

Other innovative developments concern the format of the text. For example, many of the sequences in *Virgile, non* contain extensive dialogues. This is not something previously found in Wittig's fictions. What "on dit" in *L'Opoponax* or what "elles disent" in *Les Guérillères* is only indirectly given, and the lovers of *Le Corps lesbien* do not engage in verbal exchange. Here, however, the actual utterances of Wittig and Manastabal, of some of the "âmes damnées," of the beloved, and even of the animals are quoted directly. At times this causes the text to resemble a play (which foreshadows Wittig's most recent innovative venture into the world of theatre). However, a further reversal also occurs, this time not of her own past techniques but of a literary convention: that of marking spoken discourse and the changes in speaker either by quotation marks or (in French usage) by the presence of a dash. Wittig refuses both these conventions and chooses, instead, to enclose all speeches in parentheses. On the other hand, however, she observes the conventional use of a colon. By means of such refusal and acceptance, Wittig creates yet another hybrid situation and escapes rigidity even in the domain of overthrow. This can be observed in the following example:

> Et moi de m'étonner:
> (Tu veux dire que ce n'est pas fait?)
> Elle dit:
> (Regarde autour de toi. . . . Quel mot
> te vient à l'esprit?)
> Et moi assez piteusement:
> (Beauté.)[16] (*V*, 23)

Another example of theatrical techniques used by Wittig in this text is the use of soliloquies. Usually pronounced by the "âmes damnées" (for example, IV, XXXV), they resemble the long speeches found in *The Divine Comedy* or in neoclassical tragedy, but here the setting is a modern one. This setting contributes to the hybrid character of those soliloquies, as does the language used, which is a mixture of lofty speech and slang (for examples, see *V*, 13, 119). In other instances, such pronouncements, made most frequently by Wittig (the character), resemble the harangues of orators or the discourses of heroes in didactic or historical plays. But here the tone is mock-heroic, and such utterances are usually deflated by derisive comments. For example, Wittig (the character) states: "j'ai adopté le genre noble" (*V*, 14) or "essayant mon style noble" (*V*, 15)[17] before pronouncing her speech, but the narrator shows that her words have no effect, indeed that they produce the opposite of the reaction desired, and necessitate a retreat that is far from noble (*V*, 18–19). Only the soliloquies of Manastabal have an authority, a nobility, and a simplicity that distinguish them from the diatribes of the damned or from the often foolish, inflated or ineffectual utterances of Wittig (the character). Despite their mixture of lofty language and slang (*V*, 9–10, for example), or perhaps because of it, Manastabal's soliloquies have great power and show that hers is a superior wisdom, as befits a guide or sage. Only slowly, as

Wittig gains in understanding—moving from naïveté (which echoes that of a Simplicissimus or a Candide) to compassion and, finally, to "passion active"—do her soliloquies either approach those of Manastabal in form and content or cease entirely. They either give way to questioning or to silence. Thus, soliloquies, which by their nature are monologues (and as such a form of solipsistic utterance indifferent to others), give way to dialogue (communication, or a link with others) and, finally, to a wordless state that accompanies profound feelings or indicates an encounter with the ineffable. This wordless state can be seen most clearly in the sequence that signals the approach of paradise. There, Manastabal, asked by Wittig to tell her everything about this goal of their quest, answers, "Regarde plutôt" (*V*, 88).[18] Evidently, words have become unnecessary. Only mute wonder seizes Wittig at the radiant vision of the beloved who, herself, does not utter a word (*V*, 89). And in paradise, language has given way to music. It takes the form of an opera, with recitatives, duos, trios, and choral interludes—all varieties of "chants." In many ways this evokes works from the baroque era, yet many of the instruments described are modern and are used in jazz, such as drums, trumpets, and saxophones (*V*, 110–11). In the final sequence of *Virgile, non* (*V*, 136–38), which depicts the ultimate festivities in paradise, angels who resemble jazz musicians are joined by a chorus of birds who add their voices to this hybrid, marvelously varied opera, which also includes the voices of a group of angelic motorcyclists who sing the song from *Alice in Wonderland* mentioned earlier. All these produce a musical effect that both subverts and recreates the music of the spheres.

The progression that leads from monologue to dialogue to silence and, ultimately, to music is extremely significant. It parallels the progression that leads from narcissism or self-involvement to compassion or communication to wordless wonder and musical celebration. In this sense, it is another form of voyage that leads from hell to limbo to paradise. Thus, the various stages that language must pass through are once again seen as destruction and recreation, death and rebirth. Certain types of utterances are shown to be empty or ridiculous and are annihilated in order to make way for a new form of expression. It therefore becomes clear that the journey undertaken in this work is also that of language. This should not be surprising considering the importance that Wittig (the writer) attributes to this domain. And it also suggests that *Virgile, non* has as its fundamental subject (as did her previous works) the question that is most significant for literature: the matter of words.

This is apparent too in descriptions of the language of the angels—as, for example, in the following dialogue between Wittig and Manastabal:

> (Quelle est donc la langue des anges?)
> Et Manastabal, mon guide, de dire qu'à cette même question Jeanne d'Arc a répondu à son tribunal: "mais plus belle que la vôtre"[19] (*V*, 48)

Thus, the ideal language—that of the angels and that spoken in paradise—is more beautiful than ordinary speech or probably more poetic. However, Manastabal adds that it is as language "sans paroles," that is to say, ineffable. Yet at the same time she encourages Wittig to write it, saying, "Ecris-donc l'opéra toi-même, Wittig" (*V*, 48).[20] This is a particularly interesting remark, for to transcribe a language without words is indeed difficult, if not impossible. It must remain in the realm of the ideal, existing perhaps as pure sound or music that is beyond the reach of words. On the other hand, if "opéra" (in Manastabal's second statement) means not only an opera but also a work of art, an opus, then Wittig, in the role of the writer, acts not only as a participant in the book's journey and a witness to its events, but as a chronicler or scribe who uses the power of her own words to communicate the insights gained and the illuminations encountered.

To write, therefore, is an act as important, or more so, than any of the actions represented in the work. It is the action par excellence, the best way to manifest "passion active." This is another way of celebrating the power of the word, and of affirming that language at its best can both kill and give life (as was stated in the *Brouillon pour un dictionnaire des amantes*) or, as is seen here, can both damn and save. Perhaps this is also the meaning behind the various opposing tones that characterize different sequences in *Virgile, non* and that are achieved through diverse types of writing. There are, for example, passages that are filled with ferocious invectives and with verbal violence that attains a veritable paroxysm of hatred so great that it seems it could kill (*V*, 113–15). There are others, full of sadness and mourning (for example, *V*, 81–82, 97), that evoke a dirge; and still others, that are full of such joy, exuberance, and vitality that they suggest either the dawn of creation or the birth of an ideal world that is both an end and a beginning (*V*, 21, 47, 88, 111, 135, 137–38).

But there is yet another tone that language is used to achieve in this text. It differs from all the above and even from those found in Wittig's previous works (except in isolated passages). It is one of fierce irony and is heard in the words of the narrator, who witnesses and chronicles the various outrages perpetrated on the (willing and unwilling) victims by the tormentors. This particular voice can best be observed in such sequences as "Parade 1" or "Les cartes à jouer" (*V*, 53–57, 58–59).[21] The first depicts a procession of women, all of whom are engaged in ludicrous or demeaning activities and who lend themselves willingly to such debasement. They are described in a fashion that mimics objectivity or even the observations of someone confronted by a strange spectacle for the first time. There are women with feathers attached to their rear and head, those who sport the ears and little tails of rabbits (obviously Playboy Bunnies), and those who wear evening gowns slit to the waist and advertise various types of beer, cars, and refrigerators. All of them walk in a peculiar fashion, as if on tip-toes, and at an absurd angle. This "slave flesh" is followed by those who belong to various pornographic institutions and wear the signs of their specialties prominently displayed: chains, chastity belts, whips, nail-studded clubs, and brands on their flesh. A "hideous sort of ecstasy" appears on their faces. It can thus be seen that irony is achieved in this sequence by means of descriptions in which the point of view is that of an observer who is unused to such spectacles and who reacts to them as would a traveler confronted with odd customs of the natives in a foreign land. Only such interjections as "slave flesh" or "hideous ecstasy" reveal the attitude of the narrator and somewhat reduce the ironic dimension.

Irony is much more powerfully maintained in the second sequence mentioned, "Les cartes à jouer" (which incidentally appears to be a takeoff on the Queen of Hearts episode in *Alice in Wonderland*). Here, a two-dimensional world is depicted in which women have no more reality or human attributes than playing cards. They fall over at the slightest provocation, jostle each other, trip, and collapse into a heap. If a three-dimensional individual passes them, they efface themselves or lie flat on their faces. They allow others to walk on them, without even realizing that they have been trampled. They flatten themselves to such an extent that they are often invisible or nothing but a thin line. They will do anything to avoid collision, disappearing into walls, hallways, and sewers. A policeman can easily gather a whole lot of them lying face down on the ground and turn them over one by one, saying, "Alors, on va être sage comme des images, n'est-ce pas?"[22]

Not only irony is apparent, however, in the above mentioned sequences. There is also the presence of gallows humor. This type of humor allows Wittig to achieve some of her most powerful effects. It is most useful for portraying painful, even unbearable, experiences and allows an author to confront the reader with truths that would otherwise be too shocking and too inexorable. It provides momentary (comic) relief and a certain distance, yet permits a writer to continue recounting hideous facts. At the same time, it constitutes a renversement of categories of emotions by joining laughter and terror (habitually opposed or, at least, separated). In making use of gallows humor, Wittig joins a long line of modern writers who excel at this very form of laughter—a line that extends from Laforgue to Beckett, from Rimbaud to Genet, from Jarry to Céline, from Lautréamont to Ionesco, and so forth. It marks a progression in terms of her own fictions, however, since it appears with much greater force and frequency in *Virgile, non* than in any of her previous writing.

But this kind of humor is also balanced by its very opposite—compassion, or better still, "passion active," an intense form of love. This emotion demands an entirely different tone and is achieved by another set of techniques. Among the best examples in this text are the sequences "Le lac" and "Parade 2" (*V*, 76–82, 92–97). The first revealing indication of compassion is that these sequences are much longer than any from the preceding category, and the pace is much slower, as if the rhythm mimed the emotion. The language has become more sober, and the tonalities are not strident, as before, but muted (as in a dirge). This is entirely fitting since "Le lac" describes the despair of the victims and their decision to commit suicide as the only alternative to an unbearable existence. This they do in total silence, through reciprocal strangulation, after a ritual exchange marked by courtesy and gratitude. No words of appeal, protest, or complaint pass their lips. So moved is Wittig (the protagonist) by their plight and their nobility that she is tempted to join them in death. When gently admonished and encouraged by Manastabal, she mourns them by weeping. It is in "Parade 2", however, that the last circle of hell is reached—or as Manastabal calls it (*V*, 97), "le point limite de l'existence."[23] This sequence describes a long procession of victims that resembles that of "Le lac." It is an enumeration of all the horrors perpetrated on them, accompanied by the slow beat of a drum. There are those whose feet have been mutilated and whose bodies have been deformed in various ways; those subjected to various hideous forms of excision; and those who have been beaten and broken, and who are on the verge of dying. They pass before the travelers in total silence, without even a sigh, like the living dead. This is indeed the true end of night.

In some striking ways, this incident recalls the lowest circle of hell in *Voyage au bout de la nuit*, which Céline calls "le bout à tout," in which a child victim is tortured by her parents for purposes of sexual stimulation.[24] But the difference between the two can be measured not so much by the contents, for in both cases the fate of the victim(s) is deeply shocking, but by the tone used by each of the two writers. While Céline uses a tone of detachment (that of a chronicler who records the horror he sees for that is his mission) but also one of resignation, Wittig's tone is one of compassion and of admiration for the animal strength (as Manastabal calls it) or lifedrive of these victims.

"Passion active," the final state of feeling to be achieved, manifests itself in still other sequences, and the tone used there is suitable to this emotion. It is neither ironic nor mournful. It is, as the term indicates, an active form of response. Sometimes it is expressed through harsh invectives directed at the tormentors of the victims (V, 113–15). At other times it leads to efforts to save the victims, either by verbal admonition (V, 67, 72) or by physical action (V, 91, 101). But it is also necessary to learn that the vanquished sometimes attack and mutually destroy each other (V, 73). "Passion active" is arrived at by stages, by a progressive gaining of insight, and it becomes clear that this is one of the important aims of the journey undertaken by Wittig and Manastabal. The former moves from anger and disdain at the victims' servility or passivity (V, 36, 37, 39, 55, 59) to an understanding that does not condemn them but attempts to gain insight into their motives (V, 53, 79, 87) and, finally, to help them by showing them a better way, by saving the wounded, and by mourning those that are lost (V, 44, 81, 122). More than compassion, although this must first replace outrage and mockery, it is the desire to make suffering cease that leads to active—and useful—passion. Or as Manastabal puts it:

Le malheur qu'on veut faire cesser n'arme-t-il pas?
. . . Se pâmer, gémir, gesticuler ou vitupérer même font montre de beaucoup de sentiment, mais cela ne suffit pas. C'est pourquoi je suis ici avec toi.[25] (V, 35)

This statement by Manastabal reveals that all of Wittig's past reactions—to faint, to moan, to gesticulate, and to vituperate—although they are proof of deep feeling, do not suffice and that it is her role as guide to lead Wittig beyond this state, to arm her against the misfortune she wishes to conquer, and to lead her out of the hell of suffering into a paradise that she defines as affirming "la liberté des vivantes" (V, 125).[26] Not that this journey is easy, nor even that the arrival at a better state can be predicted for the near future. As a matter of fact, Wittig exclaims, "Ah! Manastabal mon guide, c'est pas demain la veille qu'on sera en paradis" (V, 109).[27] But it is the attempt to reach paradise, the passion with which an individual strives for it, that matters. And even if the penultimate and ultimate sequences of Virgile, non ("L'arrivée" and "La cuisine des anges") depict only a fantasy of that paradise, it has the power of a vision and a prophesy.

That is probably what gives such vitality to these sequences and such vivacity to their imagery. By the power of
the writing alone, they are given reality and attain a luminous
presence that balances the somber, harsh, and painful passages with which the text abounds. And whereas in earlier
sequences concerning paradise only brief or partial glimpses
of felicity were possible, in the two final sequences this state
is revealed in all its exultant plenitude. A form of felicity,
exuberance, and plentitude is characteristic of all the joyous
passages in Wittig's fictions and is thus merely a more complete version of the various sites and situations of fulfillment
already represented in earlier works. Paradise in *Virgile, non*
resembles the dream voyage of the lovers (accompanied by
Baudelaire's "L'Invitation au voyage") in *L'Opoponax;* the
scenes of harvest and festivity, the games and fairs, and the
edifice at whose summit one hears the music of the spheres
in *Les Guérillères;* the luminous moments of encounter and
fusion between the lovers in *Le Corps lesbien;* and the "jardin
terrestre" and the "âge de gloire" in the *Brouillon pour un
dictionnaire des amantes.* However, in the present text it is even
more fully developed, perhaps because access to it has been
more difficult and could only be attained after having gone to
the farthest reaches of hell in a night journey that involves
death and resurrection. The exultation that marks the final
"chants" of *Virgile, non* is thus, in some ways, a renversement
of the title, or at least of its second part, for *no* has turned into
a joyful *yes* and negation has become affirmation.

All this can best be seen in the imagery and language used
in this end/beginning. "L'arrivée" begins with a description of
the same desert found at the start of the journey undertaken
by Wittig and Manastabal: a wasteland of sand, flat and windswept, an empty circular zone. A large crowd moves across
this space, fighting against a powerful wind. Suddenly the
wind is stilled, and a brilliant fog envelops the figures. From
between the clouds of mist, another landscape emerges of
which the narrator says, "je [le] reconnais aussitôt à ses formes
et ses couleurs" (*V,* 135).[28] It is thus a place that has always
existed, and it is instantly recognized, in a form of anamnesis
or in a return to the origins. This landscape, as it is described,
is flooded with brilliant light. The air is filled with pleasant

odors. The ground has an elasticity all its own. Here, the body becomes weightless. Jubilantly, the narrator exclaims, "Qui aurait cru qu'il serait aussi simple d'entrer au paradis" (V, 136).[29] And indeed, simplicity is one of its most striking traits. Among its other important characteristics, it is "palpable sensible" (V, 136), a paradise in which an individual participates with all his/her senses, and where all the joys of the living body can be fully realized. Not a pale abstraction, a purely spiritual concept, or the abode of disembodied spirits, it is a concrete reality, palpable and full-fleshed. This has already been hinted at in earlier episodes concerning paradise, where it was established that angels do have a sex and that it is female (V, 21); that laughter can be shared with angels (V, 89); that they live in a land of sunshine (V, 110); and that, in the celestial city, joyous music, even jazz, is heard (V, 111). But it is in this end/beginning that all these characteristics are the most fully developed.

The setting for the arrival in paradise is the countryside. It overlooks the ocean (incidentally the Pacific) and the "porte Dorée" (that is, the Golden Gate), which here has the double advantage of being both a real landmark and the gates of heaven. Angels arrive on motorcycles. Some sing the song from *Alice in Wonderland* (thus adding to the playful anachronisms used). Others set up an outdoor kitchen for a celestial feast that also resembles a typical American barbecue. But animals are not the victims here, for it appears to be a meatless feast. Flies and bees swarm about, touched by rays of sunlight. The hills are full of rainbow colors. Light transforms the trees into prisms, is refracted by them, and becomes smooth, impalpable, and sparkling. It allows those present to see the immensity of the sky, which is concave here—a renversement of the expected convex shape of the sky, which seems to suggest that the view here is from above, from heaven or paradise. All sorts of birds, coming from every part of the globe, fly through the air, and their song joins the song, music, and serene speech of the angels. The angels themselves combine unusual attributes. They are sexed beings who ride motorcycles, sing, play instruments, and also cook.

This last activity dominates the final tableau of *Virgile, non*, which is fittingly entitled "La cuisine des anges." Cooking is significant on a number of counts, mostly because of the meanings Wittig has chosen to emphasize or subject to renversement. One of the most down-to-earth occupations, it is here performed by heavenly creatures. It is no longer one of the forms of enslavement for women, but a free and joyous act. It involves a series of sensual pleasures (tastes, odors, and colors). And it is an act of metamorphosis that transforms the raw into the cooked by the action of fire (which here appears in its creative rather than its destructive aspect).

As in the previous sequence, the accent is on sense experiences, and Wittig's descriptive techniques are designed to evoke these in a pleasurable fashion. She appeals to the visual sense through the images of the angels, who are presented, as in a painting, in the full array of their skin tones—illuminated by the glow of the flames as in a Georges de La Tour canvas (incidentally skin tones of black and golden—colors suggestive of the beloved in *Le Corps lesbien,* but also of their various races). The sense of smell is pleasured by the evocation of the various herbs used in the preparation of the feast. And one can almost taste the vast array of fruits cited.

When all is ready (in an exact reversal of the dreadful trumpet calls sounded by the angels of the Apocalypse to announce the end of the world), a naked cherub sounds a trumpet to announce that everything is ready for "la cuisine des anges" and that the feasting in paradise can begin. By concluding her work in this way, Wittig does more than just portray the goal of the quest voyage of her protagonists as a feast of the senses. She portrays it as a paradise that exists here and now. This is one of the meanings that can be found in the pronouncement made by Wittig (the character) when she says, "c'est ici et maintenant que prend fin ma longue pérégrination dans l'enfer" (*V,* 136).[30]

The end of *Virgil, non* accentuates the simplicity of paradise, the simple joys that are within our reach, not in some abstract ideal or supernatural realm, but here and now. However, this notion is not expressed in a treatise on the subject, nor even in a statement of a fundamental truth such as is frequently made at the end of a hero journey. Instead, simplicity is reflected in the entire character of the work and primarily (as could be expected) in its language. The latter is a great deal simpler than in Wittig's previous texts. Nowhere in *Virgile, non* is there erudite vocabulary (like that found in *Le Corps lesbien,* for example) or learned allusions (such as were fairly frequent in *L'Opoponax* or *Brouillon pour un dictionnaire des amantes*), except for the obvious one to Dante's famous work. Even the use of quotes from other literary texts has been limited to one from *Alice in Wonderland* (a book for children). Neologisms are also few and playful (*ulliphant* and *bourlababu*). Spoken language and slang predominate. "Figures of style" are denounced and/or eliminated.

All this is, of course, a conscious choice. There is ample proof that Wittig's skill as a writer permits her to do anything she wishes in terms of "word work." If she has opted for a striking simplicity of style in this work, it is certainly related to the notion explicit in Manastabal's answer to Wittig's exclamation at the end of their journey:

> (Qui aurait cru qu'il serait aussi simple d'entrer au paradis?)
> Le commentaire de Manastabal, mon guide, est:
> (Le plus court chemin d'un point à l'autre est la ligne droite.)[31] (*V,* 136)

This "straight line" that leads from one point to another and allows the protagonists to achieve the goal of their quest is the very one that Wittig, the writer, has so successfully taken in the creation of *Virgile, non.*

Epilogue

*L*ooking back at the corpus of Wittig's fictions from the past twenty-five years reveals that hers has been a constant journey, indeed a *voyage sans fin.*[1] A continual quest for renewal, it has led her to abandon known territories, established traditions, past discoveries, and even domains successfully conquered, in order to push on to other explorations, and to further new ventures. In this pulling up of stakes, or forsaking of outworn modes of perception and creation, renversement proved to be a most useful travel accessory, the fitting accoutrement for a voyage of upheaval, overthrow, and transgression, as well as the ammunition for the functioning of her "war machine," the weapon concealed in the body of her "Trojan Horse."

But what of the present—and the future? Over five years have elapsed since the publication of her latest work, *Virgile, non.* It is natural to wonder what further renversement her next work will contain or how "it will sap and blow out the ground where it was planted" (*T*, 45). At the present moment, the only answer to these questions is silence.

However, knowing that lacunae, intervals, and instances of nonenunciation do not denote sterility or defeat—either in her individual fictions or in the course of her literary career— but instead, indicate a turning point that leads to renewal, it can be expected that this period of silence is simply a time that must elapse before words can pour forth afresh. This is in keeping with numerous occurrences of a similar kind found in Wittig's fictions: the cyclical patterns of destruction, pause, and regeneration in *Les Guérillères* in regard to the "féminaires," objects linked to women's "histoire," literature, and even language itself; the fragmentation and reconstitution of the pronoun *I* (*J/e*) and the dismemberment and reassemblage of the beloved's body that is symbolic of the actions of the lover (the writer) upon the body of the beloved (literature), in *Le Corps lesbien;* the frontal attack on the repository of language in order to arrive at a positive transformation, or the destruction of words that have lost their power and must die in order to be reborn—either in the form of neologisms (or even a neolanguage)—in *Brouillon pour un dictionnaire des amantes;* and finally, the decade of silence (which most closely resembles the present one) that occurred before the publication of *Virgile, non*. In addition, the use of phrases in English, which appears for the first time in Wittig's fictions in *Virgile, non,* (*V*, 50, 51) is a clue to the renversement par excellence that Wittig is now contemplating;[2] for her newest "war machine" is the intention to write fictions in English instead of in her native French.[3]

This would indeed be a major upheaval, a schism so radical as to resemble a cataclysm. It would certainly "sap and blow out the ground where it [her work] was planted," for it would indicate a break with an entire literary tradition (an Old World in terms of language), the abandonment or destruction of tools she had perfected as a writer, and the refutation or even annihilation of her first language, her "mother tongue." So drastic is such a move, that it could be compared to the end of a civilization, indeed a world. For any writer, but especially for Wittig, who has been so preoccupied with "word work," this change would be astounding and certainly more audacious than any renversement she has undertaken to date.

Few writers have been daring enough to undertake such action. Joseph Conrad and Vladimir Nabokov are among them. But the example of Samuel Beckett seems most pertinent in this case. His well-known switch from English to French is one of the most arresting phenomena of modern literature.[4] It is especially striking since he had already produced such fine works as *Murphy* and *Watt* in his native tongue and was thus abandoning an idiom in which he had achieved mastery. The result of this switch, however, was a series of even greater writings admired the world over, beginning with *En attendant Godot*.

Some of Beckett's reasons for the change of language (although these have rarely been stated and are frequently mystifying)[5] might also apply to Wittig, although she has given no explanation for the action she is contemplating. In her case, it is best to turn to her fictions for clues. These are more meaningful than any declaration of purpose, for they contain many references to the necessity for destroying an existing language, so that after an interval of silence either a renewed awareness of language may occur or "word work" so radical that it would produce the effect of words "being read for the first time" (*T,* 48)—as if language were participating in the dawn of creation.

In the case of both Beckett and Wittig, the decision or the intent to write in a new language is evidently also based on the refusal of too facile an approach, of too great an ease in using a language that might have become habitual or automatic, or that might result in the display of virtuosity for its own sake. Both are too demanding of their craft and too intransigent in their pursuit to allow this to happen. Amputation, dismemberment, even "execution" do not seem too great a price to pay in order to avoid facility, atrophy, and rigor mortis.

Furthermore, a change in language by a writer is more than a renversement. It can even be compared to an eschatological act, for it implies both an end and a beginning, the total annihilation and recreation of the writer's entire world. Not only does the death and rebirth of the writer's native tongue take place within his/her own language (already a major cataclysm), but it is also a split from an entire world of words, followed by the setting out into an uncharted domain of language, something akin to a cosmos newly created after an interval of nothingness (or silence). In this sense, it resembles the universal myth pattern of eschaton and cosmogony.

Even contemplating such an action takes great courage (and audacity). This is especially so since this particular eschaton is self-imposed, and not determined by circumstances, opportunism, or divine decree. The risks of such an undertaking are great. But then Wittig has shown on numerous occasions and in every one of her past fictions that she accepts, even invites, dangerous exploits so that she may destroy dead forms, old and worn-out traditions, and even her own former endeavors, subject them to positive transformation, and forge continually new creations.

The last of these, and probably the most exciting, may grow out of this period of silence. It remains for the future to determine what form they will take. But already an aura of expectation enhances this interval, which is surely still another turning point. There is every reason to believe that Wittig will produce even finer fictions than those of the past—and in a new language.

Notes

Bibliography

Index

Notes

Prologue

1. "The execution . . . of a certain type of literature" (Duras, 283). All translations from the original French in text and in the notes, are by the author. Translations from Monique Wittig's work are by special agreement with Wittig.

2. Josselin, 59. Other critics, such as Marthe Rosenfeld, see a resemblance between Wittig's literary practices and those of the "new novelists," albeit recognizing that her work goes beyond the latter's aesthetic inventions. For a detailed discussion of this point, see Rosenfeld's "Vers un langage," 56.

3. Cluny, " 'Le Corps lesbien' de Monique Wittig," 14.

4. Wittig's works were published in translation in a number of countries: *L'Opoponax* in England, the United States, Sweden, Germany, Italy, Japan, Holland, Spain, Yugoslavia, Czechoslovakia, and Finland; *Les Guérillères* in England, the United States, Holland, Japan, Sweden, Germany, and Spain; and *Le Corps lesbien* in England, the United States, Italy, Germany, Holland, Japan, and Spain.

5. The dates of publication of these works were, respectively, 1969, 1973, 1976, and 1985.

6. For example, Madeleine Chapsal, Jean-Michel Cluny, André Dalmas, Marguerite Duras, Raymond Jean, Jean-François Josselin, Mary McCarthy, Jacqueline Piatier, and Claude Simon.

7. For example, Sally Beauman, Laura C. Durand, Mary Beth Pringle Spraggins. Even some of the most recent, and best, critics, such as Noni Benegas, Diane Griffin Crowder, Marthe Rosenfeld, and Namascar Shaktini, tend to interpret Wittig's fictions primarily in terms of militant feminism. Wittig, however, denies that this is her major aim ("Point of View," 69).

8. Especially Sturrock, 20; also Josselin, who defines this "scan-

dal" as being "le scandale . . . dans ce 'plaisir du texte' dont Roland Barthes a si bien parlé" ("the scandal . . . of that 'pleasure of the text' so well discussed by Roland Barthes"), 59.

9. First published in English in *Feminist Issues* 4, no. 1 (Fall 1984): 45–49. The French version, "Le Cheval de Troie," appeared in *Vlasta,* 4 (1985): 36–41.

10. The American universities were Cornell, Harvard, Mount Holyoke, Smith, University of Massachusetts, and University of Southern California.

11.   To lose
But truly to lose
To make room for findings.
(Guillaume Apollinaire, "Toujours")

12. See, for example, the critics mentioned in note 7.

13. Such as, "On the Social Contract," "One Is Not Born a Woman," "Category of Sex," "Mark of Gender," "Point of View," and "Straight Mind."

1. The First O

1. McCarthy, 90.

2. See, for example, Didier, 19, 24–25.

3. "A masterpiece [because] it executes ninety percent of the books that have been written about childhood," Duras, 283.

4. *Dictionnaire alphabétique et analogique de la langue française,* 4th ed., s.v. "opoponax."

5. Stampanoni, 93.

6. McCarthy, 94.

7. Weightman, 25.

8. Stampanoni, 93.

9. McCarthy, 91.

10. McCarthy, 91. See also Wittig's statements concerning *on* and personal pronouns ("Mark of Gender," 7, 8).

11. "a tide of children"; "a tide of little girls" (Duras, 284).

12. "I am no longer I, but neither am I a certain little girl: I *become* childhood itself" (Simon, 70).

13. Shaktini, "Le déplacement du sujet phallique," 74.

14. "The fall into time" (incidentally also the title of one of E. M. Cioran's books) has been treated most extensively by Mircea Eliade. Eugène Ionesco has also written about this experience in *Journal en miettes* and *Le Solitaire.*

15. "After so many texts by so many adults who have tried in

vain to 'express' their childhood memories, how did Monique Wittig succeed in *telling* childhood?"; "*brings back* childhood for us. . . . That is to say, childhood is not related, but actually recreated" (Simon, 70).

16. McCarthy, 91.

17. "all alike, as anonymous as the world of adulthood itself"; "in the shadow of their pious activities, there is the pagan scrutiny" (Duras, 286).

18. "so brilliantly youthful and blooming."

19. These associations could suggest a reference to Proust, who also links art and the love object, as well as sexuality and transgression.

20. "She lies on a wild black white gray horse . . . her loosened hair flies in the wind, her fingers are entwined in its mane and her knees are bare, she is all covered with sweat . . . her mouth is open, her teeth show. . . . she is far away, drawn by the movement of the stars she wanders, one sees her in the distance, like a whirling circle of frost, voyaging as does a galaxy."

21. "purely descriptive material"; "purely objective language" (Duras, 284).

22. "can stretch out" or "can be extended."

23. "one cannot describe it [the opoponax] since it never assumes the same shape. Realm: neither animal, vegetal, nor mineral, in other words undetermined. Humor: unstable. It is not advisable to have dealings with the opoponax."

24. "soft scent, but all too bitter taste" (*O*, 239). The original French phrase in Wittig's text comes from Maurice Scève's poem, *Délie*, X, 11. It is overlooked by critics, even those who note the use of a line from the same poem at the very end of *L'Opoponax*.

25. "One can see Orpheus turned toward Eurydice and taking her hand, their heads their rounded cheeks resemble each other, their necks have the same curve as they turn toward each other, Orpheus' arm in front of Eurydice's hand is around one of her breasts."

26. Mademoiselle Caylus, one of the schoolmistresses.

27. "I so loved her that in her I live still." This verse, from Maurice Scève's *Délie*, XLIX, 41, was not "touched" in the published English translation, which Wittig considers "a pity since it is the key to the whole text" ("Mark of Gender," 10). It should also be noted that here, as in the previous use of a phrase from Scève's poem (mentioned in note 23), Wittig does not use quotation marks to distinguish it from her own text.

28. This point is made by Wenzel ("Le discours radical," 50). She

makes no mention of Wittig's use of Scève's poem, however, but treats the phrase as if it were the narrator's own.

29. Duras, 284.

30. Notably, Balakian, 3; also Weightman, 25.

31. Wittig, "Mark of Gender," 8. It is interesting to note also that Wittig speaks here of "the comical nature of the device."

32. Wenzel, "Le discours radical," 50.

33. See the last section of the Prologue.

34. *Fougerolles* suggests *fougères* (ferns) or the diminutive thereof; *Rivajou* suggests a combination of *rivière* (river) and *jouer* (to play).

35. Consider what an error or grave limitation it would be to concentrate solely on homosexual relationships in Proust's *A la recherche du temps perdu* or Gide's *Les faux monnayeurs*, for example, and to ignore the much more fundamental questions treated by these writers. While this approach in regard to these works would hardly occur to critics, such an approach has too frequently flawed discussions of Wittig's fictions. See also, her statements on this subject in "The Trojan Horse," 49 and in "Point of View, 65.

2. *From 0 to* O

1. In this respect, there is a resemblance between Wittig and Gide, who also proceeded to abandon each of his fictions as he went on to the next. In his case this was part of his doctrine of "disponsibilité," while for Wittig it is connected with the notion that each new work must "sap and blow out the ground where it was planted" (*T*, 45). Moreover, Wittig goes further than Gide by abandoning not only her past works but also the literary genres and writing styles that she previously used.

2. Didier, 19.

3. See the cover of the Avon edition of *Les Guérillères*.

4. "the poetic flower is absent from all bouquets" (Mallarmé, *Igitur*, 251); "the guérillère is absent from all wars."

5. Duras, 284.

6. See also Wittig's remarks concerning her use of *elles* ("Mark of Gender," 9).

7. Wittig mentions the impact of Nathalie Sarraute's use of *elles* (while emphasizing the difference between Sarraute's work and her own) and considers her use of this pronoun an "example of intertextuality" ("Mark of Gender," 12n.5).

8. "WHICH DISTINGUISHES THEM AS DOES THE EYE OF THE CYCLOPS."

9. Rosenfeld, "Vers un langage," 56.

10. *Les Guérillères* was published at the height of the militant phase of the women's liberation movement. For examples of sensationalist exploitation, see the covers of *Les Guérillères* and *The Lesbian Body* in the Avon editions.

11. Jean, 22.

12. "a break in levels [of experience], discontinuity, a passage to another order" (Chevalier, "Introduction," in Chevalier and Gheerbrant, 1:xii).

13. "the symbol is truly innovative [and] brings about an indepth transformation" (Chevalier and Gheerbrant, 1:xviii).

14. Chevalier and Gheerbrandt, 1:xv.

15. "universal language" (Chevalier and Gheerbrandt, 1:xxxiii).

16. Chevalier and Gheerbrant, 2:290.

17. "the song evokes the vulval ring, as does everything that recalls the 0, the zero, or the circle."

18. Neumann, 39–47, 132–33. See also, plates 27a, 28b, 33a.

19. "a mouth that speaks and throws the living words on paper" (Jean, 22).

20. Sepharial, 5–6.

21. "the instant of reversal. . . . cyclical regeneration . . . the interval before generation" (Chevalier and Gheerbrant, 4:417).

22. Chevalier and Gheerbrant, 1:302–09.

23. Chevalier and Gheerbrant, 4:338. See also Franz, *Number and Time*, 101, 104, 109.

24. Chevalier and Gheerbrant, 4:238–39.

25. Wittig, quoted in Shaktini, "Displacing the Phallic Subject," 37.

26. "the infinite sphere whose center is everywhere and whose circumference is nowhere."

27. "in all its modalities."

28. Rosenfeld, "Vers un langage," 56.

29. Tyrell, especially 18–34.

30. Jacqueline Piatier, in "Les débuts de Monique Wittig," is the first to have commented on the author's humor. Sally Beauman, in "Les Guérillères," speaks of her wit. Laura C. Durand, in "Heroic Feminism as Art," mentions irony as the sole form of humor found in *Les Guérillères*. None of these critics, however, attribute a great deal of importance to laughter in Wittig's fictions. Yet the author herself speaks of the "comical nature of the narrative," which already exists in *L'Opoponax* ("Mark of Gender," 7).

31. See Wittig's pronouncements on this subject ("One is Not Born a Woman," 53; "Category of Sex," 67).

32. "It is useless to open it to the first page and to look for an order in its arrangement. One can consult it at random and find something that concerns one."

33. "They cover them with blue green red paint and assemble them into grotesque grandiose miraculous compositions to which they give names."

34. Yaguello, especially 32–45.

35. "a new species in search of a new language."

36. "there is no reality before words . . . have given it form."

37. Shaktini, "Le déplacement du sujet phallique," 65. For Wittig's specific objections to the position of Jacques Lacan, see "Straight Mind," 104, 109.

38. Rosenfeld, "Vers un langage," 58.

39. "They say that to begin with the vocabulary of all languages must be examined, modified, totally overthrown, that each word must be put to the iron test."

40. NO / SIGNS THAT REND
ARISE VIOLENCE FROM WHITENESS
FROM THE VITAL BEAUTIFUL PRESENT
WITH A GREAT DRUNKEN WING BEAT
TORN TATTERED THE BODY
(INTOLERABLE)
WRITTEN BY DEFAULT

ARISE NO / SIGNS ASSEMBLED
EVIDENT / THE DESIGNATED TEXT
(BY MYRIAD CONSTELLATIONS)
IS LACKING

LACUNAE LACUNAE LACUNAE
AGAINST TEXTS
AGAINST MEANING
THAT WHICH IS TO BE WRITTEN VIOLENCE
OUTSIDE THE TEXT
IN ANOTHER FORM OF WRITING
URGENT MENACING
MARGINS SPACES INTERVALS
UNREMITTINGLY
GESTURE OVERTHROW.

41. The line from Mallarmé's poem reads as follows: "Tout son col secouera cette blanche agonie" ("His whole neck will shake off this white agony"). However, the swan does not succeed in freeing

himself, and the end of the poem suggests exile, immobility, and impotence.

42. This manifests itself precisely in the intervals . . . it can be sought in the lacunae . . . in everything that is not continuous in their utterances, in the zero, the 0, the perfect circle of your invention."

43. It should be noted that the correct translation of this key phrase is "THAT WHICH IS TO BE WRITTEN" and not, as the existing translation reads, "WHICH IS TO WRITE" (Avon edition, 143).

3. *J/e est une autre*

1. This term is translated as "THE JUICE" in the published English edition of *The Lesbian Body* (26). The original French term, "LA CYPRINE," is a more poetic and far less slangy word for the secretion that accompanies erotic arousal in the female. It already appears in Wittig's earlier fiction, *Les Guérillères* (42), but in *Le Corps Lesbien* it heads the list of anatomical terms and is also found in several central sequences—always in a poetic context (*C*, 19–20, 49, 157). See note 34 for further discussion of the term *cyprine*.

2. Wittig, "Author's Note," *The Lesbian Body*, ix.

3. Wittig states that separatism would destroy her intention, which is above all "to create a literary work," ("Point of View," 65).

4. Wittig, "Author's Note," x.

5. Wittig, "Author's note," ix–x.

6. Wittig, Author's Note," x.

7. In my experience reactions to this work are quite extreme—even among graduate students of literature. The only comparable reactions I have noted are those concerning the work of Louis-Ferdinand Céline.

8. Thus, Wittig emphasizes transgression through her own methods, without resorting to such lurid cover illustrations as in the Avon edition.

9. Wittig, "Author's Note," ix.

10. Crosland, iv.

11. Wittig, "Author's Note," x.

12. Wittig, "Author's Note," x.

13. "Added to 10 which symbolizes a complete cycle, 11 is the sign of excess, immoderation, overflow . . . incontinence, violence, outrage . . . the start of renewal, but also disorder . . . rebellion . . . the transgression of laws." (Chevalier and Gheerbrant, 3:321–22).

14. "a part that forms a whole within a whole, a microcosm

within the macrocosm which distinguishes and individualizes . . . a group within a set." Chevalier and Gheerbrant, 1:298–99.

15. "I am the three-horned one who lowes, I am the triple one, I am the dreaded the benevolent the infernal one, I am the black the red the white one. . . . I thunder in my three voices: the screaming the serene the strident."

16. Wittig, "Author's Note," x. The fragmentation, the alienation, the exile even—expressed with such force and economy by the slash that divides the first person pronoun—unfortunately can not be rendered in English. The typographical implausibility of splitting the monosyllabic *I* makes it impossible. Fortunately, the possessive adjective and pronoun do not present the same problem in translation. Yet they are not as vital for the understanding of Wittig's position as is the *J/e*, since the latter applies to the speaking subject and is therefore of paramount importance.

17. Wittig, "Author's Note," x.

18. Wittig, "Author's Note," x.

19. Wittig, "Mark of Gender," 11.

20. "The experience . . . of the woman writer is completely schizophrenic. One is always torn between two approaches: on the one hand, to use a language that is not ours . . . and on the other, the battle one fights to break all this up, in order to do something else through and in language," (Wittig, quoted in Josselin, 59).

21. Wittig, "Authors Note," ix. This observation was confirmed during a recent conversation with Monique Wittig, who stated that she now renegs on a number of the statements made in the "Author's Note." Moreover, it seems to be confirmed by the fiction in question.

22. "a passionate and savage song" [accompanying] "a battle without pity [in which] violence, rending . . . are so great that they cause the destruction and decomposition of the beloved's body" (Dalmas, "Contre l'ordre masculin," 18).

23. Chapsal, 12.

24. Wittig, "Author's Note," ix–x.

25. "They say that they take total possession of their bodies."

26. Rosenfeld, "Vers un langage," 56.

27. "world without end"; "so be it"; for all eternity, Amen."

28. Shaktini, "Le déplacement du sujet phallique," 74.

29. "a mixture of signs"; "situates herself, as well as her text . . . outside the masculine-feminine system." (Shaktini, 74)

30. "possessed the power of the living Verb, [a] power greater than that of Ra, the divine sun king . . . the power of naming thanks to which one can symbolically fragment and unify the world" (Shaktini, 72).

31. "the green Cytheras"; "the black and golden Lesbos [plural]."
32. Chevalier and Gheerbrant, 3:50–51.
33. "I am forbidden to enter the city where you live. There I do not have the right to go"; "I have no right of entry to the place where you live."
34. "Farewell black continent you set sail for the isle of the living."
35. *Cyprine* was described in the following manner in *Les Guérillères* (45): "Elles disent que la cyprine a été comparée à l'eau de mer salée et iodée" ("They say that cyprine has been compared to seawater that is salty and full of iodine"). This shows that the secretion associated with female erotic pleasure is linked to Aphrodite, or Cypris (another of her names), and to Cyprus (her birthplace). But it is also linked with *eau*, its homonym *O*, and the vulval ring (as will be remembered from the association of these images). Moreover, to be precise, this *eau* is seawater and thus a reminder of Aphrodite's birth from the sea. The sea is a key image that appears all throughout this text and indeed in most of Wittig's fictions. An ancient and universal symbol, the sea is the source of life from which all being arises.
36. See, *C*, 35, 49, 58, 60, 77, 78, 90, 105, 107, 109, 119, 130–32, 133, 147, 148, 153, 154, 158, 165, 179, 181, 187.
37. "At a gesture from Aphrodite, the felicitous one, all of them . . . exchange their colors. Leucothea becomes the black, Demeter the white, Isis the blonde, Io the red, Artemis the green, Persephone the violet one, the transformations overtake them one by one, the rainbow of the prism passes across their faces."
38. Eliade, *Aspects du mythe*, 231–32; *Mythes, rêves et mystères*, 35–36.
39. *Écriture du corps* is a term frequently used by critics to describe the work of women writers, and it is also considered a trait specific to such work. Moreover, it is emphasized by some contemporary women writers themselves. See, for example, the remarks of Hélène Cixous in *La jeune née* and "La venue à l'écriture." In the case of *Le Corps lesbien*, this "writing of the body" is more complex in that it reiterates the death-life thematics, for the term *corps* can be taken in its double meaning—cadaver, and living, desiring body.
40. Eliade, *Le Sacré et le profane*, 21–59, especially 21–24.
41. "[XX + XX = XX]" (*C*, 144).
42. A comparison with a kabalistic notion—that of the human body as a replica of the universe—might be suggested here. However, in this instance also, Wittig subverts the original notion by substituting a female body for the male one found in the Kabala.

43. Wittig, "Author's Note," x.

44. Didier, 17, 32, 141.

45. For the best examples of these types of poetry, see the following: lyrical, *C*, 92–93; elegiac, *C*, 165–66; dithyrambic, *C*, 59, 81–82; surrealistic, *C*, 76–78; scientific, *C*, 79–82, and the entire list of anatomical terms.

46. Cluny, " 'Le Corps lesbien' de Monique Wittig," 14.

47. Rolin, 8.

48. Piatier, "Monique Wittig," 15.

49. Chapsal, 12–13.

50. "pitiless combat . . . destruction and decomposition of the beloved's body . . . its sacrifice" (Dalmas, "Contre l'ordre masculin," 19).

51. "perverse laying on of hands that overwhelms and torments you" (Josselin, 59); "A work that is audacious . . . visceral," (Rosenfeld, "Vers un langage," 59); "radically subversive," (Crowder, "Une armée d'Armantes," 73).

52. With the possible exception of such poems by Baudelaire as "À une charogne" or "À celle qui est trop gaie." However, his group of poems, "Les Femmes damnées," dealing specifically with lesbian love, are not characterized by this ferocity of tone. Many more parallels exist between certain works of Duras and this text of Wittig. This is especially true of recent works by Duras, such as *L'Homme dans le couloir*; or *L'Amant*, where, as one critic states it, she "displays the complex connection between sexual pleasure and violence" (Willis, 7).

53. Such as Crowder, Shaktini, and Wenzel. In contrast, see Wittig's statement in "Point of View," 65.

54. In this, Wittig rejoins other modern masters of this art, such as Beckett, Céline, Genet, and Ionesco.

55. For a very interesting treatment of this aspect of Wittig's writing, see Rosenfeld, "Vers un langage," 57.

56. "I follow you I come to you"; "I am you you are me" (Wittig, *The Lesbian Body*, 89, 118). The full effect of the French original can not be rendered in English, since several of these verbs are not reflexive in traditional French usage. They have been made reflexive by Wittig, thus producing a very novel effect.

57. Rosenfeld, "Vers un langage," 58. It should also be noted that Freud stated that the essential characteristic of desire is its mobility, the ease with which it passes from one object to another (24).

58. Crosland, viii.

59. "my most forbidden one."

60. "my very delectable one"; "execrable madwoman"; "my most

somber one"; "my most solar, heavenly one"; "my beautiful proto-zoa, my green brew, my violent little vortex."
61. "What is happening here . . . has no name."
62. The elimination of commas in past works of Wittig has al-ready been analyzed, but here it assumes an additional meaning that is not immediately evident. In French, the comma is called *virgule*, the diminuitive of *virga*, or *verge*, (penis). Thus, by eliminating it, a symbol of the male is eliminated.
63. "mother, mother, why have you forsaken me."
64. Rosenfeld, "Vers un langage," 56.
65. Shaktini, "Le déplacement du sujet phallique," 72.
66. Meunier, 51.
67. Meunier, 50.
68. Chevalier and Gheerbrant, 4:170–78. The universal symbol-ism of the number seven is shown by its recurrent importance in almost every culture and religion.
69. "the accomplishment of a cycle . . . a positive renewal." (Chevalier and Gheerbrant, 4:174).
70. Chevalier and Gheerbrandt, 4:174, 176.
71. Neumann, 31, 286, 291.
72. "I seek you, my dazzling one, in the crowd."

4. The Living Word

1. For influence of language on societal outlook, see Yaguello, especially Part 2, Chaps. 1–4. For the effect of language alteration on attitude, see Yaguello, Part 2, Chap. 7.
2. Yaguello, 192–93.
3. "chiseled like prose poems" (Wittig, *Brouillon pour un diction-naire des amantes*, Jacket copy).
4. "extraordinary mixture of erudition, lyricism and roguish-ness" (Wittig, *Brouillon pour un dictionnaire des armantes*, Jacket Copy).
5. "In the beginning, if there ever was a beginning."
6. Eliade, *Le Sacré et le profane*, particularly 60–61, 67–70, 90–98.
7. "the arrangement of the dictionary allows one to eliminate the elements that have twisted our history. . . . It's what could be called a lacunary arrangement. It also lets one use the lacunae in the same way as an understatement . . . to say the least in order to say the most."
8. "a thematic study . . . is made difficult by the complexity of the text"; "the amazons, the lovers, and the mothers" (Crowder, "Une armée d'amantes," 83).

9. Wenzel, "Le discours radical," 45.

10. "the ancient goddess Vac . . . who incarnates language."

11. "did not need to use language"; "endless exegesies and . . . deciphering of meaning."

12. "a language that is both much simpler and much more complicated than those we have known since."

13. "was capable of creating life or, on the contrary, of 'striking' dead."

14. "it is unimaginable that this language had a structure and a syntax as rigid, rigorous, repressive as those that we know."

15. "the voice sustaining . . . and O . . . it's not a sentence, it's a modulation." One might suggest that there are parallels with a mantra in this description.

16. "Because of all the displacements of meaning, the shifts and losses of meaning which words tend to undergo there comes a time when they no longer relate to reality or realities. One must then reactivate them. This is not a simple operation and it can take all kinds of forms. The most widespread is the one practiced by the bearers of fables . . . they recount . . . the metamorphoses of words. They themselves change the versions of these metamorphoses, not to make things more confusing, but because they have noted these changes. The latter prevent words from becoming fixed in meaning."

17. "fixity of meaning for words."

18. Meunier, 49–51.

19. Sapho, "Ode à une aimée" in *Sapho et Ancréon: Oeuvres connues,* 59–60.

20. "*Library,* a collection of books and fragments from the past, rescued by the lovers during the last period of chaos."

21. "The lovers are those who feel violent desire for each other, live/love among various nations, follow the precept of Sappho 'in beauty shall I sing of my lovers.' The nation of lovers, of the lovers, gathers the entire culture, the past, the inventions, the songs, and the ways of life."

22. For examples of this repetition (with some variations), see: *D,* 40–41, 49–50, 73, 102–03, 105–06, 109–10, 155, 159–60, 161, 163–64, 177–78, 182–83, 215–16, 223–24, 227–28, 229–30, 246–47.

23. "watched their bellies grow"; "plenary-mother, mother-who-engenders."

24. "those-who-engender-first-and-foremost." For further descriptions of a similar nature, see the entry "HISTOIRE" (*D,* 125–26).

25. "image bags"; "the kaleidoscopes which contain the most disparate materials are those that permit the best compositions."

26. Both Wenzel and Crowder analyze, primarily, the ideological

battle raging in the MLF (Mouvement pour la Libération des Femmes) in France, which arose from the schism that opposed the two main factions in the movement (the *mères* and the *amazones* or the *maternalistes* and the *lesbiennes*) and coincided with the time of publication of the *Brouillon pour un dictionnaire des amantes*. Wenzel concentrates on the opposition between Cixous and Wittig ("Le discours radical," 45), and although she mentions Wittig's refusal of an ideology that establishes sex categories, she does not situate this refusal within the larger framework of Wittig's refusal of *all* categories in her fictions. Wittig's refusal of sex categories can best be seen in her article, "La pensée straight."

27. "the lovers of the age of glory treat their shadows as living beings."

28. The most striking examples in modern French literature include Gide and Proust (among prose writers) and Bonnefoy, Saint-John Perse, and Valéry (among poets).

29. Also the title of Roland Barthes' famous work, *Le Plaisir du texte*.

5. Dante, No

1. *Virgile, non* was published in 1985, ten years after *Brouillon pour un dictionnaire des amantes*.

2. "to coil [like a serpent] in order to better create" (Saint-John Perse, letter to Archibald MacLeish, 8 Feb. 1960, 954).

3. "a great poem in 42 cantos comparable to the 'vita Nuova' " (Benegas, 96).

4. "a happy outcome . . . as in the poem that Dante called 'comedy' because it ends well."

5. "the automatic laundry," "the central station," "the shooting galleries."

6. "I address Manastabal, my guide, and ask her if the automatic laundry is the first circle of hell. She says: (I don't know, Wittig, if the circles of hell are numbered. Does it matter? I don't intend to make you visit them in order anyway.) I need a lot of energy to retort: (O.K. then, let's do it in disorder)."

7. "(What would you do with a horse in hell, Wittig? Remember we're not in a Western [movie]. Sometimes your confusion of genres is really something barbaric.)"

8. At about this time as well, Wittig wrote "The Trojan Horse"—originally in English—which indicates a break with former language

habits and also a refusal of the traditional notion that writers must limit themselves to the use of their "mother tongue."

9. "Wittig, it's not time yet. . . . I tell you, don't let yourself get carried away by words. . . . I assure you, Wittig, this isn't the place where you can fly into extasy by figures of style."

10. "(Only active passion, Wittig, leads one to this place, although the words to express it don't exist. One generally speaks of it as compassion. But what I'm talking about can't be expressed by that word. For it [active passion] burns, ferments, explodes, exalts, fires on, agitates, transports, moves one, exactly like [the passion] that links one to her who is one's likeness. It has the same violence and tension. The passion that leads to this place, just as the other, makes one's arms and legs tremble, knot's one's stomach, weakens the knees causes nausea, twists and empties the intestines, troubles one's sight and hearing. But, just as the other, it gives one arms to strike, legs to run, mouths to speak.")

11. "the rottenness of men."

12. "Let's drop it."

13. "the truth about life is death."

14. See especially Campbell, *Hero with a Thousand Faces*, Part 1, Chaps. 1–3.

15. As are numerous other fabulous animals that appear in various of Wittig's fictions from *Les Guérillères* (26–27, 36, 79–80) to *Virgile, non*. As a matter of fact, an interesting study could be done on the bestiary she has created.

16. "And I, full of surprise: (You mean to tell me it isn't done?) She says: (Look around you, weigh the air that touches you. . . . What word comes to your mind?) I answer rather pitifully: (Beauty.)"

17. "I adopted the noble genre"; "trying out my noble style."

18. "Look rather."

19. "(What then is the language of the angels like?) And Manastabal, my guide, says that in answer to that same question Joan of Arc said to her judges: 'Why, more beautiful than yours.' "

20. "without words"; "Write the opera yourself then, Wittig."

21. "The Playing Cards."

22. "Well now, we're going to be good girls, aren't we?" In French, there is a play on words in the expression "être sage comme des images," which means to be obedient. Since the women are so submissive that they resemble playing cards, they can also be likened to the "images" found there, which have no more reality than pictures.

23. "the lowest point of existence."

24. "the end-all" (Céline, 265).

25. "Doesn't misfortune which one wants to stop arm one? . . . To faint, to moan, to gesticulate or vituperate are a way of showing a lot of feeling, but that's not enough. That's why I'm here with you."
26. "the freedom of the living."
27. "Ah! Manastabal, my guide, paradise isn't just around the corner."
28. "I recognize [it] instantly by its shapes and colors."
29. "Who would have thought it would be so simple to enter paradise?"
30. "It is here and now that my long wanderings in hell come to an end."
31. "(Who would have thought it would be so simple to enter paradise?) The commentary of Manastabal my guide, is: (The shortest path from one point to another is the straight line.)"

Epilogue

1. Monique Wittig's *The Constant Journey* is a play and is therefore not included among the fictions here considered. It was produced at Goddard College, in the United States, in 1984. The French version, *Le voyage sans fin*, was performed in Paris in 1985.
2. Note also that Wittig's theoretical works (since 1980) are written in English.
3. Information provided by Wittig during several conversations with the author in 1988–89.
4. For a more detailed treatment of this phenomenon and the ensuing results, see Ostrovsky, "Le silence de Babel," 190–200.
5. Ostrovsky, "Le silence de Babel," especially 190–91.

Bibliography

Primary Sources

FICTION AND DRAMA

Works in French

Brouillon pour un dictionnaire des amantes. With Sande Zeig. Paris: Grasset and Fasquelle, 1975.
Le Corps lesbien. Paris: Editions de Minuit, 1973.
Les Guérillères. Paris: Editions de Minuit, 1969.
L'Opoponax. Paris: Editions de Minuit, 1964; Le Livre de poche, 1971.
Virgile, non. Paris: Editions de Minuit, 1985.
"Le Voyage sans fin." *Vlasta* 4, Supplement, 1985.

Works in Translation

Across the Acheron. London: Peter Owen, 1987.
Les Guérillères. New York: Viking, 1971; Avon, 1973.
The Lesbian Body. New York: William Morrow, 1975; Avon, 1976.
Lesbian Peoples: Materials for a Dictionary. New York: Avon, 1979.
The Opoponax. New York: Simon and Schuster, 1966; paperback, 1976.

THEORETICAL ESSAYS

"Author's Note." In *The Lesbian Body.* New York: Avon, 1976, ix–x.
"The Category of Sex." *Feminist Issues* 2, no. 2 (Fall 1982): 63–68.
"The Mark of Gender." *Feminist Issues* 5, no. 2 (Fall 1985): 3–12.
"On the Social Contract." *Feminist Issues* 9, no. 1 (Spring 1989): 3–12.
"One Is Not Born a Woman." *Feminist Issues* 1, no. 4 (Winter 1981): 47–54.
"La pensée straight." *Questions feministes* 7 (1980): 21–26.

Bibliography

"The Point of View: Universal or Particular?" *Feminist Issues* 3, no. 2 (Fall 1983): 63–70.

"The Straight Mind." *Feminist Issues* 1, no. 1 (Summer 1980): 103–12.

"The Trojan Horse." *Feminist Issues* 4, no. 2 (Fall 1984): 45–49.

Secondary Sources

Balakian, Anna. "Child's World Without Wonder." *The Saturday Review*, 2 July 1966, 3.

Beauman, Sally. "Les Guérillères." *The New York Times Book Review*, 10 Oct. 1971, 4.

Benegas, Noni. "Virgile, non." *Vlasta* 4 (1985): 96–98.

Bliven, Naomi. "Daphne in India, Catherine in France." *The New Yorker*, 2 June 1966, 66, 68.

Chapsal, Madeleine. "L'Amour fou des amoureuses." *L'Express*, 26 Nov.–2 Dec. 1973, 12–13.

Cluny, Jean-Michel. " 'Le Corps lesbien' de Monique Wittig." *Combat*, 13 Nov. 1973, 14.

———. "Les sept cercles de Monique Wittig." *Combat*, 18 June 1985, 7–9.

Cournot, Michel. "Mille fleurs au courrier." *Le Nouvel Observateur*, 17 Aug. 1970, 48.

Crosland, Margaret. "Introduction." In *The Lesbian Body*, v–viii. New York: Avon, 1978.

Crowder, Diane Griffin. "Amazons or Mothers? Monique Wittig, Hélène Cixous and Theories of Women's Writing." *Contemporary Literature* 24, no. 2 (1983): 117–44.

———. "Une armée d'amantes: l'image de l'amazone dans l'oeuvre de Monique Wittig." *Vlasta* 4 (1985): 65–78.

———. "The Semiotic Functions of Ideology in Literary Discourse." *Bucknell Review: A Scholarly Journal of Letters, Arts and Science* 27, no. 1 (1982): 157–68.

Dalmas, André. "Contre l'ordre masculin." *La Quinzaine Littéraire*, 6 Dec. 1973, 18–19.

———. "Un Langage nouveau." *La Quinzaine Littéraire*, 16–30 Nov. 1969, 14–15.

Duffy, Jean H. "Language and Childhood: *L'Opoponax* of Monique Wittig." *Forum for Modern Language Studies* 4 (1983): 289–300.

———. "Women and Language in *Les Guérillères* of Monique Wittig." *Stanford French Review* 3 (1983): 399–412.

Durand, Laura C. "Heroic Feminism as Art." *Novel: A Forum on Fiction* 8, no. 1 (1987) 48–63.

Bibliography

Duras, Marguerite. "Une oeuvre éclatante" (Post-face), *L'Opoponax*, new edition. Paris: Editions de Minuit, 1983, 283–87. (First published in *France Observateur*, 5 November 1964.)

Freadman, Anne. "Poeta (1st decl., n., fem.)." *Australian Journal of French Studies* 16, no. 2 (1979): 152–65.

Jardine, Alice. "Pre-Texts for the Transatlantic Feminist." *Yale French Studies* 62 (1981): 220–36.

Jean, Raymond. "*Les Guérillères* de Monique Wittig." *Le Monde*, 13 June 1970, 22.

Jones, Ann Rosalind. "Writing the Body: Toward an Understanding of *l'écriture féminine*." *Feminist Studies* 7, no. 2 (1981): 247–63.

Josselin, Jean-François. "Lettre à Sapho." *Le Nouvel Observateur*, 8 Oct. 1973, 59.

Lindsay, Cecile. "Body/Language: French Feminist Utopias." *The French Review* 60, no. 1 (1986): 46–55.

McCarthy, Mary. "Everybody's Childhood." *New Statesman* 72, no. 1844 (15 July 1966): 90, 92–94.

Ostrovsky, Erika. "A Cosmogony of O: Wittig's *Les Guérillères*." In *Twentieth Century French Fictions: Essays for Germaine Brée*, ed. George Stambolian, 341–51. Englewood, N.J.: Rutgers Univ. Pr., 1975.

Peterson, Virgilia. "Re-entry into Childhood." *The New York Times Book Review*, 26 June 1966, 5.

Piatier, Jacqueline. "Les débuts de Monique Wittig: *L'Opoponax*." *Le Monde*, 14 Nov. 1964, 15.

———. "Monique Wittig, Sapho d'aujourd'hui." *Le Monde*, 15 Nov. 1973, 20.

Rolin, Dominique. "Elégie pour amazones." *Le Point*, 21 Jan. 1974, 8.

Rosenfeld, Marthe. "The Linguistic Aspect of Sexual Conflict: Monique Wittig's *Le Corps lesbien*." *Mosaic: A Journal for the Interdisciplinary Study of Literature* 17, no. 2 (1984): 235–41.

———. "Vers un langage de l'utopie amazonienne: 'Le Corps lesbien' de Monique Wittig." *Vlasta* 4 (1985): 55–64.

Sale, Roger. "Keeping Up with the News." *The New York Review of Books*, 16 Dec. 1971, 21.

Sarraute, Nathalie. Discussions with author. Paris, Nov. 1987, Jan. 1988.

Shaktini, Namascar. "Le déplacement du sujet phallique: l'écriture lesbienne de Monique Wittig." *Vlasta* 4 (1985): 65–78.

———. "Displacing the Phallic Subject: Wittig's Lesbian Writing." *Feminist Issues* 8, no. 1 (Summer 1988): 34–40.

Simon, Claude. "Pour Monique Wittig." *L'Express*, 30 Nov.–6 Dec. 1964, 70–71.

Bibliography

Spraggins, Mary Beth Pringle. "Myth and Ms.: Entrapment and Liberation in Monique Wittig's 'Les Guérillères.' " *International Fiction Review* 3, no. 1 (1985) 46–51.

Stampanoni, Suzanna. "Un nom pour tout le monde: 'L'Opoponax' de Monique Wittig." *Vlasta* (1985): 79–95.

Sturrock, John. "The Lesbian Body." *The New York Times Book Review*, 23 Nov. 1975, 13.

Suleiman, Susan Rubin, ed. "(Re)writing the Body: The Politics and Poetics of Female Eroticism." In *The Female Body in Western Culture: Contemporary Perspectives*, 7–29. Cambridge: Harvard University Press, 1986.

Waelti-Walters, Jennifer. "Circle Games in Monique Wittig's *Les Guérillères.*" *Perspectives on Contemporary Literature* 6 (1980): 59–64.

Weightman, John. "The Indeterminate I." *The New York Review of Books*, 1 Dec. 1966, 24–26.

Wenzel, Hélène Vivienne. "Le discours radical de Monique Wittig." *Vlasta* 4 (1985): 43–54.

———. "The Text as Body/Politics: An Appreciation of Monique Wittig's Writings in Context." *Feminist Issues* 2, no. 2 (Summer 1981): 264–87.

Wittig, Monique. Discussions with author. June 1987, Aug. 1987, Oct. 1988, Feb. 1989, May 1989.

Related Works

Albouy, Pierre. *Mythographies*. Paris: José Corti, 1976.

Apollinaire, Guillaume. *Calligrammes*. In *Oeuvres poétiques*. Edition de la Pléiade, 203. Paris: Gallimard, 1956.

Baudelaire, Charles. *Les Fleurs du mal*. In *Oeuvres complètes de Baudelaire*. Edition de la Pléiade. Paris: Gallimard, 1954.

Campbell, Joseph. *The Hero with a Thousand Faces*. The Bollingen Series, no. 17. New York: Pantheon, 1949.

———. *The Masks of God: Oriental Mythology*. New York: Penguin, 1979.

Carroll, Lewis. *Alice in Wonderland*. New York: New American Library, 1946.

Céline, Louis-Ferdinand. *Voyage au bout de la nuit suivi de Mort à crédit*. Edition de la Pléiade. Paris: Gallimard, 1965.

Cervantes. *Don Quichotte de la Manche*. Paris: Garnier Frères, 1961.

Chevalier, Jean, and Alain Gheerbrant. *Dictionnaire des symboles*. 8th ed. Vol. 1–4. Paris: Seghers, 1974.

Cixous, Hélène. "La venue à l'écriture." With Madeleine Gagnon and Annie Leclerc. In *La venue à l'écriture*, Collection 10/18, 9–62. Paris: Union Générale d'Editions, 1977.

Cixous, Hélène, and Catherine Clément. *La jeune née*, Collection 10/18. Paris: Union Générale d'Editions, 1975.

Dante Alighieri. *The Divine Comedy*. Trans. John Ciardi. Vols. 1–3. New York: New American Library, 1970.

Didier, Béatrice. *L'Ecriture-Femme*. Paris: Presses Universitaires de France, 1981.

Douglas, Alfred. *The Tarot*. New York: Penguin, 1973.

Durand, Gilbert. *Figures mythiques et visages de l'oeuvre*. Paris: Berg International, 1979.

———. *Les Structures anthropologigues de l'imaginaire*. 6th ed. Paris: Bordas, 1979.

Egyptian *Book of the Dead*. 2d Edition. London: Routledge and Kegan Paul, 1951.

Eliade, Mircea. *Aspects du mythe*. Paris: Gallimard, 1963.

———. *Mephistophèles et l'androgyne*. Paris: Gallimard, 1962.

———. *Le Mythe de l'éternel retour*. Paris: Gallimard, 1969.

———. *Mythes, rêves et mystères*. Paris: Gallimard, 1957.

———. *Le Sacré et le profane*. Paris: Gallimard, 1965.

Franz, Marie-Louise von. *Creation Myths*. Zurich: Spring Publications, 1972.

———. *Number and Time*. Evanston, Ill.: Northwestern Univ. Pr., 1974.

Freud, Sigmund. *An Outline of Psychoanalysis*. New York: Norton, 1949.

Guers-Villate, Yvonne. *Continuité/Discontinuité*. Brussels: Editions de l'Université de Bruxelles, 1985.

Hindu Myths. New York: Penguin, 1976.

Ionesco, Eugène. *Journal en miettes*. Paris: Mercure de France, 1967.

———. *Notes et contre-notes*. Paris: Gallimard, 1962.

———. *Le Solitaire*. Paris: Mercure de France, 1973.

Jung, C. G. *The Archetypes and the Collective Unconscious*. Princeton: Princeton Univ. Pr., 1980.

Jung, C. G., and C. Kerenyi. *Essays on a Science of Mythology*. Princeton: Princeton Univ. Pr., 1969.

Jung, Emma. *Animus and Anima*. Zurich: Spring Publications, 1972.

Keppler, C. F. *The Literature of the Second Self*. Tucson: Univ. of Arizona Pr., 1972.

Knapp, Bettina L. *Women in Twentieth-Century Literature: A Jungian View*. University Park and London: Pennsylvania State Univ. Pr., 1982.

Bibliography

Labé, Louise. "Sonnets." In *Louise Labé*. Ecrivains d'hier et d'aujourd' hui. Paris: Pierre Seghers, 1962.

Livingston, P., ed. *Disorder/Order*. Stanford: Stanford Univ. Pr., 1983.

Mallarmé, Stéphane. *Igitur, Divagations, Un coup de dès*. Paris: Gallimard, 1976.

————. *Poésies*. Paris: Gallimard, 1945.

Marini, Marcelle. *Territores du féminin avec Marguerite Duras*. Paris: Editions de Minuit, 1977.

Meunier, Mario. "Prologomènes." In *Sapho et Anacréon: Oeuvres connues*. Paris: Editions d'aujourd'hui, 1982, 8–54.

Neumann, Erich. *The Great Mother: An Analysis of The Archetype*. Princeton: Princeton Univ. Pr., 1963.

Ostrovsky, Erika. "Louis-Ferdinand Céline: Creator and Destroyer of Myths." In *Critical Essays on Louis-Ferdinand Céline*, ed. William K. Buckley, 92–100. Boston: G. K. Hall, 1989.

————. "Le silence de Babel." In *L'Herne: Samuel Beckett*, eds. Tom Bishop and Raymond Federman, 190–200. Paris: Les Editions de l'Herne, 1976.

Perse, Saint-John. *Oeuvres complètes*. Paris: Gallimard, 1975.

Rank, Otto. *The Double*. Chapel Hill: Univ. of North Carolina Pr., 1971.

Sapho. "Poésies." In *Sapho et Anacréon: Oeuvres connues*, ed. Mario Meunier. Paris: Editions d'aujourd'hui, 1982.

Sarraute, Nathalie. *L'Ere du soupçon*. Paris: Gallimard, 1956.

Scève, Maurice. *Délie*. Paris: Hachette and Cie., 1916.

Scholem, Gershon. *On the Kabbalah and Its Symbolism*. New York: Schocken, 1977.

Sepharial. *The Kabala of Numbers*. Hollywood: Newcastle Pub., 1974.

Tyrell, William Blake. *Amazons: A Study in Athenian Mythmaking*. Johns Hopkins Univ. Pr., 1984.

Vierne, Simone. *Rite, roman, initiation*. Grenoble: Presses Universitaires de Grenoble, 1973.

Willis, Sharon. *Marguerite Duras: Writing on the Body*. Urbana and Chicago: Univ. of Illinois Pr., 1987.

Yaguello, Marina. *Les Mots et les femmes*. Paris: Payot, 1987.

Zéraffa, Michel. "Ordre mythique, ordre romanesque." In *Claude Lévi-Strauss*. Paris: Gallimard, 1979, 361–94.

Index

Erika Ostrovsky was born in Vienna but educated mostly in the United States and France. She is the author of such books on contemporary French writers as *Céline and His Vision, Voyeur Voyant: Portrait of L.-F. Céline,* and *Under the Sign of Ambiguity: Saint-John Perse/Alexis Leger.* Her other publications include numerous studies in collections of critical essays devoted to Samuel Beckett, Louis-Ferdinand Céline, Jules Laforgue, Saint-John Perse, and Monique Wittig. She is Professor of French at New York University and has frequently taught in that university's program in Paris. Her research interests include the contemporary novel, women writers, and myth criticism. At present, she is writing a book on new women dramatists and theatre directors in France.